INTRODUCTION TO METRICS

SLAVISTIC PRINTINGS
AND REPRINTINGS

edited by

C. H. VAN SCHOONEVELD

Indiana University

LVIII

1966

MOUTON & CO.

LONDON · THE HAGUE · PARIS

V. ŽIRMUNSKIJ

INTRODUCTION
TO METRICS

THE THEORY OF VERSE

Translated from the Russian by

C. F. BROWN

Edited with an Introduction

by

E. STANKIEWICZ *and* W. N. VICKERY

1966

MOUTON & CO.

LONDON · THE HAGUE · PARIS

PRINTED IN THE NETHERLANDS BY MOUTON & CO., PRINTERS, THE HAGUE

EDITORS' PREFACE

The growing scholarly interest in poetics makes it appropriate that Žirmunskij's *Introduction to Metrics* should be made available to a wider circle of readers than heretofore. The Russian original was published in 1925 in a small edition of 2200 copies and has never been republished; consequently many students of Russian verse have been denied the privilege of reading the book. At the same time others, interested in the comparative aspects of poetic language, have been kept away from it by the language barrier. It is for these reasons that the decision was taken to republish *Introduction to Metrics* in an English translation.

Despite the lapse of almost forty years, Žirmunskij's book has lost none of the exceptional qualities which made it stand out as one of the most solid contributions to the study of Russian versification at the time of its appearance. Composed in that post-revolutionary atmosphere of Russia, in which the study of poetic language was posited, perhaps for the first time, as a scientific problem, and reached unprecedented heights, Žirmunskij's book remains an example of lucidity of exposition, a mine of historical and comparative information, and the most exhaustive synthesis of the achievements of the Russian school of poetics which has become identified with the so-called Formalist movement. But the book is not the fruit of an eclectic mind; on the contrary, the reader will come across many polemic passages, expressing views, some of which have with time gained general acceptance, while others may still be regarded as controversial and one-sided.

To the student interested in the development of Russian poetic theory these passages afford, however, an invaluable insight into the crystallization of those ideas which have helped to shape our modern conceptions of poetic language, in particular of problems of verse. Although Žirmunskij's approach is not always free from psychological or naturalistic overtones, his rejection of the subjective interpretations of rhythm put forward by Belyj and his followers, as well as of the crude empiricism of some Russian and Western theoreticians (known best under the name of "Ohrenphilologen") has lost none of its actuality, particularly in the West, where a revival of metrical studies has been accompanied by a naïve and utterly exaggerated attention to phonetic detail, which confuses oral delivery with the structure of verse. The study of Žirmunskij shows at the same time how intimately the structure of a poem is connected with the structure of a given language, and how inseparable is the link between poetics and linguistics.

Žirmunskij's *Introduction* is free from abstract or abstruse theorizing. One of its chief merits is, in fact, the broad comparative framework, which reveals interesting convergences in the evolution of Russian, French, German, and English versification. The student of European versification will also find of inestimable value the references to the works of Western and Russian scholars, and the sizeable bibliography appended to the book. The student of Slavic poetry will not, however, fail to notice the striking gap in Žirmunskij's panoramic survey: the lack of reference to any Slavic versification system other than Russian. This gap, which is consistent with the dearth of such studies at the time of the publication of the book, has since been filled by a number of valuable works on the structure and history of Czech, Polish, Serbo-Croatian, and Bulgarian verse, which have made their appearance particularly in the post-war period. To the student of Russian versification it must also be a heartening thought that the stimulating insights and contributions of the scholars dedicated to the scientific exploration of verse in the twenties are being revitalized and advanced in Russia, after years of suppression, in the sixties.

In editing the English version of Žirmunskij's book the editors have taken some liberties with the text, which they believed would enhance its clarity. The style of the Russian original is often choppy; names of authors and titles of books and journals are frequently abbreviated and lack the customary bibliographical information. These shortcomings have been repaired, whenever possible. Some incomplete references were, however, left in the same form as in the original, for lack of a solution. For the benefit of those unfamiliar with Russian, accent marks have been added to the quotations of Russian verse.

The editors have tried as far as possible to preserve Žirmunskij's terminology, which is a part of the Russian poetic tradition. Thus "syllabo-tonic" and "tonic" have been used in preference to "syllabo-accentual" and "accentual". In discussing Russian, French, German, and English verse, the term *stress* has been preferred to the more generic term *accent*. We have also dispensed with the terms *metrical stress* and *actual stress* and have introduced the terms metrically *strong* and *weak syllables*. It should be noted that in speaking of the intrusion of the *syllabic* principle into *tonic* verse, Žirmunskij (and other scholars whom he quotes) generally means the adoption of the *syllabo-tonic* principle; the same principle is, of course, referred to by the author, when he speaks of the intrusion of the *tonic* principle into purely *syllabic* verse.

The editors have deemed it advisable to omit translations of the foreign titles and examples, including the Russian. Even a competent and faithful rendering of the poetic excerpts would have failed to meet their true purpose, which was to illustrate the metrical and rhythmic organization of verse. The student of Russian consulting this book, will, we believe, have a sufficient command of the language to do without the translations, while the general reader interested in versification will still derive some profit, even if he be denied the pleasure of comprehending the original poetic passages.

All Russian examples are given in a transliteration which is now standard in American linguistic publications.

The editors wish to acknowledge with gratitude the generosity of Indiana University, which made possible the translation of the Russian text under the auspices of the Research Center in Anthropology, Folklore, and Linguistics. We are also indebted to Professor Hugh McLean for his participation in editing a section of the book.

January 1964

E. Stankiewicz   W. N. Vickery
University of Chicago University of Colorado

TABLE OF CONTENTS

FOREWORD

This book is devoted to the theory of verse. It is intended to serve as an introduction to a series of works by the author dealing with the field of metrics (*Rhyme: Its History and Theory*, 1923, and *The Structure of Lyrical Poetry*, 1921). It originated, as did the books preceding it, from a course on poetic theory which I gave several times from 1920 to 1923 in various philological and art institutes, principally in Leningrad University and in the Russian Institute of Art History. The basic tenets of this work were laid down when I attempted such a course for the first time in the winter and spring of 1920. Chapters II, IV and V were written for the most part during the summers of 1921 and 1922.

In accordance with the general plan of a projected book on metrics, separate parts of which have been published at various times, I have set myself here a double task — to present a systematic exposition of the entire subject of metrics and in addition to explore certain special problems which up till now have not been investigated or have caused considerable disagreement and dispute. As before, I shall base my account mainly on facts drawn from the history of Russian verse, but, wherever possible, I shall amplify these facts with comparative-historical material; otherwise, an exposition of the problems of Russian metrics, in the present state of that science, would inevitably be dogmatic and one-sided. It scarcely needs to be pointed out that the disputes about rhythm and meter which arose in Russia as a result of the investigations of A. Belyj and the rejection of the traditional "classroom formulas" and "logaoedic" theories of verse correspond exactly to developments in the work of German and English scholars. Further, I consider it impossible, in a work dealing with theoretical problems, to limit the description to the classical, so-called syllabo-tonic, Russian versification. Here also, as in the history of rhyme, the most recent critical period in the development of the Russian lyric (1890-1920) raised many new questions of principle, questions which must be explained in the context of analogous phenomena in Western European metrics (not excluding, where necessary, the earlier stages of development). This applies, for example, to the problem of "purely tonic" verse (cf. Chap. V). Finally, inasmuch as the modern science of verse is abandoning abstract metrical schemes in favor of the study of actual rhythm, the phonetic examination of accentual relationships has become the foremost task of Russian metrics. In the "heroic period" of Russian metrics — when, for the most part, it was the poets themselves and critics of poetry (e.g. A. Belyj, V. Brjusov, S. Bobrov, V. Čudovskij, and others) who were concerned with verse theory and made many interesting and revitalizing discoveries in the field of Russian versification — it was precisely in phonetic questions that the most completely unscientific dilettantism prevailed. While I do not consider my remarks on Russian prosody (Chap. III) in any way final or exhaustive, I should at least like to hope that they will excite an interest in these questions among linguists, who are more experienced in this regard than the author himself.

The basic problem of the theory of verse out of which the entire book grew, is the opposition between rhythm and meter — an opposition which A. Belyj was the first to formulate clearly for classical Russian poetry in his famous works on the iambic tetrameter (*Simvolizm*, 1910). My views on this question were developed long ago in the course of extensive arguments in which I tried to defend the concept of meter against a group of theoreticians of Russian verse who were more or less consistently attempting to destroy the traditional metrical schemes — iambic, trochaic, etc. — considering them the heritage of so-called "classroom metrics" (N.V. Nedobrovo, V. A. Čudovskij, K. V. Močul'-skij — in several unprinted works, and others; cf. § 11). This was the reigning school of thought until recently, and even today it has many adherents. I formulated my own point of view on this fundamental question of the theory of verse as follows: "Rhythm is the actual alternation of stresses in verse, resulting from the interaction between the inherent properties of the linguistic material and the ideal norm imposed by the meter" (*The Structure of Lyrical Poetry*, p. 98). From this point of view, there can be no rhythm without meter. In his book *Russian Versification* (1923), B. V. Tomaševskij discussed a slightly different aspect of this question in his critique of the so-called "logaoedic theory" of Russian verse. It is, however, just this side of the problem which seems to me rather a matter of terminology than of principle.

Thus the theoretical discussion of rhythm and meter, based on the example of Russian "syllabo-tonic" verse and analogous Western European systems (Chap. II), is in this study combined with an analysis and criticism of the metrical ideas of Andrej Belyj and his followers, as well as the ideas of their predecessors in the eighteenth and nineteenth centuries (Tred'jakovskij, Lomonosov, Vostokov, and others). The more general aesthetic foundations of the system which I advocate are briefly noted, where necessary, in the introductory chapter.

I should like to express my profound gratitude to all those who have kindly consented to share with me their knowledge of certain questions touched on in my book, especially to S. I. Bernštejn and G. A. Gukovskij. I am indebted to the friendly aid of G. A. Gukovskij for many examples from the Russian poets of the 18th century.

5/XII/1924

I. BASIC CONCEPTS

1. THE FUNCTIONS OF METRICS

Poetic speech is distinguished from prose by the regular ordering of its phonetic material. Let us take as an example a poem by Bal'mont:

> Oná otdalás' bez uprëka,
> Oná celovála bez slóv.
> — Kak tëmnoe móre glubóko,
> Kak dýšut krajá oblakóv!
>
> Oná ne tverdíla: "Ne nádo",
> Obétov oná ne ždalá.
> — Kak sládostno dýšet proxláda,
> Kak táet večérnjaja mglá!
>
> Oná ne strašílas' vozmézd'ja,
> Oná ne bojálas' utrát.
> — Kak skázočno svétjat sozvézd'ja
> Kak zvëzdy bessmértno gorját!...

The principal feature which we observe in this poem, as distinguished from prosaic speech, is the regular alternation of strong and weak (stressed and unstressed) syllables. Each phonic sequence (line) has a stress on the second, fifth and eighth syllable; thus, before the first stressed syllable there stands an unstressed syllable, and between each stressed syllable there are two unstressed syllables. After the last stress in the odd-numbered lines there follows one more unstressed syllable; in the even-numbered lines a stressed syllable stands at the end. There are thus nine syllables in each odd-numbered line, and eight in each even-numbered line: together they form a longer sequence, a unit of a higher order — the period (9 + 8 = 17 syllables). The odd and even lines are connected with each other by endings of similar phonetic shape (rhymes): the final sounds coincide, beginning from the last stressed syllable (uprëka : glubóko, etc.). Thanks to the rhyme, the periods form pairs which yield a still longer sequence, the unit of the highest order in the given poem — the stanza. The poem has three stanzas of identical construction. The *most important* factor distinguishing this bit of poetry from a sample of prose is the orderly arrangement of syllables and stresses within the limits of the line, the period and the stanza.

In addition to the fundamental alternation of stress, there exists also a secondary organizing phonetic principle. There is, for example, an arrangement, of a very free sort, of the qualitative elements of sound, a patterning of vowels and consonants ("verbal orchestration"). Thus, the harmonizing endings (rhymes) are repeated at corresponding places in the line; the distribution of stressed vowels in the first two lines of the first stanza is identical ("vowel harmony"): a — a — o, a — a — o; the third line has three identical vowels: o — o — o; note also lines one and three in the second stanza: a — i — a, a — y — a; in the third stanza, line two: a — a — a, and so on.

But not only the phonetic form of the verse follows a regular pattern; there is also, against the background of corresponding phonetic alternations, an artistic arrangement of syntactic and semantic elements. Each line forms a closed and complete syntactic unit, the sentence. Within the stanza neighboring lines (1-2 and 3-4) are linked by syntactic parallelism and by repetition of the initial words ("anaphora"). This division of the stanza into two syntactically isolated periods extends throughout the entire poem, while the chain of syntactic correspondences and the use of anaphora unite the periods both at the beginning of each stanza and at the end. This is matched by the semantic grouping: the first and second tell the story of a woman whom the poet loves; the third and fourth, which stand apart from them and contrast with them, contain a picture of nature in the form of lyrical exclamations. Within each period, moreover, the second line usually constitutes a semantic variation of the preceding line (semantic or "interior" parallelism). It is this regular rhythmic-syntactic structuring of the stanza that produces, in addition, a certain uniformity in the intonational movement, i.e., in the raising and lowering of the voice ("melodics of verse"), the laws of which have hitherto been insufficiently studied.[1]

Poetic language is, therefore, more or less subject to artistic laws governing the alternation of its constituent elements. But all these types of arrangement occur against the background of one fundamental and uniquely obligatory alternation: the regular arrangement of strong and

---

[1] Cf. B. Èjxenbaum, *Melodika stixa* (Petersburg, 1922), and V. Žirmunskij, "Melodika stixa. Po povodu knigi B. Èjxenbauma", *Mysl'*, No. 3 (1922).

weak syllables, which determines the structure of the simplest phonetic sequence (the line) and of the sequence of a higher order (period, stanza).

The term *metrics* is usually taken to mean the study of the regular alternation of strong and weak sounds in verse (i.e. the study of "quantitative relationships" in the broadest sense). But the word metrics has still other meanings — both narrower and wider. In the narrower sense, metrics is the study of meter (or meters) as opposed to rhythmics, the study of rhythm; in this sense meter has to do with general laws governing the alternation of strong and weak sounds, while rhythm concerns specific, concrete cases of the application of these laws and of variations on the basic metrical scheme. Metrics, in the wider sense of the term, includes all questions pertaining to artistic regularity in the phonetic structure of verse (including orchestration and melodics). It is in this wider sense that the term is used in the works of Ed. Sievers and his school.[2] In what follows, we shall use the term metrics in its narrower, traditional meaning, noted above, pertaining only to the alternation of "quantitative" elements.

Scientific metrics must be based on phonetics, the science of the sounds of language. The central fault of school metrics is the failure to understand the actual phonetic characteristics of the linguistic material with which it deals. However, metrics should not be identified with phonetics, not even with the phonetics of poetic language. Phonetics studies *facts*; metrics studies the *norms* which govern the phonetic facts of poetic language. In this sense, *phonetics* is a part of general linguistics, the science of linguistic facts, considered as *data* possessing *causal* relationships. *Metrics*, on the other hand, is a part of poetics, the science of the *norms* of artistic speech determined by artistic intention (teleologically). In certain areas metrics and phonetics, as well as poetics and linguistics, overlap, or, to be more exact, they study the same linguistic *material*. But their approaches to the subject are different: phonetics (as a part of the science of language) studies the factual data of speech; metrics (as a part of poetics) studies the *selection* — in obedience to artistic intention — of certain elements of the data, and the basic principles involved in this selection.[3]

---

[2] Ed. Sievers, *Rhythmisch-melodische Studien* (Heidelberg, 1912), demonstrates that the subject studied by metrics is "the phonetic form of poetic art" (lautliche Kunstform der Poesie), p. 37. Cf. also Fr. Saran, *Deutsche Verslehre*, p. 2, where he asserts that metrics in the broad sense (Verslehre) includes the study of rhythm, melody, rhyme and instrumentation (Sprachklang).

[3] The following writers identify the poetic study of artistic speech with linguistics: R. Jakobson, *Novejšaja russkaja poèzija* (1921), pp. 5-11; V. Vinogradov, "O simvolike

The study of metrics is divided into several parts. *Theoretical metrics* studies the basic principles governing the regular arrangement of syllables of varying intensity. It must explain the interrelationship between the ideal metrical scheme operating in a given poem, and its actual implementation. Theoretical metrics constructs that system of concepts which are used by other branches of this science in their classification of metrical devices. The aim of *descriptive metrics* is to describe the types of meter used by a given writer or in a specific historical period, to provide classification of these meters, and to ascertain the incidence of various concrete rhythmical variations. *Historical metrics* studies the change of metrical forms or the history of particular systems of versification, meters, etc. In the following pages only problems of theoretical metrics will be considered; descriptive-historical material, taken chiefly from the history of Russian poetry, will be cited to illustrate general principles. But metrical problems are solved in a particular way within the limits of any given language, and this largely depends on the inherent phonetic nature of the linguistic material. Along with the Russian examples, therefore, the more characteristic phenomena of other national literatures will be introduced as a basis for the comparative historical study of metrical forms. Without such a study any treatment of theoretical metrics will inevitably suffer from dogmatism and narrowness of view.

2. METER AND RHYTHM

Problems of metrics, i.e., those related to the regular alternation of strong and weak sounds in artistic language, are concerned with the *structure* of the poetic work.[4] Along with the semantic (thematic) structure, which involves, for example, the question of the subject-matter, one can also speak of a purely linguistic structure, which deals mainly with phonetic and syntactic problems. Depending on their general principles of structure, the arts fall into two groups. To the first group belong the visual

A. Axmatovoj", in *Liter. Mysl'*, No. I, pp. 91-92, and *O zadačax stilistiki* in the collection *Russkaja Reč'*, p. 195 ff. and 286 ff. Opposed to such identification: V. Žirmunskij, review of Jakobson's book in *Načala*, No. 1, 1921; "Zadači poètiki" in the same issue, p. 69, and published in a more detailed version in the collection *Zadači i metody izučenija iskusstv*, published by the Russian Institute of Art History, 1923, p. 147; *K voprosu o formal'nom metode*, the preface to the Russian translation of Prof. Oskar Walzel's book, *Problema formy v poèzii* (1923), pp. 24-25, and B. M. Èjxenbaum, *Melodika stixa*, p. 14.

[4] In this regard, cf. *Kompozicija liričeskix stixotvorenij* (1921), pp. 4, 7, and also *K voprosu o formal'nom metode*, pp. 16-19.

arts (ornament, architecture, sculpture, painting), which arrange their sensory material (visual impressions, combined in part with tactile and motor impressions) in some spatial relationship. A work of visual art is always some kind of material object: its structure is determined by the proportionality of spatial forms, i.e., by *symmetry* in the broad sense of that term. To the second group of arts (arts which for the ancients were the arts of the Muses) belong music and poetry. The sensory material of these arts (auditory impressions, also partly combined with motor impressions) is arranged in some sort of temporal sequence. Artistic structure in these arts is thus determined by the regular alternation of qualitatively different sensory impressions in time, i.e., by *rhythm* in the broadest sense. Rhythm in poetry and music is established by the regular alternation in time of *strong and weak sounds* (or movements). Thus a work of art belonging to the second group is not a material object. For its reproduction, which is realized anew each time it is perceived, it requires an intricate complex of actions (musical performance, declamation) accomplished either by the author himself or by a special performer acting at the behest of the author (in specific instances the performer and the perceiver may be the same person). For this reason the study of a work of poetry or music (regarded as the work itself, in some unrealized, ideal form) must be strictly separated from the study of the devices used in its *performance*. In dealing with a poem we distinguish its metrical characteristics, as such, from the various devices employed in its declamation, which may depend to a considerable extent on the completely separate *art of the performer*.

For the sake of a full and exact classification, we must mention the existence of a third group of arts which in large measure combines the features of the first two: to this group of *syncretic* arts belong the *dance* and the *theater*. The sensory material of these arts is constituted chiefly by movements of the human body, arranged in certain spatial relationships and in a temporal sequence. In the syncretic arts *symmetry* and *rhythm* are simultaneously the determinants of the compositional form.[5]

There is yet another, no less important, way of dividing the arts. One can distinguish between *representational* and *non-representational* arts (thematic or athematic). To the non-representational arts belong, in the first group, ornamentation; in the second, music; and in the third, the

---

[5] On Greek and Roman classification of the arts, cf. R. Westphal, *Theorie der neuhochdeutschen Metrik* (1870), §§ 1-5. August Schlegel gives an interesting development of this classification in his system of the arts: *Vorlesungen über schöne Literatur und Kunst*, pub. by J. Minor (1884) in the series *Deutsche Literaturdenkmale*, Bd. 17, 112 ff.

dance. Painting and sculpture, poetry, and the drama are representational arts. This division finds a theoretical basis in the aesthetics of Kant. "Schön ist, was ohne Begriff gefällt", asserts Kant: "That is beautiful which gives pleasure apart from its meaning" (or more exactly, "regardless of its meaning".). Kant adduces as examples of beauty: a glittering shell, the multicolored plumage of a bird, the lines of some ornament — when we ignore the practical function of the combination of lines and colors involved. He contrasts this "pure beauty" ("freie Schönheit") with "associated beauty" ("anhängende Schönheit"). Thus the beauty of the human body and face, and in art the beauty of a portrait, are both associated with the signification of the given aggregation of forms: the aggregation of forms designated as the human body and face is beautiful or ugly only with respect to its signification ("durch seinen Begriff"). A face with two noses, for instance, or a body with two heads, even though it may follow all the rules of ornamental symmetry, is nevertheless ugly *qua* human face or body because of its failure to correspond to its signification.

The division of the arts into representational and non-representational can be based on this theoretical opposition. In the case of an ornament, in music, and in the dance, we have a combination of lines, sounds and movements *without any signification* and which give pleasure *quite apart from signification*. In such arts there is the obligatory structural element, but the *thematic* element is totally absent. The material of such art, divorced from practical circumstances and free of any actual significance or use, is wholly conventional; it is completely formal, aesthetic, created for art's sake alone. The sounds used in music are tones of a certain relative pitch (distributed on one scale or another), of a definite length proportional to the length of the neighboring sounds, and of a certain limited volume. The lines of ornamental art approach pure geometrical forms (circle, rectilinear polygon, parallel lines) repeated according to simple laws of geometrical symmetry. The whole artistic efficacy of the non-representational arts is concentrated in the compositional structure of the work of art in its "formal" organization. Here we find both pure forms of symmetry and pure forms of rhythm realized, in a purely artistic medium which offers no resistance to this realization.

The situation in the representational arts is different. In painting, sculpture and poetry the material of the art is *charged with meaning*; it is not completely divorced from practical reality and therefore is not completely subject to the laws of purely artistic structure. The primary consideration in the representation of the human face or body is its "meaning", its thematic unity: the representation must resemble the thing represented. A portrait, for example, is largely oriented toward the reality to which it corresponds (e.g., "man in armchair"). Of course, every picture is organized spatially and the artist always retains the right to group his models. But the purely spatial forms in the composition of a picture are much looser, much more individual and much less clearcut. There is an absence of pure symmetry, and the unity of the picture is determined to a great extent by the semantic element or *theme*, i.e., by facts lying in part outside the bounds of the art and independent of it.

The same may be said of poetry as a verbal art. The medium of poetry, the word, is not especially created for poetry, unlike the specially designed, purely artistic medium utilized by music. The word is charged with meaning. The structure of our speech is chiefly determined by the *communicative function*, by the desire to express thought. Consequently, the alternation of speech sounds is never controlled exclusively by requirements of rhythm. In a verbal work of art unity is achieved not by the purely compositional deployment of verbal material, but by the sense of what is said, by the subject. A comparison of poetry and music makes this very clear. The sounds of a word, unlike those of music, do not have a specified pitch; they are gliding tones, and we do not have exact intervals between each tone but only raising or lowering of the voice. Speech-sounds do not exhibit a definite length, constant and proportional to each other, as do the sounds in a musical melody. Thus to create a work of art by using words in accordance with the rules of musical composition, will inevitably do violence to the nature of the verbal material, just as the use of the human body in purely ornamental art will inevitably to some extent distort its relationship to its referent.[6] There is thus no pure rhythm in poetry just as there is no pure symmetry in painting. Rhythm exists as the *interaction* of two things: the natural characteristics of the verbal *material*, and the compositional *law* of alternation, which is incompletely realized, owing to the resistance of the verbal material.

In language there exist sounds of varying length, pitch, and stress (long and short, high and low, stressed and unstressed). In normal practical speech (in so-called "prose") they are distributed in an arbitrary, irregular order: the arrangement is wholly determined by semantic requirements. In poetry, the distribution of these sounds, as we saw in the

[6] The ornamental use of a human or animal figure always leads to the distortion of its organic unity in favor of formal principles of composition (symmetry, etc.); that is why an ornamental or decorative representation might picture a human body with four arms, and so on.

example of Bal'mont's poem, is governed by a specific structural law: sounds are ordered in a certain sequence, a stressed sound recurs after a certain number of unstressed sounds, the boundary of a verse line is defined by a specific number of stressed and unstressed sounds, and the verse lines recur in accordance with a definite rule. The law regulating the alternation of stressed and unstressed sounds can be expressed in an ideal scheme (meter). The linguistic medium, however, has its own natural phonetic characteristics, independent of the metrical law, and thus the linguistic medium offers resistance to the metrical scheme. In this way poetic rhythm results from the interaction of the metrical scheme with the natural phonetic properties of the verbal material.

Let us take another example:

> Moj djádja sámyx čéstnyx právil,
> Kogdá ne v šútku zanemóg,
> On uvažát' sebjá zastávil
> I lúčše výdumat' ne móg ...

The metrical law operating in this quatrain, as we shall see below, is the metrical pattern of the iambic tetrameter, used throughout *Evgenij Onegin*. According to this law, the strong sounds (stresses) are placed in each line on the even-numbered syllables. In various lines, however, departures from this scheme can be observed: thus, in the second line the stress expected on the sixth syllable is absent (zAnemóg); in the third line, a stress is missing on the second syllable (on uvažát'); in the fourth, it is again missing on the sixth syllable (výduMAT'). In addition to this, the stresses are not all equally strong: thus, the stresses on the words *kogda* and *sebja* are weaker than the others; of the unstressed syllables, the first in the third line (the weakly stressed word *on*) is stronger than the rest. Word boundaries do not in any way coincide with the distribution of strong and weak syllables. In each line these boundaries are distributed in a special way, like melodic phrasing in music which does not correspond to the division into bars. Furthermore, the distribution of qualitative elements of sound ("orchestration") does not reveal the least regularity, and the syntactic and semantic organization is limited to the distribution of syntactically unified groups in accordance with the boundaries of the phonetic lines ("lines"). So the actual phonetic shape of the verse is determined by its metrical structure only in part and its poetic rhythm is always a compromise resulting from the resistance shown by the linguistic medium to the rules of artistic organization.[7]

[7] Rhythmical forms are regarded as the result of *struggle* and *compromise* by Fr. Saran in his *Deutsche Verslehre*, p. 134 ff.: "Every verse form results from the internal

Hence, in the study of metrics, it is essential to distinguish three basic concepts: 1) the natural *phonetic characteristics* of the given *linguistic material* ("the material to be rhythmicized" in the terminology of the classical theorists: *to rhythmizomenon*); 2) *meter*, the ideal law governing the alternation of strong and weak sounds in the verse; 3) *rhythm*, as the actual alternation of strong and weak sounds, resulting from the interaction between the natural characteristics of the linguistic material and the metrical law.[8]

3. VERSE AND MUSIC

The theoretical opposition between rhythm and meter is justified on historical grounds. In the broad sense of the term, rhythm, as an element of structure in the arts, is more ancient than the poetic word, and was superimposed on verbal material from without, under the general influence of music and the dance, for among the earliest peoples poetry was closely bound up with these arts. "All the German meters", asserts Fr. Saran, "derive from songs which were accompanied by movements. Some arose directly out of such songs in the evolutionary process of the national art, others are related to them across a series of intermediate stages as combinations or variations of traditional forms or as analogical new formations" (*Deutsche Verslehre*, 137).

Actually, as we learn from the comparative study of historico-ethnographical material (historical records concerning the earliest artistic creations of the European peoples, the evocations of everyday life in so-called "folk poetry", the arts of contemporary primitive and semi-primitive tribes) poetry is a comparatively recent outgrowth of the original syncretism which obtained in the "arts of the Muses".[9] The primitive

---

union or compromise of two elements: the phonetic form inherent in the language, and the orchestrating meter, sometimes taken over from other poetic works which arose in their turn out of just such a compromise" (p. 137). "Thus arises that struggle, unending and often encountered in the history of verse, which has as its result the diverse 'styles' of one and the same verse form" (p. 135). On the psychological premises of this struggle, together with the significance of the semantic element in poetic language, cf. in particular Meumann, pp. 397-399 (*Philos. Stud.*, X, 1894). Cf. also B. Tomaševskij, "O stixe Pesen zapadnyx slavjan", *Apollon*, 1916, No. 2, p. 33; and V. Žirmunskij, *K voprosu o formal'nom metode*, pp. 16-19.

[8] Cf. the definition of rhythm in *Kompozicija liričeskix stixotvorenij*, p. 98, note 4.
[9] On the problem of original choral syncretism, cf. W. Scherer, *Poetik* (1888); A. Veselovskij, *Tri glavy iz istoričeskoj poètiki* (*Works*, vol. I); Fr. Gummere, *The Beginnings of Poetry*.

circle song-and-dance game, accompanied by a mimetic performance, unites those elements out of which words and music, the dance and dramatic performance, were later isolated. The movements of the dance-acting in the circle game, as well as the words and melody, are united and controlled by rhythm. The precise rhythm connected with the movements of the chorus is reinforced by the simplest percussion instruments (drum, tambourine, bamboo canes) or by clapping of the hands. The circle game, in which the rhythm and the melody are more closely bound by tradition than are the words, limits itself, at its most primitive, to an emotional refrain (e.g. eio! eio!), which is repeated by all the participants. When a text does make its appearance in the song, this is — in its earliest stages of development — an extremely rudimentary sort of text, improvised to fit the occasion and then easily forgotten. In other forms of choral art — in the *work song*, which accompanies the measured movements of physical labor performed in groups, or in the *military song*, sung during a march — rhythm, which controls the movements, also takes precedence over words or melody.[10] As academician A. N. Veselovskij has shown, the verbal element becomes important and is valued for its own sake only with the emergence of the soloist and his special rôle and, afterwards, with the transformation of the leader of the chorus into a professional singer interested in preserving the vocal tradition. But there is still a long way to go from the singer to the poet: not only classical art, but also medieval poetry (e.g., the lyrics of the troubadours and minnesingers) and contemporary folksong are intimately connected with music in their rhythmic forms. It is owing to this fact that the literary poetry of modern European nations, like the verbal art of late antiquity, inherits a wealth of metrical forms invented as a result of the interaction of poetry and music.

It would not be correct, however, to suppose that these genetic relationships give us the right without further ado to consider any phenomenon of verse rhythm in the light of analogous phenomena in music. On the contrary, at the time that poetry was in the process of liberating itself from music, it was also developing a special kind of verse rhythm ("declamatory"), quite distinct from musical rhythm.[11]

We have already noted the most important features differentiating the phonetic medium of poetic speech from musical tones: gliding tones, irregular intervals, the absence of exact and proportional timing. This last factor is especially important for an understanding of the peculiar

---

[10]   Karl Bücher, *Arbeit und Rhythmus* (Leipzig, 1909⁴).
[11]   Cf. Fr. Saran, *Deutsche Verslehre*, p. 185 ff.; H. Paul, p. 45 ff.

aspects of verse rhythm. In modern tonic systems of versification considerations of temporal length are not fundamental elements of metrical
structure. More exactly, time has not a material but rather an abstract,
purely *formal* significance, as the *ideal sequential order of the structural
units*, the syllables, which are conventionally regarded as being equal to
each other. In other words, the essential factor in rhythm is the very
form itself of the sequence of strong and weak syllables and not the actual
length of each sound, metrical group (foot), or line. Thus, depending on
the situation, a person reciting poetry can, within the limits of one and
the same verse, arbitrarily accelerate or retard the tempo of his speech,
make a more or less emphatic logical pause, and so on. This does not,
however, disturb the general rhythmical impression; and the character
of the metrical form remains unchanged, just as it is also unchanged by
the less important disparities in the length of two adjacent syllables.
Unfortunately, musical theories of poetic rhythm which equate the foot
with the bar and the syllable with a single beat equal in length to other
beats have played and still play a prominent part in theoretical metrics.
This is partly due to the example of classical versification, which is
taught in close connection with music and is, indeed, based on quantity.
The distinguishing feature of all these theories is the reliance on one form
or another of "*isochronism*" (equality of time intervals) as the basic
principle of the *metrical structure* of verse.[12] The fact is, however, that
the decisive role in modern European versification is played not by
equal quantity in various parts of a poem but by the order and form of
the sequence of stressed and unstressed syllables taken as the rhythmical

---

[12] Certain students of English verse are the particular champions of "isochronism"
in the most recent times. For this point of view, cf. T. S. Omond, *English Metrists*
(Oxford, 1921²) (and also his *Study of Metre* (London, 1903), and *Metrical Rhythm*
(London, 1905), and the experimental study of P. Verrier, *Essai sur les principes de la
métrique anglaise*, vols I-III (1909-1910) (cf. also his *L'isochronisme dans le vers
français* [Paris, 1912]). On the other hand, E. Landry (*La théorie du rythme*, pp.
77-78) shows that the *count* of syllables creates the *illusion* that there is an alternation
of elements which are equal in time (if the differences in duration are not too pronounced
and if the tempo of utterance is sufficiently rapid), and the regular repetition of a
combination of *weak* and *strong* syllables gives rise to the *illusion* that there is a sequence of measures made up of temporally equivalent units; in actual fact, the temporal differences realized in declamation can be very considerable (cf. the examples on
pp. 359-61 and elsewhere). The remarks of Abercrombie (*Principles of English Prosody*,
§ 19, p. 131 ff.) are very interesting. He denies the significance of time as a measure
in tonic verse and regards as the only essential element the *order* or *succession* of
stressed and unstressed syllables. "It is essential to maintain in the line a certain
regular order (or succession) of alternations: that is the role which the sense of time
plays in tonic meter" (p. 137).

units in the abstract scheme of temporal sequence. What from the purely musical point of view appears to be an imperfection in such rhythm is explained and justified by the semantic content of the rhythmical lines. Here the unity of the lines as thematic and semantic units, that is, their semantic structure takes the place of a purely musical rhythm, just as in a portrait we have, instead of abstract symmetry, the objective unity of the human face. The example of Bal'mont's poem, quoted at the beginning of this chapter, shows how far these *secondary* (syntactic and thematic) elements of composition can be developed in a poem.

In defining poetic rhythm as the result of a compromise between the metrical law and the natural phonetic characteristics of the linguistic material, we have added to the ancient definition of rhythm a new sense, which might be labeled "unity in multiformity".[13] The *multiformity* of verse is provided by the phonetic variations in quality and quantity, height of pitch and degree of stress; the grouping of sounds into words or phraseological units of varying configurations; the diversity of syntactic formations; and finally, the momentum of the thought and of the poetic "images". In contrast to this actual multiformity of the linguistic material, the metrical law serves as the element of structural *unity*. The artistic law subordinates to itself the disparate and contradictory chaos of free linguistic elements and imposes a rhythmic structure. But the chaos is visible through the light covering thrown over it in the process of composition; it is to be found in the individual manifestations of multiformity which characterize a given line of verse and which violate strict metrical uniformity and regularity. Hence it is clear that there are two possible kinds of poetry, as there are two kinds of art in general: in one the emphasis is on formal compositional structure, unity, law; in the other — on the specific peculiarities of the thematic material which destroy any strict regularity. In modern times we can observe this typological opposition of two forms of art in the conflict between Classical and Romantic poetry. In regard to poetry in particular, Classical poetics will defend the simple, strict forms of metrical uniformity which control the multiplicity of the verbal material. Romantic poetry, on the contrary, will regard metrical forms as mere traditional conventionality impeding the lively individual multiformity of the poetic material; it will favor any sort of "deviation" from the metrical scheme, any replacement of a

---

[13] Cf. the analogous definition of rhythm given by Schiller and August Schlegel: "the constant within the change" (*das Beharrliche im Wechsel*). Cf. Schiller in his letter to Schlegel dated 10 Dec., 1795; and Schlegel in his review of *Hermann und Dorothea* (*Werke*, XI, pp. 192-3) and *Vorlesungen*, I, p. 244.

strict metrical system by a system of looser principles, any struggle against the "syllabo-tonic" method of constructing the foot, any attempt to discard a uniform, orthodox stanza pattern as, for example, in so-called "free verse". It will cultivate enjambment ("enjambement") as a deliberate violation of the "metrical" rule which seeks to make syntactic groups coincide with rhythmic groups; and it will encourage inexact rhymes as a dissonant protest against the banal habit of precise sound repetition. An understanding of this contrast can be extremely useful for the concrete history of metrical systems.

4. SYSTEMS OF VERSIFICATION

In accordance with established tradition, school metrics recognizes three systems of versification: *metric*, based on *quantity*; *tonic*, based on *stress*; and *syllabic*, based on the *number of syllables*. From the scientific point of view, this classification requires thoroughgoing revision.

The "metrical" (quantitative) system was predominant among the Greeks and Romans. According to this system, a line is constructed with a regular alternation of long and short syllables, i.e., on the principle of quantity. In classical metrics, the length of a short syllable (*mora*) is taken as the unit of time. A long syllable is equal to two short ones (in some meters there exist long syllables which correspond to three or four short ones). The length of a syllable is determined by its "quality" if it contains a long vowel, or by its "position" if it contains a short vowel followed by at least two consonants (in other words, if the syllable is closed). The *foot*, a regularly recurring group of long and short syllables, serves as the basic unit of repetition. Built on quantity, the foot of classical versification corresponds to the musical bar; so, too, the quantitative principle, in general, and, in particular, the conventionally accepted relationship of long and short syllables are to be explained by the alliance between classical poetry and music. One must bear in mind that the foot is neither a word nor a phonetic group which actually occurs in isolation, but rather an ideal unit of metrical repetition, an element recurring in an abstract metrical scheme. Feet are classified according to the number of syllables and according to the distribution of longs and shorts. In classical metrics the verse structure is noted schematically by the use of special signs: the short syllable by an arc (◡); the normal long, equal to two shorts, by a dash (–). In modern musical notation we could replace this by using a quarter note for a short syllable and a half note for a long.

Since the traditional classical terminology has been preserved in the metrics of recent times, we give below a list of the most important feet used in antiquity:[14]

DISYLLABIC-FEET: *trochee* – ◡; *iamb* ◡ –; *spondee* – –; *pyrrhic* ◡ ◡.

TRISYLLABIC FEET: *dactyl* – ◡ ◡; *amphibrach* ◡ – ◡; *anapest* ◡ ◡ –; *tribrach* ◡ ◡ ◡; *amphimacer* – ◡ –; *bacchius* ◡ – –; *antibacchius* – – ◡; *molossus* – – –.

TETRASYLLABIC FEET: *choriamb* – ◡ ◡ –; *antispast* ◡ – – ◡; *rising ionic* ◡ ◡ – –; *falling ionic* – – ◡ ◡; *paeon I* – ◡ ◡ ◡; *paeon II* ◡ – ◡ ◡; *paeon III* ◡ ◡ – ◡; *paeon IV* ◡ ◡ ◡ –; *epitrite I* ◡ – – –; *epitrite II* – ◡ – –; *epitrite III* – – ◡ –; *epitrite IV* – – – ◡; *di-iambus* ◡ – ◡ –; *ditrochee* – ◡ – ◡; *dispondee* – – – –; *procelevsmatic* ◡ ◡ ◡ ◡.

PENTESYLLABIC FEET: *dochmius* ◡ – – ◡ –.

As is clear from this list, there may be not only two to three syllables in a foot, as in modern European versification, but also four to five syllables (composite rhythms in music). One foot may include several shorts or several longs. In accordance with the basic rule of "metrical" versification, based as it is on quantity, a long syllable in the foot can be replaced by two shorts, or two shorts by one long. This system of replacement is limited only by the tradition of the given meter. Thus an iamb may be replaced by a tribrach and a dactyl by a spondee. The hexameter (a dactylic line of six feet with a final foot of two syllables, either a trochee or a spondee) admits the replacement of a dactyl by a spondee in any foot except the penultimate (fifth), according to the following scheme:

$$– \overline{◡◡} \; – \overline{◡◡} \; – \overline{◡◡} \; – \overline{◡◡} \; – ◡◡ \; – \overline{◡}$$

Thus, in composing verse according to the classical rules of versification one takes into account only the regular alternation of long and short syllables in accordance with the principles of the given meter. No order is generally imposed on the disposition of word stresses; in some cases they are distributed on the long syllables, in others — on the short. Cf. the iambics of Horace:

Beatus ille qui *procul* negotiis ...

In the poetic art of the ancient Greeks this lack of correspondence between word stress and the metrical alternation of long and short syllables could be justified on two grounds: first by a musical setting in which the

---

[14] Cf. P. Masqueray, *Traité de métrique grecque* (Paris, 1899), pp. 7-8.

rhythm of the text is subordinated to the rhythmical structure of the melody, and second, by the peculiarities of the language itself, since the stress was not signalled by increased intensity (expiratory, dynamic accent), but by raising the pitch of the voice (musical, melodic accent). In modern school practice — not only in Russia, but in the majority of Western European countries, where distinctive quantity or at least its functional significance in verse has been lost and where the musical accent has yielded to the dynamic — the alternation of long and short syllables of classical meters is usually replaced by a sequence of stressed and unstressed syllables, and the stresses are made automatically and arbitrarily to coincide with the long syllables of the original. (Beátus ílle quí procúl negótiís). This fact is of considerable significance for the history of the adoption by modern European nations of the classical meters.[15] Even in Latin poetry the quantitative principle was imported from outside, from the Greeks, and took the place of the ancient, native method of versification based on the dynamic, "tonic" (stress) principle. It is possible that this "tonic" system continued to exist in the poetry of the common people. In any case, the ancient vowel distinctions of length were in so-called "Vulgar Latin" replaced by qualitative distinctions. Likewise, the versification of those peoples who continued the tradition of the Latin language and Latin culture replaces the quantitative principle, no longer native to the language, by a new system based on the number of syllables and stresses.[16]

School metrics describes the system predominating in the poetry of the Germanic peoples and of several Slavic nations, including the Russians, as a "tonic" system of versification.

Instead of the alternation of long and short syllables, we find in this poetry an alternation of stressed and unstressed syllables (the "tonic" principle). Here also, in the tradition of classical terminology, the *foot* is recognized as the unit of metrical repetition. The "tonic foot" is a regularly recurring group of stressed and unstressed syllables. Each foot contains one stressed and one or more unstressed syllables, which produces the following five meters:

Iamb (– ´):   Moj djadja samyx čestnyx pravil...
Trochee (´ –):   Mčatsja tuči, v'jutsja tuči...
Dactyl (´ – –):   Mesjac zerkal'nyj plyvët po lazurnoj pustyne...

---

[15] Cf. A. Heusler, *Deutscher und antiker Vers* (Qu. F. 123) (Strassburg, 1917); especially p. 6 ff.
[16] Cf. E. Stengel, *Romanische Verslehre*.

Amphibrach (– $\llcorner$ –): Gljažu kak bezumnyj na čërnuju šal'...
Anapest (– – $\llcorner$):   Nadryvaetsja serdce ot muki...

Feet with two stresses are not generally used (independently, at least) since every *metrical* stress is, as we shall see later, a unit which signals by its presence the occurrence of an independent metrical group (or foot). Nor do the four-syllable feet with one stress ("paeons") form independent meters, since, for phonetic reasons, they automatically receive a heavier stress on one of the weak syllables (next but one to the regular stress) and thus become iambic or trochaic.[17]

In the so-called "syllabic versification" used in the Romance languages and in several Slavic languages (French, Italian, Spanish, Polish, and in Russian up to the time of Tred'jakovskij and Lomonosov) the meter depends on two things: the number of syllables and an obligatory stress on the last syllable. If the line is divided into two hemistichs by a regular metrical pause ("caesura"), each hemistich has a constant number of syllables with a stress on the last syllable.

Let us take as an example Victor Hugo's eight-syllable line:

> Ainsi, quand tu fonds sur mon âme,
> Enthousiasme, aigle vainqueur,
> Au bruit de tes ailes de flamme
> Je frémis d'une sainte horreur ...

or the twelve-syllable, so-called "Alexandrine" line (6+6) of A. Chénier:

> Mon visage est flétri | des regards de soleil.
> Mon pied blanc sous la ronce | est devenu vermeil.
> J'ai suivi tout le jour | le fond de la vallée;
> Des bêlements lointains | partout m'ont appelé ...

It should be noted that in counting the syllables of French poetry one takes into account the so-called "mute *e*" (*e muet*), which is not usually pronounced in the colloquial language when it occurs in a final syllable (cf. above, ailEs, saintE). At the end of a word before a vowel, mute *e* is elided, e.g., Mon visag(e) est flétri ...or, sous la ronc(e) est devenu... In Italian poetry, when two vowels are in adjacent positions, either medially in a word or at the end of one word and the beginning of the next, they are grouped together to count as one syllable.[18] Consider the ten-syllable lines of Petrarch [Žirmunskij means the Italian hendecasyllable. Ed.]:

---

[17]   For further details in this connection, cf. B. Tomaševskij, *Russkoe stixosloženie*, pp. 15-16.
[18]   On elision in Italian poetry see footnote 6 on p. 180.

Voi ch'ascoltate *in* rime sparse *il* suono,
Di qu*ei* sospir*i* ond' *io* nutriva *il* core,
In sul m*io* primo giovenil*e* errore,
Quand' er*a in* part*e a*ltr' uom da quel ch'i' sono ...

The traditional classification of metrical systems is vitiated by serious inadequacies — first of all, by the lack of any uniform principle of classification. No one can object to the distinction made between classical verse, based on quantity (i.e., the "metrical" principle) and modern systems which in one form or another take account of stress (the "tonic" principle). It is true that the question of stress is raised in classical verse, where the terms "arsis" and "thesis" bear witness to the difference between rhythmically strong and weak syllables. In a dactyl, for example, the first syllable is strong, and a spondee in the hexameter line therefore has the arsis on the first long.[19] The theoretical part of this question, however, remains up to the present extremely confused, but, no matter how it was resolved in classical metrics, there can be no doubt that the verbal material of poetry was organized according to the principle of *quantitative* alternation and not as a regular sequence of word *stresses*. As for the principle of "syllabism", that is, the counting of syllables, it constitutes a type cutting across the preceding classification: it is possible, for instance, to have "tonic" versification which either does or does not keep a strict count of the syllables. Especially in the usual variety of "tonic" versification — in tonic iambic, anapestic, etc. — the number of syllables in a line also remains constant. On the other hand, however, there exists a special form of "tonic" verse, not included in the schemes of the traditional feet, in which the number of syllables in a line is a variable quantity, the only constant being the number of stresses. Such verse is to be found in German and Russian folksongs, German ballads, and lyrics close to the folk tradition (e.g. Heine's *"Die Lorelei"* or the so-called *dol'niki* of the most recent Russian lyrics).

Compare Heine's:

> ...Die Luft ist kühl und es dunkelt
> Und ruhig fliesst der Rhein,
> Der Gipfel des Berges funkelt
> Im Abendsonnenschein ...

or Blok's translation which reproduces exactly the stress pattern of the original:

[19] Cf. B. Kazanskij, "Učenie ob arsise i tezise", *Žurn. Min. Nar. Prosv.*, Aug. 1915.

> Proxládoj súmerki véjut,
> I Réjna tíx prostór.
> V večérnix lučáx aléjut
> Gromády dál'nix gór ...

Here each line has three constant stresses ("three-stress line"). The number of unstressed syllables between stresses, as well as the overall number of syllables in the line, is variable. We shall call such verse "pure tonic". Its general metrical scheme, which depends on the *number of stresses*, is indicated by the formula: $x \perp x \perp x \perp x$ ..., where x equals a variable quantity (x = 0, 1, 2, 3...).

In other cases, both the number of syllables between stresses and the overall number of syllables in the line can be constant. We shall call such a system "syllabo-tonic" (the term is N. V. Nedobrovo's), since it is based simultaneously on syllable count and on stress accent.[20] "Tonic" iambic, trochaic, dactylic and other meters belong to this system. If x = 1, we have a group of disyllabic feet, trochees or iambs, which are distinguished from each other by different beginnings (if the line begins with a stress, $x_1 = 0$: trochaic; if the line begins with an unstressed syllable, $x_1 = 1$: iambic). If x = 2, we have a group of trisyllabic feet — dactyls, amphibrachs, anapests — which are also distinguished by the manner in which the line begins (if the line begins with a stress, $x_1 = 0$: dactylic; if $x_1 = 1$: amphibrachic; if $x_1 = 2$: anapestic).

So-called syllabic verse also belongs, in actuality, to the syllabo-tonic system, since here too the metrical structure of the verse is not determined by the number of syllables alone, but by the recurrence after a specified number of syllables of the obligatory *stress*. In verse of this type, however, only the general number of syllables remains constant: the number of syllables between stresses — in other words, the distribution of the stresses — is variable. The number of stresses is also variable. In general, all stresses except the last one, which is obligatory, belong to the province of rhythm, i.e., to the diverse variations on the metrical scheme. Under

---

[20] N. V. Nedobrovo, *Ritm i metr*, p. 15. With regard to the history of this term it is curious to note that N. Nadeždin (*Versifikacija*, p. 516) had already used it in the same sense as N. V. Nedobrovo. He considers Russian folk poetry "tonic" and the system of Tred'jakovskij and Lomonosov "syllabic-tonic": "The entire difference between our early and modern versification resides uniquely in the fact that we always maintain isosyllabism in the construction of our lines; it would be correct to call our present versification '*syllabic-tonic*'." For a contrary opinion, cf. B. Tomaševskij, *Russkoe stixosloženie*, p. 41, where the origin of the term "syllabo-tonic versification" is explained by the circumstance that in Russian poetry "there reigns a dual system of versification": in the ternary meters — tonic, and in the binary meters — syllabic (?). On this problem cf. also A. Heusler, *Über germanischen Versbau*, pp. 29-30.

these conditions, therefore, one can continue to call this more liberal system of syllabo-tonic versification by the traditional term "syllabic".

We shall now undertake the study of verse theory, beginning with the syllabo-tonic system, since that is more familiar to us from classical Russian poetry of the eighteenth and nineteenth centuries and the predominant forms of German and English poetry.

II. SYLLABO-TONIC VERSIFICATION

5. RUSSIAN THEORETICIANS OF THE EIGHTEENTH AND NINETEENTH CENTURIES

The most ancient forms of poetry among the Germans and Russians were constructed on the purely "tonic" principle. Historically, the syllabo-tonic system arose among the Germans under the influence of the classical metrical schemes. The theoreticians and poets of the Renaissance regarded the alternation of strong and weak syllables in classical metrics as "correct" and disapproved of the primitive, archaic freedom of the old national form. They also borrowed from classical metrics the nomenclature of the meters (iamb, trochee, dactyl, amphibrach, anapest) used in traditional metrics both in the West and in Russia up to the present time. It is not surprising that the demand for regularity of alternation, called forth by new artistic tastes formed on classical models, should in both German and Russian conflict with the natural phonetic properties of the linguistic medium. As a result, the actual verse rhythm tends to deviate from the metrical scheme in two ways: by the omission of metrical accents and by the supplementary stressing of syllables where there is theoretically no metrical accent.

Classical Russian syllabo-tonic versification was introduced by Lomonosov and Tred'jakovskij, who followed German models. Lomonosov borrowed from Germany the classical names for the meters, examples of which were given by him in *Pis'mo o pravilax rossijskogo stixotvorstva* (1739). However, even the earliest theoreticians of Russian syllabo-tonic verse knew very well that the actual forms of Russian poetry were not covered by the nomenclature adopted — that in the iamb and trochee, for instance, the stresses prescribed by the metrical scheme could be omitted in actual practice. In such cases the Russian theoreticians usually speak of iambic and trochaic feet being replaced by *pyrrhics* (two unstressed syllables: ∪ ∪). Tred'jakovskij, in the second edition of his

Sposob k složeniju rossijskix stixov (Chap. I, § 18), wrote: "The feet most often used in our present versification are the trochee and the iamb. For both of these feet one can always — except in certain positions in certain kinds of verse, about which see below — place the *pyrrhic* foot, consisting of two short components, without which it would be impossible to compose a single line of our poetry." Tred'jakovskij is the first to offer an explanation for this phenomenon: "Such license is inescapable on account of our polysyllabic words, without which it would be almost impossible to write a line.".... (Chap. II, § 5). The use of the pyrrhic for the iamb and trochee is also mentioned by Sumarokov in his *O stopo-složenii, Collected Works*, vol. X, p. 55: "The length of our words justifies the writer in his use of the pyrrhic, for without this license one would not be able to compose verse. Though one may play the pedant for gaudy effects, such needless niceties are contemptible, and divert the author from good taste, causing him to seek for glory in a place where it never yet was, and spend his strength, to become a laughing-stock. The examples of the pyrrhic are very numerous..." Among these early theoreticians Lomonosov himself stands alone. It was to him that Sumarokov alluded in the above excerpt; for his concern that his iambic meter should be metrically exact led him to object in his *Pis'mo* to the use of the pyrrhic in poetry of the elevated style: "Pure iambic verse, though it may not be easy to write, nevertheless tends gently upwards, and magnifies the height, splendor, and nobility of the matter. It can nowhere be better employed than in triumphal odes, which I have done in my present work ..." Lomonosov admits the license of using the pyrrhic only in light verse: "I call those verses in which one may use the pyrrhic in place of an iamb or trochee irregular and loosely constructed. Such verses I use only in songs ..." In his own practice, Lomonosov really tried to abide by his rule: the *Oda na vzjatie Xotina* (1739) is written in pure iambics with extremely few exceptions. So is his *Večernee razmyšlenie o božiem veličestve* (1743):

> Licó svoë skryváet dén';
> Poljá pokrýla mráčna nóč';
> Vzošlá na góry čёrna tén';
> Lučí ot nás sklonílis' próč';
> Otkrýlas' bézdna zvézd polná,
> Zvezdám čislá net, bézdne dná ...

Gradually, however, he too frees himself from this "pedantry", and in the famous *Oda na den' vosšestvija na prestol imperatricy Elizavety Petrovny* (1749) he uses pyrrhics in a completely free manner.

The Russian theoreticians of the early nineteenth century accepted this point of view in toto. For example, we read in Vostokov's *Opyt o russkom stixosloženii* (1817, p. 55): "In the Russian language iambic and trochaic verses are always mixed with pyrrhic, which gives them, as compared with German iambs and trochees, greater variety." In this connection, D. Samsonov (*Kratkoe rassuždenie o russkom stixosloženii, Vestnik Evropy*, 1817, XCIV) mentions the differences in the treatment of disyllabic and trisyllabic meters: "Since in our polysyllabic words there is only one stress, while conjunctions and prepositions have none, it is permitted to replace high [stressed] syllables with low [unstressed] ones in the trochaic and iambic meters, except in the last foot. However, in those verses made up of three-syllable feet and mixed feet such liberties cannot be taken, since a great number of low syllables occurring side by side produces an unpleasant impression..." (228). Samsonov also suggests that poets be required wherever possible to make sure that two adjacent lines containing deviations from the meter should not have the deviations in the same position: "The ancients made it a rule that two lines of identical structure in their hexameters should never occur side by side. It seems that in our own practice it would not be a bad idea to avoid placing next to each other those iambic or trochaic lines which contain omitted stresses in one and the same foot." (241). In the *Slovar' drevnej i novoj poèzii* (vol. III, p. 495 f.), Ostopolov defends the rhythmic wealth and variety of the iambic meter against the champions of the hexameter by referring again to the omission of stresses: "It is in vain that some biased admirers of the ancient meters assert that the iambic meter can never equal them in value on account of its monotony; for one can say with assurance that this monotonous quality is imputed to the iambic meter only because up to the present time no attention has been paid to its variety. The *pyrrhic* foot, which is included within the framework of this meter, produces in it the same alterations as do the trochee and spondee in the hexameter..." And further on (498): "From these examples it is easily seen that our iambic verse, especially when it comes from the pen of a skillful writer, is not monotonous, and that other feet enter into its composition..." Finally, throughout the nineteenth century, even such "scholastic" authors as Klassovskij, Perevlesskij and others, writing at a time when Russian verse theory was at a low ebb, make more or less detailed reference to that same group of phenomena mentioned earlier by Tred'jakovskij and his contemporaries.

Thus in his *Simvolizm* (1910) Andrej Belyj's articles on the Russian iambic tetrameter did not contribute anything absolutely new to the theory of Russian verse. Belyj's contribution consists only in his having been the first to draw the necessary conclusions from the generally known fact of "deviation" and in his having subjected the structure of Russian verse to systematic investigation from this point of view. By his efforts he resuscitated the study of Russian versification and concentrated scholarly attention not on uniform and abstract metrical schemes, but on the vital multiformity of the real rhythm of Russian verse, which deviates in various directions from the particular prescribed scheme.

6. THE THEORY OF ANDREJ BELYJ

Andrej Belyj proceeds from the above-mentioned peculiarities of Russian iambic tetrameter. Let us look once more at the opening lines of *Evgenij Onegin*:

> Moj djádja sámyx čéstnyx právil,
> Kogdá ne v šútku zanemóg,
> On uvažát' sebjá zastávil
> I lúčše výdumat' ne móg ...

It has already been noted above that only the first line fulfils the requirements of the metrical scheme of iambic tetrameter, i.e., it stresses all four even-numbered syllables. In the second line a stress is omitted on the sixth syllable (zAnemog); in the third line the required stress is missing on the second syllable (on uvažat'); and in the fourth line it is again the sixth syllable which departs from the metrical pattern (vydumAT'). Andrej Belyj uses the term *rhythm* to designate the *sum total of deviations* from the metrical scheme.[1] There are many possible kinds of "deviation" in iambic tetrameter. The only indispensable stress in the line is the last one (the one on the eighth syllable), which signals the end of a line and is further marked by rhyme. Deviations may occur at the beginning or in the middle of a line; and, when considered in the context of adjacent lines, they may form various patterns with other deviations. Belyj believes that the rhythmic wealth and originality of any given poem are determined by the abundance of such deviations, by their variety and their rare and unexpected combinations.

Let us consider some examples of various "deviations" (more exactly, rhythmical variations) in iambic tetrameter.

1) The stress is most frequently omitted on the sixth syllable (i.e., on the third foot) — according to Belyj's calculations, in 40-60 % of all lines, on

[1] For the definition of rhythm as a system of deviations, cf. in particular *Simvolizm*, p. 396, and also pp. 259-260, 394.

the average. This mobility of stress on the penultimate foot results necessarily from the obligatory nature of the final stress. Cf. "I sé Minérva udarjáet" (Lomonosov); "Zlatája plávala luná" (Deržavin); "Bogát i sláven Kočubéj" (Puškin); "Beléet párus odinókij" (Lermontov); and many others.

2) The omission of the stress on the fourth syllable (i.e., on the second foot) is more frequently encountered, according to Belyj's observations, in Russian poets of the eighteenth century, more rarely in those of the nineteenth. Cf. "I klásy na poljáx gustéjut" (Lomonosov); "Na lákovom polú moëm" (Deržavin); "Gde róza bez šipóv rastët" (Deržavin); "Caréviču mladómu Xlóru" (Deržavin); "Vzdyxája, podnosít' lekárstvo" (Puškin); "Vzryvája, vozmutíš' ključí" (Tjutčev); and others.

3) On the other hand, the omission of the stress on the second syllable (i.e., on the first foot) distinguishes the poets of the nineteenth century from those of the eighteenth. Cf. "Dlja beregóv otčízny dál'noj" (Puškin); "Napominájut mné oné" (Puškin); "Iz gorodóv bežál ja níščij" (Lermontov); "Gromokipjáščij kúbok s néba" (Tjutčev); and so on.

Belyj believes that omitting the stress on the second syllable produces the impression of a quickening in the tempo (allegro), while a missing stress on the fourth syllable is perceived as a slowing down (andante) (263). Belyj's calculations indicate that in the poetry of the eighteenth century the second type occurs in about 20 % of all lines and the first in only 2-6 %. In the nineteenth century (beginning with Žukovskij) the incidence of the first type increases to 15-25 %, while that of the second decreases to 8-1 % of the lines. Of course, considerable fluctuation is to be observed in the work of individual poets who fall within these periods.[2]

---

[2]   In agreement with Belyj are the observations of P. Verrier, I, p. 67: if the stress falls at the end of a rhythmical group (accentuation croissante), the tempo is speeded up, but if it falls at the beginning (accentuation décroissante) the tempo is slowed. For a contrary view: R. Jakobson, "O češskom stixe", p. 22, where he points out the existence of various linguistic habits in this regard (e.g., in German and French). V. Čudovskij, *Neskol'ko myslej*, p. 68, considers this problem in connection with the general rhythmical inertia of the iambic tetrameter: "1) a line with an omitted stress on the third position shows a natural, easy support of the rhythm; 2) but a line with four stresses shows a forced support, a deliberately emphatic premeditation; 3) a line in which the first stress is left out has variety without abruptness, but it excludes any possibility of great expressiveness; 4) a line which omits the *second* stress reveals a rhythmical *contradiction*, which becomes very extreme when the line begins with a four-syllable word..." Similar observations on the rhythmical structure of the iambic tetrameter are made by F. Korš in his article on *Rusalka*, p. 724. B. V. Tomaševskij (*Ritmika četyrëxstopnogo jamba*, p. 156) calculates that in *Evgenij Onegin* 26.6 % of the lines have stresses 1, 2, 3, 4; 47.5 % — 1, 2, 4; 9.7 % — 1, 3, 4; 6.6 % — 2, 3, 4; 9 % — 2, 4; and about 0.5 % on 1, 4. A. Belyj's calculations are not expressed by him in percentages (pp. 286-287) and are given here in round numbers.

More rarely, one encounters lines in which two stresses are omitted simultaneously.

4) Stresses omitted on the second and sixth syllables (first and third feet): "Bogopodóbnaja carévna" (Deržavin); "Nižegoródskij meščanín" (Puškin); "I na porfírnye stupéni" (Tjutčev); "Kak nezažžënnoe kadílo' (Sologub); and others.

5) Stresses omitted on the fourth and sixth syllables (second and third feet): "Vozljúblennaja tišiná" (Lomonosov); "I klánjalsja neprinuždënno" (Puškin); "Kak démony gluxonemýe" (Tjutčev); and others.

Belyj found that the majority of eighteenth-century writers used the first type in only 1% of their lines, while those of the nineteenth century increased its usage to 5-12%. The second type is, on the contrary, generally very rare. In nineteenth-century poets there are only scattered examples of it, and in the eighteenth century it may have accounted for 1-2% of the lines. There is no record at all of a line in which the stress is omitted simultaneously on the second and fourth syllables (first and second feet). Belyj himself composed an artificial example: "I velosipedíst letít".

Belyj's terminology for this group of rhythmical variations in iambic meter is rather unstable and is fashioned after the tradition of old Russian metrics. Sometimes he speaks not of an omitted stress but of a *half stress*, sometimes of an *acceleration* of the foot in question, more often of the replacement of the iamb by a *pyrrhic*, which, as was demonstrated earlier, can occur in the second, fourth, or sixth foot. In some cases Belyj considers two iambic feet to be a larger unit — an iambic *dipody* (see below, § 13 and 25); then, when a stress is omitted, one has instead of two iambic feet a four-syllable foot — either *paeon I* or *paeon II* — with a stress on the second or fourth syllable.

In addition to omitting a stress, one can also shift it from a metrically strong (even) to a metrically weak (odd) syllable, or give more prominence to an odd syllable by placing a supplementary stress on it. Belyj terms the first instance the replacement of an iamb by a *trochee* ($\perp$ –); the second he regards as the use of a *spondee* (two stressed syllables: $\perp \perp$). In both cases the supplementary stressing of a metrically weak (odd) syllable occurs only when that syllable is a monosyllabic, stressed word. In the great majority of cases it occurs in the first syllable of the line.

Examples:

Supplementary stress on the first syllable (*spondee* instead of iamb): "Švéd, rússkij, kólet, rúbit, réžet" (Puškin); "Smért' dščér'ju t'mý ne nazovú ja" (B.); "Dúl séver, plákala travá" (F.); "Gúl táncev c gúlom razgovórov" (B.); "Drúg čéstnosti í drúg Minérvy" (Deržavin); and others.

Shift of the stress from the second syllable to the first (*trochee* instead of iamb): "Bój barabánnyj, kríki, skréžet" (Puškin); "Mýsl' izrečénnaja est' lóž'" (Tjutčev); "Dén' večeréet, nóč' blizká" (Tjutčev); "Vnóv', osněžĕnnye kolónny" (Blok); "Kázn' oskorbíteljam svjatýn'" (Brjusov).

7. THE GRAPHIC METHOD

For the purpose of ascertaining the reciprocal relationship of rhythmic deviations in a poem Belyj proposes a special graphic system. The rhythmic variations are entered on a grid in which each horizontal row represents one line of verse and each vertical column represents a foot. Each omitted stress is plotted according to the foot in which it occurs. Straight lines are then drawn connecting the plotted positions, both from one line of verse, to the next and within the same line (if there are two omitted stresses in one line). The sum total of the deviations — that is, the rhythm of the given poem — is shown by the resulting curve. Take for example the lines of Tjutčev:

> Osénnej pózdneju poróju
> Ljubljú ja Carskosél'skij sád,
> Kogda on tíxoj polumglóju
> Kak by dremótoju ob"ját.
> 5. I belokrýlye vidén'ja,
> Na túsklom ózera steklé,
> V kakój-to nége onemén'ja
> Kosnéjut v ètoj polumglé ...
> 9. I na porfírnye stupéni
> Ekateríninskix dvorcóv
> Ložátsja súmračnye téni
> Oktjábr'skix ránnix večeróv.
> 13. I sád temnéet, kak dubróva,
> I pri zvezdáx iz t'mý nočnój
> Kak ótblesk slávnogo bylógo,
> Vyxódit kúpol zolotój.

If we now consider the rhythm of this poem as represented graphically on the accompanying chart (Fig. 1), we see a continuous broken line showing considerable fluctuation, which is typical of the "luxurious rhythm" of Tjutčev. When the rhythmic deviations are "meager", the line straightens out on the third foot, where omissions are especially common, or it is interrupted at those rows which constitute orthodox

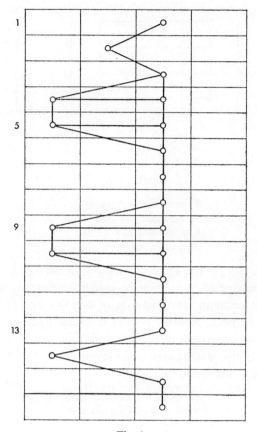

Fig. 1

metrical lines (i.e., verses without any deviations: for example, "Moj djádja sámyx čéstnyx právil"). When the rhythmic deviations are exceptionally "meager", there are only solitary points interspersed among numerous metrical lines. Take, for instance, Brjusov's lines: (the omission is in the first foot of the second line).

> I ráz moj vzór suxój i strástnyj
> Ja uderžát' v pylí ne móg;
> I on skol'znúl k licú prekrásnoj
> I óči béglo ej obžëg ...

Deviations in adjacent lines form various "figures" on the diagram. Thus (returning to the Tjutčev lines) lines 4-5 and 9-10 are united to form a "square" (pyrrhic on the second and fourth foot: 2, 4—2, 4). [Sic. Žirmunskij clearly means, as he indicates on the diagram, that the pyrrhic

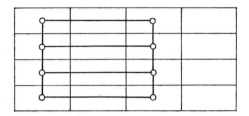

Fig. 2

is on the first and third foot, *Ed.*] Several "squares" one after the other constitute a "ladder". Cf. Sologub's lines (Fig. 2):

> Ty nezamétno proxodíla,
> Ty ne sijála i ne žglá.
> Kak nezažžënnoe kadílo
> Blagouxát' ty ne moglá ...

In lines 3-4 or 8-9 [of the Tjutčev] we have, in Belyj's terminology, the figure of a "rectangle" (more exactly, a right-angle triangle), where the "pyrrhic" feet occur in the third foot of one line and in the first and third feet of the next. Another type of the same figure is to be seen in lines 5-6 or 10-11 (pyrrhics in the first and third feet of one line and in the third foot of the next). Lines 1-3 compose a "small angle", lines 13-15 a "large angle". Lermontov's lines:

> Ne ángel li s zabýtym drúgom
> Vnov' povidát'sja zaxotél

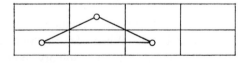

Fig. 3

are an example of what Belyj calls a "roof" (Fig. 3). The lines by Puškin:

> I Táne už ne ták užásno,
> I, ljubopýtnaja, tepér'
> Nemnógo rastvoríla dvér' ...

are recorded as a "diamond" (Fig. 4). Each figure, composed of lines of various types, has its own rhythmical effect, just as did separate lines containing different rhythmic variations. According to Belyj, the rhythmical style of each poet is determined by an unconscious preference for

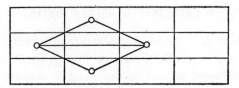

Fig. 4

lines or figures of a certain type. Belyj examines an identical sample
from each poet (arbitrarily set at 596 lines) and, by counting the number
of lines of various rhythmic constructions and the number of figures,
derives a numerical indicator which serves to characterize the rhythmical
style of any given poet. The abundance, variety and rarity of the figures
chosen distinguish poets with "rich", original rhythm. Tjutčev stands
first among the poets of the nineteenth century in this regard, and,
among our contemporaries, Sologub. As examples of poets with "meager"
rhythm, Belyj cites A. K. Tolstoj, Brjusov, and several others. If the
number of lines of a given type or figures of a given type in one poet come
close to those of another poet, then the two poets are regarded by Belyj
as having affinities. Such comparisons may indicate either simple
resemblance in rhythmic style or the existence of a definite tradition.
Thus, "on the basis of the main criteria determining rhythm", Sologub
resembles Fet on the one hand and, on the other, Baratynskij. Baratynskij
and Jazykov parallel each other in a great many rhythmical devices and
therefore "belong to one rhythmical school". The similarity of their
numerical indices to those of Puškin show that "this school, of course,
is that of Puškin". But both types differ from Puškin in, for example,
"the extremely large number of accelerations in the first foot (164 and
126, respectively)" and in "the extremely small number of accelerations
in the second foot (4 and 13)". The corresponding figures for Puškin are
110 and 33 (p. 347). One of the characteristic traits of Tjutčev is his
tendency to return to the style of Deržavin. Among the poets of the
Puškin epoch it is Tjutčev who most frequently employs the "pyrrhic"
in the second foot (the "andante" type habitual with the poets of the
eighteenth century), which causes a corresponding increase in the number
of figures containing a "point" in the second column (e.g., the "roof";
p. 353). Such comparisons showing degrees of similarity or divergence
among various poets constitute for Belyj the basic "comparative rhythmical morphology" of Russian iambic tetrameter (cf. pp. 330-395).

8. CRITICISM OF BELYJ'S SYSTEM

It is impossible to deny the great importance of A. Belyj's work for the study of Russian verse. Belyj was the first to challenge the abstract schemes of traditional metrics by disclosing to students of poetry the actual multiformity of rhythmic variations within the Russian iamb, variations which completely determine the individual rhythmical style of a given author or work. For the study of rhythm Belyj developed a method which is, in essence, altogether correct: rhythm, conceived of as changing and individual, is examined *against the background* of meter, which is general, constant, and unalterable. Furthermore, Belyj himself undertook a systematic description of iambic tetrameter in Russian poetry from the eighteenth to the twentieth centuries and attempted to formulate his results statistically. Belyj's undoubted contributions are, however, inseparable from certain basic methodological shortcomings and mistakes which have exerted great influence on the further development of Russian metrics. On the one hand, some superficial blemishes have concealed the outstanding merits of the book and have laid it open to the harshest criticism; on the other, Belyj's students and followers have erected his mistakes into a fullblown system which in its onesidedness is no less pernicious for the theory of Russian verse than was the abstract schematism of traditional metrics. Thus, one must criticize Belyj's work if only for the purpose of freeing the fruitful and significant *kernel* of his theory from the external *accretions* which are an obstacle to the proper solution of the problems broached by him.[3]

1) The most successful feature of *Simvolizm* is the graphic method and the calculations connected with it. The principal shortcoming of the graphic method as proposed by Belyj is that it allows no possibility of registering, along with "omissions" of stresses, the "supplementary stressing" of weak syllables, which is no less essential from the point of view of rhythm. Even if we noted the additional stresses by a special sign (by an asterisk *, for example) we should not be able to include them in the general system of notation, which takes account only of figures formed by the omission of stresses (pyrrhics). This, of course, is the radical inadequacy of the whole graphic system: it notes not the presence of stresses but only their absence ("omissions, deviations"). Furthermore, Belyj's tables indicate nothing about the division of poems into stanzas.

---

[3]   Cf. for example the harsh review by V. Brjusov, *Apollon*, 1910, No. 11, p. 52; and also V. Čudovskij, *Neskol'ko Myslej*, p. 56.

But rhythmical figures are grasped most clearly within lines belonging to one stanza. The boundaries between stanzas considerably weaken the connection between consecutive lines, and the bringing together of such lines into one rhythmic figure is hardly more than a conventional graphic device, in no way reflecting the actual perception of the rhythm (cf. the "rectangle" in lines 4-5, 8-9 [*Sic.* Žirmunskij means in 3-4, 8-9. It should be noted that of these two figures, which Žirmunskij has more correctly labeled "right angle triangles", the first is within a stanza while the second straddles the boundary of two stanzas. *Ed.*]

2) Belyj based his work on the completely correct assumption that the individual rhythmical style of a poet is expressed in his unconscious preference for certain rhythmic variations over others. In the same way, long before Belyj, Sievers and his students used statistical analysis of certain rhythmic types of four-stress alliterative verse as an auxiliary means of determining the authorship and chronology of old Germanic poems.[4] But the statistical method is meaningful only when applied to "large numbers". In his statistics, however, Belyj deals with comparatively small samples of 596 lines in which figures of a certain kind sometimes occur 5 or 10 times. It is quite possible that such small differences result from the operations of chance.[5] Nor are we guaranteed against accidental fluctuations arising out of the heterogeneity of the material studied: different poetic genres — odes, elegies, epistles, songs, epic, or long lyric poems — can have their own rhythmical characteristics, which are ignored in Belyj's analyses; and this is all the more important since such characteristics depend directly on the form and size of the stanza (compare the stanza of *Evgenij Onegin* or of long lyric poems with the ordinary stanza of four lines). All these considerations render the statistics of the figures wholly dubious. In individual cases where the rhythmical deviations are especially sharp and characteristic, this method can of course point out those traits which are actually inherent in the verse of various poets. The statistical analysis of the different types of line is more convincing; although, in view of the limited number of such types,

[4] For Sievers' statistical method, cf. his *Zur Rhythmik des germanischen Alliterationverses* (*Beowulf*); Paul-Braune, *Beiträge zur Geschichte der deutschen Sprache und Literatur*, X, pp. 209 ff., and also M. Cremer, G. Herzfeld, F. J. Mather and others on the question of the authorship of *Kynewulf* (M. Trautmann, *Kynewulf*, 1898, p. 6).
[5] On the statistics of the figures cf. B. Tomaševskij, *Pjatistopnyj jamb Puškina* (in the collection *Očerki po poètike Puškina* [Berlin, 1923]). According to Tomaševskij, the figures are the result of a fortuitous combination of lines of various types: in any given poet the number of figures always coincides with a number that can be calculated in advance for the given combination on the basis of probability theory.

it is not especially fruitful for the characterization of an individual rhythmical style.

3) From the theoretical point of view the fundamental defect of Belyj's work lies in those subjective evaluations which recur again and again in *Simvolizm*, interrupting the objective scientific description of rhythmical types. For Belyj some figures are "more harmonious", others are less "refined to the ear" (pp. 273, 316). The "square" turns out to be "more perfect" than the figure of the "roof" (324), the "ladder" still better than the "square". A zig-zag fluctuating line "is a mark of rhythmical wealth" (267) while isolated points or an entirely straight line testify to poverty of rhythm. The more varied the rhythmical deviations from the meter, the more unusual and complicated the figures produced by the deviations, the "richer" is the poet's rhythm, — that is, not only objectively more hetero-geneous but also "better" in an artistic sense. The classification of Rus-sian poets into four categories according to the merits of their rhythmic patterns is based on the number and variety of the figures showing on Belyj's graphs (275). It must, however, be clear that there are in essence no good or bad rhythms, just as there are no worthy or unworthy metrical forms. The poet is free to choose a trochee or an iamb depending on what his artistic purpose is. In exactly the same way the rhythmical purpose of the poet might at one time be best accomplished by using the rhythms of Tjutčev, rich in "deviations", but at another time by emulating the poems of Brjusov, with their great number of metrical stresses.[6] In its place the metrically "correct" line: "I grjánul bój, Poltávskij bój!" is just as perfect as a deviation like "I velosipedíst letít" might prove to be in another context. We grasp Puškin's particular rhythmical intention when he brings the poem *Obval* to a close by heaping up metrically orthodox lines:

> ... I pút' po něm širókij šël
> I kón' skakál, i vlëksja vól,
> I svoegó verbljúda vël
>   Stepnój kupéc,
> Gde nýne mčítsja liš' Èól,
>   Nebés žiléc. . .

Furthermore, not only in the abstract theory but also in the poetic practice of Belyj and his students, this appraisal of rhythmical deviations led to a chase after "pyrrhics" and "paeons", after extraordinary and totally unmotivated rhythmic devices. The historical reason behind such

---

[6] Cf. V. Žirmunskij, *Valerij Brjusov i nasledie Puškina*, 1922, pp. 42-44.

subjective preferences on the part of Belyj and many of his contemporaries is completely clear. It is allied to the general tendency of the period toward the rhythmical deformation of syllabo-tonic verse, toward eliminating the tedious uniformity of "correct" metrical stresses and the equally tedious rhythmical deviations of the more usual sort (e.g., dropping the stress on the third foot). In the work of contemporary poets this tendency appears under one guise in the development of the so-called *dol'niki*, i.e., in the struggle against the syllabic principle. It is evidenced again in the sharp deformation of the iambic tetrameter, which is to be noted in the preference for the less usual omission of stresses on the fourth and sixth syllables of the same line (the so-called combination of "paeon II" and "paeon IV"), or even in the use of a trochaic word initially in an iambic line, which was inadmissible in classical Russian metrics (cf. V. Brjusov: "Tajna? — Ax, vot čto! Kak v romane ja" or Sergej Bobrov: "Voin, moi prezrevšij gromy"). Hence also the subjective preference shown for the unusual rhythms of Tjutčev. Even in the reading of classical iambs or ternary meters one can recognize the characteristic aesthetic preferences of our time: for example, in the apportionment of a special rhythmical stress to metrically weak syllables ("V *čas* nezabvennyj, v čas pečal'nyj"). Note also those cases in which a supplementary stress falls on a totally insignificant word, which is probably very far from any accord with the feeling for rhythm of the Puškin era (e.g., "*Kak* nad gorjačeju zoloj" or "*On* uvažat' sebja zastavil"). But even if the preferences of Belyj and his contemporaries are perfectly admissible as an expression of the tastes of our age and its creative tendencies in poetry, it is nevertheless altogether inadmissible from a scientific point of view that the subjective aesthetic prejudices of today should be elevated to the status of an objective criterion for judging the past or even into a self-styled theoretical system. Andrej Belyj and his followers begin with the assertion that lines like "Ty nezamétno proxodíla, / Ty ne sijála i ne žglá" (the "square" chart) are *better* than lines like "Oná vošlá stopój nespéšnoj / Kak tól'ko žrícy vxódjat v xrám" (two "metrically correct" lines), that is, that "*rhythm*" is better than "*meter*". This is only one step away from the doctrine according to which meter does not exist at all, since meter is merely a fiction thought up in textbooks on versification; according to which there is only rhythm which — unlike meter — genuinely exists and produces an esthetic impact. The confusion in this idea is aggravated by the ambiguity of the word "rhythm", which is not clarified in Belyj's *Simvolizm*; on the one hand rhythm is defined in a wide and indeterminate sense as "the expression of the natural lyricism of the poet's soul (the spirit of music)" (p. 244); on the other hand, rhythm is defined in a more exact and technical way as the sum-total of deviations from the meter (p. 397). The unwarranted identification of these two concepts leads to the conviction that the poet demonstrates the natural lyricism of his soul, the spontaneous freedom and originality of his talent, by his "*violations*" of the monotonous, abstract schemes of so-called "school metrics".

In the light of this it becomes especially obvious that one must revise the very definition of rhythm proposed by Belyj: "By the term poetic rhythm we understand a symmetry in deviations from the meter, that is, a certain complex homogeneity of deviations" (p. 396). The unusual definition of rhythm as "deviations", i.e., the use of a purely negative criterion, grew quite naturally out of the methods employed in studying rhythm, regarded as an individual, changeable phenomenon against the background of a stable and generalized metrical scheme. The corresponding positive side of this idea was discussed earlier: rhythm is the actual alternation of stresses in verse and results from the interaction of an ideal metrical pattern with the inherent phonetic characteristics of the given linguistic material. The definition of rhythm as the actual alternation of stresses in verse as opposed to meter — an ideal regularity, an abstract scheme — is in complete accord with Belyj's basic idea, and it saves that idea from the unsuccessful formulation which has occasioned much misunderstanding and some unjust attacks.

4) Special attention has to be devoted to the terminology used by Belyj in discussing rhythmical "deviations": "paeons", "replacement" of an iamb by a pyrrhic, spondee or trochee, etc. We shall consider this question in the light of its broad theoretical significance somewhat later when we are not limited to the work of Belyj and his students. The problem of how stresses are to be counted also has general theoretical importance, since this considerably influences the results of statistical analysis (in the poem quoted above consider, for example, such dubious cases as "KAK BY dremotoju ob"jat" and especially the compound words, "...CARSKOsel'skij sad ... tixoj POLUmgloju ... BELOkrylye viden'ja"). This will be treated in greater detail in Chap. III.

9. RHYTHM AND METER IN BINARY METERS

The methodological principles expounded in *Simvolizm*, where they were related to the iambic tetrameter, can be used as the basis for studying other meters of Russian poetry. In doing so, one discovers considerable difference between the rhythmical characteristics of the binary meters (two-syllable feet — iambs and trochees) and those of the ternary meters (three-syllable feet — dactyls, amphibrachs, anapests).

In all binary meters the rhythmic variations consist, in most cases, of weakening the stress on certain metrically strong syllables ("omission" of metrical accents). The last stress, however, which marks the line boundary and is itself marked by rhyme, always remains intact. The stress is most frequently dropped on the next to last foot, the penultimate; other stresses are more rarely discarded, their omission depending on the character of the meter itself or on the rhythmical style of a given poet.

In the iambic trimeter, where the stress on the sixth syllable remains intact, it is the stress on the fourth syllable which is most often omitted. A line of six syllables bearing stresses on the second and sixth is the most usual variation of the iambic trimeter. It is extremely rare to encounter an omitted stress on the second syllable.[7] Consider Puškin's epistle to his sister *K sestre*:

> Ty xóčeš', drúg bescénnyj,
> Čtob já, poét mladój,
> Besédoval s tobój,
> I s líroju zabvénnoj,
> 5. Mečtámi okrylënnoj,
> Ostávil monastýr'
> I kráj uedinënnyj,
> Gde neprerývnyj mír
> Vo mráke opustílsja,
> 10. I v pústyni gluxój
> Bezmólvno vocarílsja
> S ugrjúmoj tišinój!...

Lines 1 and 2 have three metrical stresses, line 8 is the rare example of an omitted stress on the second syllable, and the other nine verses are of the predominating type (with the stress dropped on the fourth syllable).

The iambic hexameter is divided by a regular metrical cut ("caesura") into two hemistichs which can each be regarded as an independent iambic trimeter verse ($- \acute{} - \acute{} - \acute{} / - \acute{} - \acute{} - \acute{}$). For the second half-line all the rules of the ordinary iambic trimeter are in effect: the stress on the twelfth syllable is always intact, the stress on the tenth is most frequently dropped, and the eighth syllable loses its stress comparatively rarely. These rules cannot be applied to the first half-line without special reservations. The

---

[7] According to the calculations of G. Šengeli (*Traktat*, p. 138) Puškin's *Gorodok* has all three stresses in 41.5% of the lines, stresses 1 and 3 in 57.1%, and 1 and 2 in 1.4%. [*Sic*. Žirmunskij means that feet 2 and 3 were stressed in 1.4% of the lines. *Ed.*]

reason for this is that the stress before the caesura is in Russian poetry not so absolutely indispensable as is the last stress in the line. In those poems where it is more or less stable, the middle stress (on the fourth syllable) of the first hemistich is discarded with a proportional frequency. As for the initial stress (on the second syllable), it is usually rather stable $(- \acute{\;} - - - \acute{\;})$. In other poems where the stress before the caesura (on the sixth syllable) is less regular, the stress on the fourth syllable becomes correspondingly more regular $(- \acute{\;} - \acute{\;} - -)$. Ordinarily, of course, there is a mixture of both types with one or the other predominating. Cf. Puškin's *Osen'* (Type 1):

> Oktjábr' už nastupíl; ‖ už róšča otrjaxáet
> Poslédnie listý ‖ s nagíx svoíx vetvéj;
> Doxnúl osénnij xlád, ‖ doróga promerzáet;
> Žurčá eščë bežít ‖ za mél'nicu ručéj,
> 5. No prúd užé zastýl; ‖ soséd moj pospešáet
> V ot"éžžie poljá ‖ s oxótoju svoéj —
> I stráždut ózimi ‖ ot béšenoj zabávy,
> I búdit láj sobák ‖ usnúvšie dubrávy.

In the second hemistich there is a clear predominance of the type with a stress missing on the middle syllable: cf. lines 1, 3-8. Line 2 has all three stresses. There is no example of a stress omitted from the initial foot (on the eighth syllable). In the first halfline the predominating pattern also shows absence of stress on the middle foot ("poslednie listy"): cf. lines 1, 2, 6, lines 3, 4, 5, and 8 have all three stresses, but in two cases (lines 4, 5) the middle stress is also weakened and the line approximates closely the predominant type ("Žurča *eščë* bežit ... No prud *uže* zastyl"). There is only one instance of a line in which the foot before the caesura bears no stress (7 "I stráždut o*zimi* ‖ ot bešenoj zab**a**vy): at the outset of the final couplet of the octave this unexpected rhythmical effect is utilized as an individual sort of cadence. (Cf. the analogous device in line 15: Kogd**a** pod sobo*lem* ‖ sogreta i sve**ž**a ...).

Puškin's epistle *K vel'može* can serve to exemplify type II:

> Ot sévernyx okóv ‖ osvoboždája mír,
> Liš' tól'ko na poljá, ‖ strujás', doxnët zefír,
> Liš' tól'ko pérvaja ‖ pozelenéet lípa, —
> K tebé, privétlivyj ‖ potómok Aristíppa,
> K tebé javljúsja já, ‖ uvížu séj dvoréc,
> Gde církul' zódčego, ‖ palítra i rezéc
> Učënoj príxoti ‖ tvoéj povinovális'
> I vdoxnovénnye ‖ v volšébstve sostjazális' ...

In the second hemistich the predominating type (with a stress on the eighth and twelfth syllables) is shown by lines 4, 6, 7 and 8. Lines 2 and 5 have all three stresses. The rarer form with omission of the initial stress (on the eighth syllable) is to be seen in lines 1 and 3 ("... osvoboždaja mir").

In the first hemistich three stresses are encountered in line 5. The absence of the middle stress, normal for type I, is to be noted only in lines 1-2. The omission of the stress before the caesura, which is characteristic of type II, occurs four times (lines 3, 4, 6, 7: cf. "liš' tol'ko pervaja ..."). In addition, line 8 shows the lack both of the caesura stress and of the first stress (on the second syllable): "I vdoxnovennye..." $(- - - \acute{} - - \, || \, ... \,)$.[8]

In iambic pentameter the arrangement of stresses is more complex. With the final stress (on the tenth syllable) remaining constant the most frequent stress to disappear is the penultimate (on the eighth syllable). The three other stresses are distributed differently in different kinds of verse. In this connection one must distinguish two varieties of iambic pentameter: in one the line has a caesura after the second foot (after the fourth syllable) as, for example in *Boris Godunov* and *Gavriiliada*; in the other there is no constant caesura in the line, as in Puškin's *Rusalka*, *Domik v Kolomne*, the little tragedies, and other poems. (Concerning the caesura see below, § 24). Of the first three stresses the most frequently omitted is the second (on the fourth syllable), especially in the caesural iamb: cf. in *Boris Godunov*: "Svidételem || gospód' menjá postávil ... On, kážetsja, || pokínul vsë mirskóe... Ty výmučit' || odná moglá priznán'e"; in *Mocart i Sal'ieri*: "Ne sméja pomyšljat' eščě o sláve... I nóvoj vysotý eščě dostígnet". Even more often, especially in lines with the caesura, one encounters the simultaneous omission of stress on the fourth and eighth syllables $(- \acute{} - - \, || \, - \acute{} - - - \acute{})$. Cf. in *Boris Godunov*: "I létopis' || okónčena mojá... Pečál'naja || monáxinja caríca... Deržávnymi || zabótami naskúčil... I knížnomu || iskússtvu vrazumíl... Pravdívye || skazán'ja perepíšet..." It is rarer to find a stress omitted on the second syllable in caesural iambic: "Narjažený || my vméste górod védat'..." Especially rare is the omission of a stress on the sixth syllable: "Ja znáju tvój || gosepriímnyj dóm..." Equally rare are lines in which these omissions (in the second and eighth syllables) occur together or with one of the above types: "A za grexí, || za témnye deján'ja" or "I nakonéc

---

[8]   G. Šengeli (p. 171 ff.) obtained the following results. For the first hemistich: stresses 1, 2, 3 in 28.5% of the lines, stresses 1, 3 in 30.6%, stresses 1, 2 in 30.9%, stress 2 in 5%, stresses 2, 3 in 5.2%. For the second hemistich: stresses 4, 5, 6 in 34.6%, stresses 4, 6 in 62%, stresses 5, 6 in 3.6%. Cf. further G. Šengeli, *Morfologija russkogo šestistopnogo jamba* (*Kamena*, Khar'kov, 1918, No. 1).

|| po mílosti svoéj". In lines without the caesura these variations occur considerably more often. In particular, there is a notable rise in the number of lines containing a weakened sixth syllable — for example, in *Mocart i Sal'ieri*: "Rebënkom búduči, kogdá vysóko... Dostígnul stépeni vysókoj. Sláva..." The presence of a constant caesura forces the poet to choose words of particular rhythmical form and measure and, by the same token, imposes greater uniformity on his use of rhythmical variations.[9]

Supplementary stressing of weak syllables occurs in all varieties of iambic lines, but principally, as was demonstrated, in the first foot. One must distinguish between *displacement* of the stress from the second to the first syllable (in Belyj's terminology, substituting a "trochee" for an iamb) and the supplementary stressing of a metrically weak syllable, in which case the following syllable *keeps* its stress (exchanging a "spondee" for an iamb). Type I: *Vsë* za edínyj blagosklónnyj vzgljád... *Zját'* palačá i sám v dušé paláč... *Rús'* obnjalá kičlívogo vragá... (Puškin). Type II: *Vést'* vážnaja i ésli do naróda... *Dní* pózdnej óseni branját obyknovénno... *Spój*, Mèri, nám unýlo i protjážno... *Króv'* bródit, čúvstva, úm toskóju stesnený... *Zvúk* líry Bájrona razvléč' edvá ix móg... (Puškin).

In the second case the additional stress must of necessity always fall

[9]   Cf. the figures arrived at by G. Šengeli (p. 156 ff.) for Puškin's noncaesural iambic pentameter in the "small tragedies":

All five stresses	25% of the lines
1, 2, 3, 5	22.8%
1, 3, 4, 5	13.4%
1, 2, 4, 5	10.3%
1, 3, 5	11.1%
2, 3, 4, 5	7%
2, 4, 5	2.2%
2, 3, 5	6.4%
others	1.7%

For the caesural iambic pentameter of *Boris Godunov*:

All five stresses	19.2%
1, 2, 3, 5	30.7%
1, 3, 4, 5	9.3%
2, 3, 4, 5	7.3%
2, 3, 5	9.2%
1, 3, 5	19%
1, 2, 4, 5	3.3%
2, 4, 5	1.1%
1, 4, 5	1.4%

B. Tomaševskij's work on Puškin's iambic pentameter is known to me only through a lecture read at the Russian Institute of Art History.

on a monosyllabic word, which must be sufficiently independent to maintain its own special stress (concerning the reduction of stress in monosyllables cf. § 18). But in the first case also, where one could expect at the beginning of the line disyllabic or trisyllabic words, one finds in fact only monosyllables. It is possible, for instance, to have "*Bój* barabánnyj, kríki, skréžet" but impossible to find "*Kríki* pobédy, smértnyj skréžet". A reasonable explanation of this would seem to be that the monosyllabic word in the first example, even though it is independent in meaning and undoubtedly stressed in pronunciation, can be subordinated to the dominant syntactic (and metrical) stress on the fourth syllable, while in the disyllabic word (kríki) the first stressed syllable clearly prevails over the following unstressed syllable, and the distortion of the meter is much more perceptible. In Russian poetry of the eighteenth and nineteenth centuries there is no example of the use of a disyllabic trochaic word appearing in the initial position in an iambic line.[10] Among twentieth century poets, however, one can find isolated attempts at such artificial distortions of the iambic meter: Brjusov, "'*Tajna*?' — Ax, vot čtó! Kak v románe ja...;" Sergej Bobrov, "*Žízni* cvetúščie zabóty"; Adalis, "*Zóri* begút čerez ozëra" and so on.

Supplementary stressing of weak syllables in the middle of an iambic line is encountered far more rarely. Thus in all of *Evgenij Onegin* B. Tomaševskij counted only 19 cases where the stress is indisputably on an autonomous monosyllabic word. Cf. Puškin's lines: "Pod néj *snég* útrennij xrustít... Monastyrjá *víd* nóvyj prinimál... Plenít' umél *slúx* díkix parižán..." and several others. Somewhat more frequent in iambics is the positioning of a hypermetrical stress on an odd syllable after the caesura, though this is still not so common as at the beginning of the line: thus the beginning of the hemistich is subject to rules analogous to those which operate at the beginning of the entire line. Cf. in the iambic hexameter: "Skučná mne óttepel' || *vón*', grjáz', vesnój ja bólen..., I části setovál || *sám* jásno vídel ón..., Byl nékto Ándželo || *múž* ópytnyj, ne nóvyj..." Or the iambic pentameter: "*Vsem* vól'nyj vxód, || *vsé* gósti dorogíe..., Dimítrija? || *Kák*? Étogo mladénca?..., Kljanús' tebé! — || *Nét*, Šújskij ne kljanís'..." Sometimes, even without a caesura, a strong syntactic pause midway in the line is sufficient to compel us to perceive

---

[10] On stress shift in the disyllabic prepositions and conjunctions, and also in compound words, cf. §§ 19-20, and the following works: B. Tomaševskij, *Ritmika četyrëxstopnogo jamba*, pp. 173-74; *Russkoe stixosloženie*, p. 27; G. Šengeli, p. 38 ff., p. 50 ff.; R. Jakobson, "O češskom stixe", p. 29.

the beginning of a sentence as the beginning of a rhythmical unit permitting hypermetrical stress. Cf. in *Mednyj vsadnik*:

> ... Ráz on spál
> U névskoj prístani. — Dní léta
> Klonílis' k óseni ...

Or in *Andželo*: "No kák? — *Zló* jávnoe, terpímoe davnó..." and so on.

Hypermetrical stresses on metrically weak syllables are encountered
much more frequently in some poets of the eighteenth century. Deržavin
is an example of this, and that is why his poetry often impresses us as
being labored and, as it were, retarded by rhythmical interruptions.
Consider, for example, *Evgeniju. Žizn' Zvanskaja*:

> Baráškov v vózduxe, v kustáx *svíst* solov'ëv,
> *Rëv* kráv, *gróm* žëln i konej ržán'e ...

Or, from the same source: To v másle, to v sotáx *zrjú* zláto pod vetvjámi...
Rumjano-žëlt piróg, *sýr* bélyj, ráki krásny... Žnecóv pojúščix, žníc
pólk ídet s polosý... Or again: Bez žálosti *vsë* smért' razít... V šinkí *pít'*
mëdu zajezžáju... and many others.

In the trochaic, as in the iambic, the last stress is obligatory and the
stress on the penultimate foot is most often left out; in the trochaic
tetrameter, for instance, the most frequently omitted stress is that on the
fifth syllable. Also very common in the trochaic tetrameter is a lessening
of the stress on the first syllable, so that the trochaic line is not infrequently limited to two stresses — on the third and seventh syllables.
(In Belyj's terminology: the trochaic tetrameter is transformed into two
feet of the paeon III type). Cf. Puškin's lines:

> Skvoz' volnístye tumány
> Probiráetsja luná.
> Na pečál'nye poljány
> L'ët pečál'no svét oná.
> Po doróge, zímnej, skúčnoj,
> Trójka bórzaja bežít.
> Kolokól'čik odnozvúčnyj
> Utomítel'no gremít ...

The dominant type (with a stress on the third and seventh syllables) is to
be seen in lines 1, 2, 3, 7, 8. Omission of the stress only on the fifth
syllable: line 6. Only on the first syllable: line 5. All stresses in place:
line 4. There is no example in this excerpt of a stress omitted on the fourth
syllable ("paeon I") [Sic. Žirmunskij obviously means third syllable], and
this in general is an extremely rare occurrence in the trochaic tetrameter.

Cf. in Puškin's verse tales (*skazki*), for example: Mésjac pod kosój blestít... Zá morem žit'ë ne xúdo... and several others.

A special role is played in the trochaic meters by the shift of the first stress to the second syllable (replacement of the first trochaic foot by an "iamb"). This rhythmical variation occurs in verses which imitate the folk tradition with its rhythmically more liberal handling of the verbal material. Cf. Kol'cov's lines:

> ... *Krasávica* zór'ka
> V nébe zagorélas'...
> ...Já sam drúg s tobóju
> *Slug*á i xozjáin...

Or Nikitin's *Dolja Bestalannaja*:

> Dólja bestalánnaja
> *Ves' dén'* potešáetsja,
> Rastolkáet sónnogo,
> *Vsju nóč'* nasmexáetsja.
> *Grozít* múkoj-bédnost'ju
> *Sulít* dní tjažëlye.
> *Smotrét'* velít sókolom
> Pésni pét' vesëlye...

Or Nekrasov's *General Toptygin*:

> ...Pribežáli toj porój,
> *Jamščík* i vožátyj...
> ...Zavoróčalsja v sanjáx
> *Mixájlo* Iványč...

When it is sung — especially this is true of the modern *častuška* — the iambic beginning of a song [Sic! Ed.] frequently undergoes a reversal of the stresses ("Na goré stoít aptéka — *Ljúbov'* súšit čelovéka...") This applies particularly to words that bear little stress. Brjusov exhibits this device in his urban songs:

> *Óna* sérdce ne vzjalá
> I s drugím gulját' pošlá...
> Prosižú do útra v skvére
> *Óna* výjdet iz toj dvéri...

Cf. also Nikitin's: *Ódna nóčen'ka bezzvëzdnaja.*[11]

[11] G. Šengeli (p. 176) reports the following results for Puškin's trochaic tetrameter in his verse tales:

All four stresses	23.3%
1, 2, 4	31.7%
2, 3, 4	19.9%
2, 4	23.1%
others	2.2%

On *Rusalka*, cf. F. Korš, p. 645 ff.

Of the binary meters the iambic is much more widespread in Russian poetry than is the trochaic. For the poets of the eighteenth century the iambic hexameter was for the most part regarded as heroic verse: it was used in the epic and in high tragedy, but also in the lyric genres, e.g., in the elegy and the idyll (cf. Sumarokov). In Russian poetry, as in German, paired iambic hexameter couplets take the place of the French Alexandrine line. The iambic tetrameter was originally the meter of the ode; at the end of the eighteenth and the beginning of the nineteenth century it gradually took over the lyric genres (at first the comic tale, and later the romantic poem written in the grand style). During the Puškin era it was the predominant meter. The iambic pentameter is chiefly adapted to the drama (dramatic blank verse, under the influence of the Shakespearian play) and also to the stanzaic forms deriving from Italy such as the sonnet, octave, terza rima (the Italian "decasyllabic" [*endecasillabo*, *Ed.*]). In English poetry iambic pentameter couplets replace the heroic line of the era of classicism. As for the trochee, after Tred'jakovskij's ill-fated attempt to have it adopted as the heroic meter (in the first edition of his *Novyj Sposob*), it retained an independent but very limited function in lyric poetry. From the second half of the eighteenth century on the trochee is used, among other places, in verse written in imitation of Russian folk poetry and this determines its choice as the meter for such ballads as Puškin's *Besy* and *Utoplennik* as well as in his fairy tales in verse.

10. TERNARY METERS

In contrast to the binary meters, the ternary meters do not, as a general rule, omit metrical stresses. Only in exceptional cases is the metrical stress discarded from a lightly stressed syllable of some polysyllabic word (most often, from a compound word); but even then such a syllable, surrounded as it is by two syllables bearing no stress at all, receives a slight stress. Cf. Nekrasov's verses:

> Trevolnén'ja mirskógo dalëkaja
> S nezemným vyražén'em v očáx.
> Rusokúdraja goluboókaja,
> S tíxoj grúst'ju na blédnyx ustáx...

The only more or less customary weakening of the metrical stress occurs in the first foot of a dactylic line. Cf. Fet's

> V véčer takój zolotístyj i jásnyj,
> V ètom dyxán'i, vesný vsepobédnoj

> *ne* pomináj mne, o drúg moj prekrásnyj,
> *ty* o ljubví našej, róbkoj i bédnoj...

In the second line the stress on the first syllable is already greatly weakened; in the third and fourth lines the weakening is even more noticeable.

Again from Fet:

> Drúg moj, ja zvëzdy ljubljú
> *i* ot pečáli ne próč'...

And again:

> Mne tak otrádno s tobój!
> *ne* otxodí ot menjá...

Similarly an excerpt from Nekrasov's *Saša*:

> *iz* pererúblennoj stároj berëzy
> Grádom lilísja proščál'nye slëzy
> *i* propadáli odná za drugój
> Dán'ju poslédnej na póčve rodnój...

Or, from the same source:

> ...V *ne*doumén'i taščát murav'í
> Čto ni popálo, v žilíšča svoí...

This variety of dactyl with a regular lessening of the initial stress is sharply distinguished, so far as rhythm is concerned, from those lines which always begin with a fully stressed word:

> Mésjac zerkál'nyj plyvët po lazúrnoj pustýne
> Trávy stepnýe unízany vlágoj večérnej.
> Réči otrývistej, sérdce opját' suevérnej.
> Dlínnye téni vdalí potonúli v ložbíne...

On the other hand, the ternary meters differ from the binary in allowing much wider scope to hypermetrical stressing of metrically weak syllables. Especially common is the supplementary stressing of the first (unaccented) syllable in the anapest, both in monosyllabic and disyllabic words. The additional stress in this case varies in strength depending on the degree of independence and the semantic weight of the initial word in question.

Cf. the lines of Fet:

> Unosí moë sérdce v zvenjáščuju dál',
> Gde, kak mésjac za róščej, pečál'!
> V *ètix* zvúkax, na žárkie slëzy tvoí
> *Krótko* svétit ulýbka ljubví.
> O, ditjá, kak legkó sred' nezrímyx zybéj

Doverját'sja mne pésne tvoéj!
Výše, výše plyvú serebrístym putĕm,
Budto šátkaja tén' za krylóm...

The strongest additional stress occurs on the initial dissyllabic words in lines 4 and 7, where we find the completely independent *krótko* and *výše*. The stress in lines 3 and 8 is weaker on *v ètix* and *budto*. In comparison with the following unstressed syllable, the weakly stressed monosyllables *gde* and *o* in lines 2 and 5 show a slight strengthening. Cf. lines taken from other poems by Fet: *Nóč'* lazúrnaja smótrit na skóšennyj lúg... *Trét'ja* s námi — lazúrnaja nóč'... *Sérdce* róbkoe b'ĕtsja trevóžno... *Dólgo* snílis' mne vópli rydánij tvoíx... *Dén'* prosnĕtsja i réči ljudskíe... Note the following from Nekrasov's *Rycar' na čas*: *Žáždoj* déla dušá zakipáet... *Sóvest'* pésnju svojú zapeváet... *Mésjac* pólnyj plyvĕt nad dubrávoj... *Vódy* járko blestját sred' poléj. Cf. also, from Puškin's *Budrys*, the beginning of both hemistichs in which there is a strong caesura:

...*Déneg* s célogo svéta, ‖ *súkon* járkogo cvéta...
...*Snég* na zémlju valítsja, ‖ *sýn* dorógoju mčítsja...

This strong opening of the line, when it is more or less consistently maintained throughout an entire poem, becomes as it were part of the metrical scheme (in Brjusov's terminology: anapest with a trochaic *base*). Cf. Puškin's

P'jú za zdrávie Méri,
Míloj Méri moéj.
Tíxo záper ja dvéri
I odín, bez gostéj,
P'jú za zdrávie Méri.
Móžno kráše byt' Méri,
Kráše Méri moéj,
Ètoj málen'koj péri,
No nel'zjá byt' miléj
Rézvoj, láskovoj Méri...

This sort of supplementary metrical stress is also encountered internally within the body of the line, both on monosyllabic and disyllabic words. Cf. Fet's: Ne tebé *pésn'* ljubví ja pojú... Liš' odín v *čás* večérnij, zavétnyj... To — Avvadón, *ángel* bézdny zemnój... Okružús' ja togdá *gór'koj* sládost'ju róz... Cf. also Nekrasov's *Rycar' na čas*: Vsjá belá, vsjá vidná pri luné... *Dá*, ja vížu tebjá, *bóžij* dóm... S golovój, *búrjam* žízni otkrýtoju... Na detéj *mílost'* bóga zvalá... and others. As an example of an unusually extreme distortion of a ternary meter N.V.

Nedobrovo (*Ritm i metr*, p. 19) cites Fet: *Vsë* sorvát' *xóčet* véter, *vsë* smýt' *xóčet* líven' ruč'jámi... ("Istrepalisja sosen..."). This line is represented schematically as follows: ⏑ – ⏑́ | ⏑ – ⏑́ | – ⏑ ⏑́ | ⏑ – ⏑́ | – – ⏑́ | – [the hyper-metrical stresses being indicated by grave accent marks]. It is, however, clear even from this example that the prevailing metrical stresses of the ternary meter, regularly recurring as they do on every third syllable, possess much greater power than does the occasional rhythmical weighting of ordinarily unstressed words. In other cases, which practically constitute a majority of the examples of "weighting" adduced by Belyj's followers, a lightly stressed word (even though it is disyllabic) is completely overshadowed by the predominating metrical stress adjacent to it and loses its independence as well as much of its stress (in varying degrees, naturally). Examples: "Prixodí, *moja*-mílaja króška... Tý o ljubví-*našej* róbkoj i bédnoj... Ja sovétuju gnát'-*eë* próč'... Zovët *menja* vzgljádom i kríkom svoím..." and so on. (Further details below, § 19).

The ternary meters were little used by the Russian poets of the eighteenth century. During the Puškin era the amphibrach and the anapest became more widespread as ballad meters, owing largely to the influence of English models; cf. Žukovskij's *Zamok Smol'gol'm*, Puškin's *Čërnaja šal'* and *Pesn' o veščem Olege* (ballad compositions). In Puškin's ternary meters supplementary stressing plays an extremely limited role. Thus, in the two poems named above there is, as an example within the line, only "S glavý eë mërtvoj *snjáv* čërnuju šál'...", and on the first unstressed syllable of the amphibrach: "*Knjáz'* pó polju édet na vérnom koné... *Knjáz'* tíxo na čérep konjá nastupíl..." Ternary meters were first given wide currency by Lermontov, then by Fet and Nekrasov, and in recent times by Bal'mont and partly by Blok. In the case of the latter they are in competition with the *dol'niki*. During the second half of the nineteenth century ternary meters become rhythmically more varied — especially in the poetry of Fet.

In the terminology of Belyj and his successors, a variation in a ternary meter is usually referred to as the replacement of one trisyllabic foot by another one equivalent to it. If, for instance, the metrical stress on the first syllable of a dactyl is omitted, they speak of the *replacement* of the first dactylic foot by a *tribrach* (– – –). When there is supplementary stressing the anapest, amphibrach or dactyl is said to be replaced — in some cases, by an *amphimacer* (or *cretic*), in others by a *bacchius* or *antibacchius*. Thus if the extra stress falls on the first syllable of an anapest we have an *amphimacer* (⏑́ – ⏑́); "*Dólgo*, dólgo za ním ja sledíl" (Nekrasov). If it falls on the first syllable of an amphibrach, an *antibacchius* results ($\overset{\perp}{-} \overset{\perp}{-} -$): "*Knjáz'* pó polju édet na vérnom koné..." The line by Fet cited above, which attracted the attention of N. V. Nedobrovo, is in this terminology an aggregation of the following feet: I — cretic, II — cretic, III — bacchius, IV — cretic, V — anapest (cf. Nedobrovo, p. 19). The terminology which is used in this book has in its favor the advantage of being brief and simple. In any ternary meter we are able to speak of a *supplementary stress* on the *first* or *second* of the metrically weak syllables *within* the line, or on the corresponding syllable preceding the first stress in the line.

A comparison of the rhythmical variations of the binary and ternary meters provides the clue for the so-called "deviations". Tred'jakovskij himself, as already mentioned, was quick to call attention to the length of Russian words. According to the calculations of the most recent theoreticians of verse, the average length of a Russian word (or more exactly, of an accentual or stress group) in a sample of ordinary prose is somewhat less than three syllables (about 2.7).[12] A Russian word of average size, therefore, is comfortably accommodated in a ternary meter; a more extended group (of four syllables, for example) can be used in combination with a two-syllable group. In the binary meters, on the other hand, if the metrically strong syllables are all stressed, longer words cannot be used: even a trisyllabic group with the stress on the first or third syllable (golová, gólovy) cannot be fitted into the iambic or trochaic metrical scheme. Thus, the "deviations" noted by Belyj arise as a result of the *resistance* of the linguistic *material*. In such cases of conflict between the metrical scheme and the natural phonetic characteristics of the language the *actual rhythm* results as a sort of compromise. Analogous examples are to be seen in the versification of other peoples (see below, § 15).

11. THE FIGHT AGAINST METER

A. Belyj's investigations into the iambic tetrameter, and also the works of his successors, have led to a reconsideration of traditional doctrines concerning Russian verse. Those parts of Belyj's teaching which have had the greatest impact on the most recent theories of rhythm and meter have proved to be those which were in tune with the general spirit of the literary era: the preference shown for original and *recherché*

---

[12] According to G. Šengeli, there is an average of 2.7 syllables for every stress in prose; according to V. Čudovskij, 2.86. Cf. Šengeli, p. 10.

rhythms and, in general, the various devices employed to deform the syllabo-tonic line, and, along with this, the unconscious identification of rhythm as the "expression of the natural lyricism of the poet's soul" with rhythm as a system of "deviations" from meter. As a result, the conviction gained ground that the very concept of "meter" and "metrics" was inherited from the days when the schoolmaster was dominant in matters of versification, that it was based on the improper application of the terms used in classical metrics, and that as a matter of fact the only thing existing in verse was its actual rhythm. This being the case, the task of the investigator consisted in describing the multiformity of the rhythmical forms without ever relating them to an abstract metrical scheme. What, really, is Puškin's iambic tetrameter (as in *Evgenij Onegin*, for instance) if this meter, conventionally regarded as uniform, actually breaks down into iambs, trochees, spondees, pyrrhics, and paeons II and IV? Or, to use other terms, what gives us the right to speak of iambs in verse where even syllables might occur with no stress, while odd syllables frequently carry supplementary stresses not prescribed by the metrical pattern? The theoretical muddle of those days was compounded by the appearance of the so-called *dol'niki*, that is, verses in which the very principle of syllable counting was invalidated (in Brjusov's work and later, especially in that of Blok and Axmatova). The theoretical confusion may be seen in various forms in the articles of N. V. Nedobrovo, V. A. Čudovskij, and several others.

In his article "Ritm, metr i ix vzaimootnošenie" (*Trudy i Dni*, 1912, No. 2) N. V. Nedobrovo quotes a great many isolated lines from Puškin, Baratynskij and Tjutčev which depart from the required metrical scheme of the iambic tetrameter, and sums up his investigations as follows: "If we seek to determine what, in any metrical scheme, constitutes the unassailable stronghold of rhythm, we see that that stronghold is nothing more than one syllable in each line, namely, the last syllable stressed according to the metrical pattern: it alone is consistently stressed while the other "accented" syllables quite often do not carry the stress, which may, on the other hand, fall on any weak syllable. But if this be true, then, from the above mentioned point of view of those who would defend metrics, one must formulate some such definition as this: the iambic tetrameter is a verse meter in each line of which the eighth syllable from the beginning carries an obligatory stress and is the last stressed syllable in the line. But by means of such metrical definitions we shall end up with purely syllabic verse. That, however, is inevitable, if we are to deny the possibility of having beautiful poetry with violated meter" (p. 19). ..."If you agree with me and say that an examination of Russian metrics forces one to admit that Russian verse is syllabic and that all the phenomena of stress properly belong to the area of rhythm, then it remains for me to demolish syllabic verse also by demonstrating that it is possible to have beautiful poetry which also violates the syllabic rules." As an example, he cites Tjutčev's *Poslednjaja ljubov'* (cf. below, § 31).

One can for the time being disregard the second part of these arguments: *Poslednjaja ljubov'* is an example of *dol'niki* written in accordance with the purely "tonic" principle of counting the stresses while leaving a varying number of unstressed syllables between them. The existence in poetry of various systems of versification does not in itself represent anything impossible (e.g. Russian literary and folk poetry), and the development of one system alongside another or even at the expense of another cannot constitute a reason for doubting the existence of the older system. The first part of Nedobrovo's arguments boils down to the assertion that in Russian poetry (especially in iambics) each syllable except the last stressed one can be indifferently stressed or unstressed and that, consequently, the meter of Russian syllabo-tonic verse is identical with that of the French so-called "syllabic" system. Although this identity is asserted in a purely hypothetical form, it poses a problem which must be solved if we are to construct a theory of Russian verse.

The most extreme point of view among those who oppose "school metrics" is held by V. A. Čudovskij (cf. especially his article *Neskol'ko myslej k vozmožnomu učeniu o stixe, Apollon*, 1915, No. 8-9). He rejects the concept of "meter", in the traditional sense of the word, as the opposite of "rhythm" — and especially the concept of the "foot". The actual rhythmical unit, he asserts, is the line. The principle of poetic composition is different for classical poetry and for that of modern European nations. In the "metrical" versification of antiquity the line was constructed "without any regard for words as such, but simply as a sequence of *arbitrary* time-units, called feet, which did not coincide with "living" words. There was likewise no account taken of the natural stress, but there was a distinction of the long and short syllables." In this system, "the foot is identical with the musical measure", and for that reason one can call classical metrics "melodic" or "odometric". In contradistinction to the "melodic" poetry of classical times, modern poetry is based on "narration" (*skaz*): in this "narrative" or "logometric" system the simplest unit is not the foot but the word. In all modern literatures the line is built as a sequence of *living spoken words*, which are completely inviolable, and the rhythm is determined by the natural stress and length of the word.".... "The line represents a combination of certain elements. The line itself is obviously indivisible; it is a unit. Of what? — Of feet, answers the school doctrine. It is my opinion that the whole trouble lies in this answer. — Not of feet. But of *words*. — The foot does not exist. There is no such thing in Russian versification." If Russian versification, says Čudovskij, had developed not in the times of Lomonosov and Tred'jakovskij, when an artificial attempt was made to import an "alien and preconceived theory", but during the time when Russian poetry was in flower, during the Puškin era, for example, then not one investigator "would ever have thought up the concept of the *foot*." And Čudovskij proposes that the modern investigator undertake the study of how verse is composed of *words* (pp. 58-60).

In the theory of Čudovskij the rejection of "school metrics" leads logically to extremes which themselves constitute the best arguments to demolish the basic tenets of his whole theory. If verse were really composed of "inviolable words" (arranged in an arbitrary order) there would be nothing to distinguish it from prose. According to this notion, any newspaper article would be constructed on the "logometric principle". It is obvious that some kind of order, some kind of general law which determines the alternation of stressed and unstressed syllables, does after all operate to distinguish poetic speech from prosaic. One must formulate this law first of all: for it determines, in our versification, the very choice of "living, inviolable words"; and that is the first task of metrics.

Even Čudovskij cannot remain altogether consistent in his rejection of the organizing role played by the metrical scheme. He says somewhat later: "The Russian verse line is a sequence of living, inviolable words, so arranged that the stressed positions partially coincide with *certain rhythmical sequences*" (!); "for example, in the so-called iambic meter the stresses fall on the even syllables, but not on each even syllable, this being left to the fairly free choice of the poet" (p. 61). Thus, after sweeping rejections, the author is obliged to return to the starting point, to the system of A. Belyj: "certain rhythmical sequences" (that *is* meter!) with which there is "partial coincidence" (apparently, along with partial "deviation" from the "scheme" of the line) of the actual (i.e. "rhythmical") stresses of the line.

And so the task of the investigator, as was noted earlier, is to define that ideal "rhythmical line" with which, in the words of Čudovskij, the stresses of the "living inviolable words" "partially coincide". By means of this we shall be able to establish the general *law* governing the alternation of stresses in the line, i.e., its abstract *metrical scheme*. In order to construct such a scheme it is necessary to indicate those minimal conditions which are sufficient to impart to the line a distinct rhythmical structure — or, in other words, those organizing elements in the absence of which verse loses its rhythm and ceases to be verse.

According to the idea expressed by N. V. Nedobrovo in hypothetical form, the Russian verse line is defined by the number of syllables and the constant, obligatory stress on the last syllable. If these conditions actually were sufficient, one could rearrange the words within the line, keeping the same number of syllables, and the stress on the last syllable, and the verse would not be disturbed by this. In the iambic tetrameter, for instance:

> Moj djádja sámyx čéstnyx právil,
> Kogdá ne v šútku zanemóg,
> *Uvažát' sebjá on zastávil*
> *I výdumat' lúčše ne móg...*

It is obvious that while the rhythmical "deviations" in the second line ("omission" of the stress on the syllable ZA — in the word "zanemog") do not change the nature of the verse, the shifting of stresses from the even to the odd syllables in the third and fourth lines (uvažat' sebja... vydumat' lučše) disrupts the iambic movement and destroys not only the meter but the rhythm itself. Thus, not any and every distribution of stresses is admissible on the first seven syllables of the Russian iambic tetrameter and in this fact we observe its difference from the "syllabic" French octosyllable.

12. THE THEORY OF RUSSIAN SYLLABO-TONIC VERSE

Wherein did N. V. Nedobrovo err in identifying Russian verse with French "syllabic" verse — in particular, the iambic tetrameter with the French octosyllabic line?

1) The followers of A. Belyj greatly exaggerate the number and significance of "deviations" from the meter. In many cases, as we shall see later, "deviations" — especially those which at first glance appear to be unusually rare — can be explained by incorrect reading or counting of stresses, or, when the reading permits various shades of emphasis, by an unconscious preference for those shades of emphasis which constitute a deformation of the syllabo-tonic pattern (cf. below, § 17). All this is related o the current trends in literary taste which were mentioned above (cf.

§ 8). In reality, even in the binary meters which permit far more "deviations" than the ternaries, there are definite rules and limitations which prevent the disruption of the meter and at the same time lend support to the rhythmic organization of the verse.

2) In the overwhelming majority of cases, the "deviations" in the binary meters amount to omissions of stress ("replacement" of an iamb or trochee by a "pyrrhic") which produce the rhythmical variation and which are least apt to disorganize the line. In a certain line the stress may be missing from a given foot, but, to compensate, it may occur in the corresponding place in the preceding and following lines (though it may be absent from the other feet in those lines); it is this which creates that "inertia" of the rhythm on even syllables in the iambic, on odd in the trochaic, which N. V. Nedobrovo mentioned, correctly regarding it as the basis for our perceiving the meter (cf. p. 22: "meter is the inertia of rhythm"). This, too, is the essence of Čudovskij's formula: "In the so-called iambic meter the stresses fall on the even syllables, but not on each even syllable, the choice being left fairly free." Of course not on each even syllable; nevertheless, as is proved by the work of A. Belyj, Tomaševskij, Šengeli and others, the stresses in binary meters are, with the exception of the penultimate stress, omitted in relatively few cases. (Šengeli calculates that, for instance, Puškin in his longer poems written in iambic tetrameters shows the following average frequency of stress omissions: on the second syllable — 13 to 17.5%; on the fourth — 4.5 to 11%). The stresses that are present are thus completely sufficient to establish the impression of rhythmical inertia on the even syllables. Each even syllable in the iambic meter, even though it does not in fact bear a stress, is perceived by us as a syllable *stressed in principle* because of the rhythmical inertia of the whole poem. This is obvious if only from the fact that every displacement of stress from an even to an odd syllable is felt to be a violation of the metrical pattern and a deformation of the rhythm. This perception of a syllable as *stressed in principle* applies also, of course, to the penultimate stress in iambic or trochaic lines. Although in the iambic tetrameter the sixth syllable loses its stress in at least 50% of all lines, it would nevertheless be inaccurate to consider the metrical scheme of the so-called iambic tetrameter as consisting of two iambs with a paeon IV ($- \acute{-} - \acute{-} - - - \acute{-}$); there are always sufficient stresses present for us to regard the sixth syllable also as *stressed in principle* and as participating in the general iambic movement of the line. A displacement of the stress to the adjacent odd syllable is in this case also perceived as a violation of the metrical law.

3) The supplementary stressing of metrically weak syllables ("replacement" of an iamb by a "trochee" or "spondee") is simply a corroboration of these general principles. As has already been shown, such hypermetrical stressing is subject to a great many conditions and limitations, which protect the general rhythmical movement of the line from being disrupted. The chief limitation on the distribution of such stresses is that they occur only in monosyllabic words: one encounters the line "*Dní pózdnej óseni branját obyknovénno*" but not such a line as "*Rádosti óseni branját obyknovénno*". Furthermore, a monosyllabic word, even one with a full lexical meaning, can in a syntactic construction be subordinated to the predominating syntactic stress of the adjacent word (e.g. bòj-barabánnyj..., gùl-táncev s gulom razgovorov), while a disyllabic or a polysyllabic word ("radosti oseni...") has so precise a hierarchy of prosodic elements within the word itself as to render impossible any toning down — in line with metrical conformity — of the hypermetrical stress. Moreover, as was said earlier, the majority of the examples with a supplementary stress on an odd syllable show such stressing on the *first syllable* in an iambic line; *within the line* this phenomenon is limited to a few scattered examples. Besides, the first foot of the most diverse meters — not only in Russian verse but also in German, English and others — plays a special role, being to a certain degree metrically "ambiguous": the movement of the rhythm has not yet been unequivocally laid down, since it is only from the second foot that a regular repetition of a definite movement can be said to have begun. In any case, at the beginning of the line the rhythmical stressing of a metrically weak syllable and even the shift of a stress are much less perceptible than in the body of the line. Finally, and this is most important, displacement of stress or the presence of an additional stress in a metrically weak position (even when such precautions and limitations are observed), is always felt by us to be an individual rhythmical deviation from the norm. A line such as "V *čás* nezabvénnyj, v cás pečál'nyj" is perceived by us as a deformation of the normal rhythmical movement, as an impediment to the regular alternation of stresses, as a "displacement" confirming the presence in our consciousness of a definite metrical norm, in accordance with which we read each line. Such displacements are common when special emphasis is required, when an emotional or logical stress falls on a metrically weak syllable in order to bring out the word in question: "V *čás* nezabvénnyj, v *čás* pečál'nyj". For that reason it is most common in dramatic poetry, where emphasis, rhetorical stressing or logical foregrounding of a word may enhance the expressiveness of an idea, for the sake of which the

metrical regularity of the line is disrupted: "*Dá*, Dón-Guána mudrenó priznát'..." Or: "*Któ* podkupál naprásno Čepčugóva? *Któ* podoslál obóix Bitjagóvskix?..." Or: "*Vsém* vólnyj vxód, *vsé* gósti dorogíe!..." Of course, the impression of "divergence" from the norm is heightened when the rhythmical stresses occur on odd syllables within the line: it is for this reason that we feel Deržavin's verse, as compared with that of Puškin, to be especially "encumbered". If some contemporary poets begin an iambic line with a disyllabic trochaic word, a device which Puškin and his contemporaries did not permit (Brjusov: "*Tájna*? Ax, vót čto! Kak v románe já..."), it is to be interpreted precisely as a deformation of the line, i.e., it is one more exception confirming the rule. As is clear from German and especially from English verse, our rhythmical consciousness is in this respect very flexible, and is conditioned by the literary tradition in question; the presence of a metrical norm can still be felt when the deviations from the metrical norm are far greater than is the case in Russian iambics (cf. below, § 15).

Hypermetrical stresses on unaccented syllables (i.e. in metrically *weak* positions) in ternary meters (e.g. at the beginning: "*Dólgo* snílis' mne vópli rydánij tvoíx" or, more rarely, in the middle: "Okružús' ja togdá *gór'koj* sládost'ju róz"), are likewise perceived as an interruption of the rhythm, as an impediment to the regular movement of the line. It must be mentioned, however, that in the ternary meters the rhythmical inertia of the stresses, regularly recurring on every third syllable, is much more strongly felt than in the iambic or trochaic meters, and the metrical stress generally overshadows the supplementary stress, except in a few cases where a special logical emphasis is required (cf. below § 19). A reading which highlights all the hypermetrical stresses in such a line as "*Vsë* sorvát' *xóčet* véter, *vsë* smýt' *xóčet* líven' ruč'jámi" is a fashionable affectation (again characteristic of the modern inclination to deform the "correct" syllabo-tonic meters).

4) The arguments of N. V. Nedobrovo and others who deny the real significance of metrical schemes are usually based on isolated, anomalous, but artistically beautiful verses which violate the metrical regularity of alternating stressed and unstressed syllables. But no line taken in isolation, out of the context of the whole poem, can reveal the metrical pattern. Only the entire poem exhibits that inertia of the rhythm, that general rhythmic impulse, those regularities of rhythmic movement which we call meter. As a matter of fact, an isolated line not only has no meter, but it does not even show the presence of rhythm; all it shows is the alternation of the natural word stresses. This is clear from the examples

of metrically ambiguous lines which have been repeatedly adduced by theoreticians. Let us take the line, "V zavétnuju *ix* citadél'." Considered outside its poetic environment, as a bit of prosaic speech, this phrase has two strong stresses on the second and eighth syllables and another considerably weaker one on the fifth (*ix*). When put into the context of amphibrachic verse it becomes an amphibrach line: because of the metrical inertia of the stress on every third syllable, the stress on the word *ix* becomes heavier.

> Kak nýne sbiráetsja véščij Olég
> V zavétnuju íx citadél'...

In a poem written in iambics the same phrase is perceived as an iambic tetrameter, with the hypermetrical stress on *ix* weakened as much as possible. Thus, in Tjutčev's lines *A. F. Gilferdingu*:

> V akademíčeskie stény,
> V zavétnuju ix citadél'...

Regardless of the fact that this line actually occurs in an iambic poem by Tjutčev, taken from the poem it becomes metrically neutral; its rhythmical interpretation depends wholly on the rhythmic inertia of the poem. In one case it is an amphibrachic trimeter with a slightly reduced second stress, in another it is an iambic tetrameter with "omission" of the stress on the fourth and sixth syllables. Moreover, as has already been mentioned, the reading itself is altered basically. More important, however, is the change in our perception of the linguistic material and of its rhythmical groupings: in one instance this material is perceived in accordance with a specific rhythmic sequence having a stress on the second, fifth and eighth syllables, i.e., on every third syllable; in the other instance, in accordance with a totally different rhythmic sequence, with the stress on every second syllable. Only our consciousness of the metrical rule, to which we *relate* a given sequence of syllables, creates *rhythm*, i.e., converts the natural alternation of speech stresses into a regular cadence.

The same phenomenon may be observed in any other example of a word-group consisting of eight or nine syllables with predominant stresses on the second and eighth syllables, e.g. "Kak démony gluxonemýe..." or "I klánjalsja neprinužděnno..." and so on. Divorced from their proper contexts these lines are rhythmically ambiguous, amorphous; but in iambic or amphibrachic poems they carry the corresponding rhythmical movements. Cf.:

Iambic:

Kak démony gluxonemýe
Vedút besédu mež sobój

or:

Legkó mazúrku tancevál
I klánjalsja neprinuždënno.

Amphibrachic:

Kak démony gluxonemýe
Besédu vedút mež sobój

or:

Mazúrku legkó tancevál
I klánjalsja neprinuždënno

G. Šengeli adduces analogous examples for the ternary meters and for purely tonic verse (*Traktat o russkom stixe*, 2d. edition, pp. 66-68). One and the same phrase is given different rhythmical interpretations, depending on whether it occurs in the context of an *anapestic* pentameter or dactylo-trochaic *hexameter* (concerning this latter see § 32 below).

Anapest:

Poburévšie l'dý razošlís', rasstupílis' pred úst'em,
I polúdennyj vétr polyxáet vesénnim teplóm, —
Nyne čërnyj korábl' na svjaščënnoe móre nispústim...

Hexameter:

Býstro k nemú obratjás', veščál Agamémnon mogúčij:
Síl'nyx izbrávši grebcóv, na korábl' gekatómbu postáviv,
Nýne čërnyj korábl' na svjaščënnoe móre nispústim...

In the first case the word *nýne* has the customary hypermetrical stress on the first syllable of the anapestic pentameter; in the second case the word covers the entire first ("trochaic") foot of the dactylo-trochaic hexameter line.

Consider another example of the same kind:

Anapest:

Opustílis' tjažëlye túči
Šël ves' dén' utomítel'nyj dóžd'...

Hexameter:

Túči Kroníon sgustíl, i pod xládnym dalëkim Boréem
Šël ves' dén' nad ravnínoj, izmúčennoj žáždoju, líven'...

This shows that such metrically ambiguous phrases as "*Nyne čërnyj korabl'*" or "*Šël ves' den'*", taken in isolation, are rhythmically amorphous; *they have no rhythm*. Rhythm appears only through the subordination of the natural word stresses to a definite metrical pattern, i.e., it exists only in the poem as a whole, in the interrelationship between a given line and the analogous rhythmical cadence of a whole group of lines.[13]

In actual practice, of course, this does not mean that the meter or rhythm of a poem emerges only in reading the entire poem, strophe or group of strophes. Within an established literary tradition we always have sufficient experience to recognize the meter at once, that is, to interpret correctly a given alternation of stresses by relating it to a known metrical type. For example, the variations of the iambic tetrameter are sufficiently common for us to immediately perceive and assimilate as iambs such diverse alternations of stress as "Na lákovom polú moëm" or "I v vysoté iznemoglá", or "V čás nezabvénnyj, v čás pečál'nyj", or "I grjánul bój, Poltávskij bój". It is this fact which makes possible poems of one line, the so-called "monostich", constructed on the basis of a familiar and clearly defined metrical system. Cf., for example, the monostich of Ausonius (hexameter): "Rím zolotój, obítel' bogóv, mež gradámi pérvyj" (translated by Brjusov, *Opyty*, 123). If, however, we were to put ourselves in the place of a reader who has never heard Russian iambs (for instance, of a reader unaccustomed to the frequent omissions of stress) we would understand the metrical nature of a given poem, (and consequently the rhythmical significance of separate lines) only after gaining an impression of the whole, an impression which would be gained with considerable hesitation and difficulty on our first being confronted with the differing rhythms of separate lines. It is in such a position as this that we ap-

---

[13] L. Abercrombie (p. 118) cites the following examples of ambiguous lines from the modern English poet J. Thomson:

> O mellow moonlight warm
> Weave round my love a charm!

These lines occur with a dactylic dimeter measure (cf. Nightly to leave thee, dear.), but out of context they might be interpreted as iambic trimeter with masculine endings. A German example is cited by R. M. Meyer, *Grundlagen des mittelhochdeutschen Strophenbaus* (*Qu. F.* IV, p. 6):

> Gib dich so wie du bist,
> Weil das die Form doch ist ...

These lines also occur in dactylic dimeter surroundings, but might be read as iambic trimeter in the company of such a line as the one which follows: Die Gott dir hat gegeben...

proach new and original rhythmic cadences which deform sharply the traditional system: in order to grasp their rhythical peculiarities we must think of them as variations of a definite metrical pattern. We experience this sort of difficulty to an even greater degree when faced with a new metrical system: that is why the *dol'niki* of Blok and, in particular, the purely tonic verse of Majakovskij were and are considered by many people brought up on traditional syllabo-tonic metrics as non-rhythmical creations. Those readers who regard the poems of Majakovskij as formless prose have difficulty in finding a metrical common denominator in lines varying so widely in their syllabic structure; not sensing the meter, i.e., the inertia of the rhythmical movement, they lose the feeling for the rhythm itself, as the organized arrangement of syllabic sequences within a specific metrical pattern.

5) Thus the existence of rhythmical variations in verse does not in any way preclude the presence of a metrical scheme to which these variations are subordinated. We have defined rhythm as the actual alternations of stress in verse, alternations which arise from the interaction of the natural phonetic characteristics of the linguistic medium with the metrical scheme. The presence of a metrical scheme in verse is perceived by the reader as the *inertia* of *rhythm* (a stress missing from a given line is present in a strong position in many preceding and following lines). From the point of view of the author or the performer of the poem this metrical scheme or law can be described as a sort of *impulse* dominating the given linguistic material. In more abstract terminology we speak of a metrical *design* or of a metrical *law*. The presence of a metrical law in our consciousness is proved by the fact that every metrically strong syllable, even though it bears no stress *in actuality*, is for us *stressed in principle*; displacement of a stress (e.g. from an even to an odd syllable in an iambic) is always perceived as a *deformation* of the verse. Only the presence of the metrical scheme converts the neutral alternation of prose stresses into poetic rhythm, which can be demonstrated by the example of metrically ambiguous lines. And so, *without meter there is no rhythm*; rhythm in a line arises only through the apperception of a given (metrically regular) alternation of stresses, i.e., through its relation to the metrical scheme and through its correlation with other lines which are but individual variations of one and the same metrical type.[14]

---

[14] In *On the concepts of rhythm and meter*, Fr. Saran, pp. 146-47, includes in the concept of meter only the most essential general features of a given rhythmical form, features which might be expressed by an abstract pattern of the meter and conventional scansion. "Thus, meter is a general concept (Begriff), a combination of features which, it is true,

13. TERMINOLOGY

The terminology of Belyj and his closest followers has played a considerable role in the confusion which has arisen over the concepts of meter and
rhythm. As was mentioned earlier, Belyj spoke of the "replacement" of
an iamb by a trochee, spondee or pyrrhic; of the "replacement" of two
iambs by a paeon II or IV; and the same terminology is employed by
N. V. Nedobrovo, V. Brjusov, G. Šengeli and many others. In just the
same way they discover in the anapestic meter the presence of cretics,
bacchii, tribrachs, and so on. For these theoreticians, therefore, all
Russian meters turned out to be, as Lomonosov called them, "mixed",
i.e., composed of heterogeneous feet. It was this circumstance which
caused B. V. Tomaševskij to label as "logaoedic" all those verse theories
which followed the principle of "replacement" of feet and used the
corresponding terminology (by analogy with the mixed "logaoedic"
meters of classical lyric poetry; cf. below, § 33).[15]

---

belong to concrete, individual phenomena, but which, taken together, are only part of
the total characteristics of those phenomena. Meter is always something abstract,
something called forth by the requirements of classification, unreal... Meters are
abstract rhythmical forms, general types of rhythms (Allgemeinrhythmen)." A.
Heusler (*Über germanischen Versbau*, pp. 24-25) distinguishes the metrical "frame" of
verse and its "content" (metrischer Rahmen — Versfüllung). The abstract metrical
structure (*das abstrakte metrische Gerüste*) underlying every verse form, according to
Heusler, has pure rhythm (*hat ungemischten Rhythmus*). When the metrical "frame" is
filled with verbal material "there arises the mixed rhythm of concrete lines". (p. 22).
According to R. Jakobson ("O češskom stixe" p. 35), "for the reader of syllabo-tonic
verse" the prescribed sequence coexists alongside the actual accentual sequence since
the "periodicity of the dynamic stress" inherent in the syllabo-tonic line "causes one to
expect its repetition after a certain interval of unstressed syllables". L. Abercrombie
also points to the existence of an ideal rhythm which is the "base" or "rhythmical
pattern" for the variations of the actual rhythm: "the actual speech rhythm" is "heard as
conforming to the base... referred to the constant scheme of an ideal pattern... actual
speech-rhythm heard not only as actual sound, but also as conforming to the ideal
blank-verse pattern — the base" (cf. pp. 41 ff., 86ff,96 ff, 138 ff.). B. V. Tomaševskij,
(*O stixe Pesen zapadnyx slavjan*, pp. 33-35) came out in his turn against the "logometric
theory" of V. Čudovskij. For Tomaševskij "the tonic pattern is not a result of the
realization of the poetic speech, but, on the contrary, the *prerequisite* of such realization" (p. 33). "Nor does rhythm arise out of the narrative [skaz] any more than in
general it arises out of the actual forms of the verse. On the contrary, both the narrative
and the actual verbal forms arise out of the rhythm and undergo the constant influence
of the rhythm" (p. 35). "It is not that the rhythm flows out of the word combinations,
but rather that the words fall into such and such combinations under the influence
of the poet's rhythmic instinct" (p. 33).
[15] For a more detailed criticism of "logaoedic" theories, cf. B. Tomaševskij, *Russkoe
stixosloženie*, pp. 28-33. The principle of the "replacement" of feet and the "logaoedic"
system are used in the analysis of English iambics by Mayor and in particular by
Saintsbury (cf. *Manual of English Prosody*, the theoretical chapters, pp. 3-37).

The "logaoedic" terminology of most recent Russian metrical theory is based on a confusion of the concepts of rhythm and meter. The foot is not really an element in the actual phonetic realization of the line and consequently does not belong to the province of "rhythm"; it is an abstract unit of repetition, a pattern of alternation established for the metrical scheme and applied only in relation to the meter of the poem. For this reason, the line "I klánjalsja neprinuždënno" — which has only two stresses, on the second and eight syllables — is just as much a representative of the *iambic tetrameter* within the context of *Evgenij Onegin* as is a line with four stresses: "Moj djádja sámyx čéstnyx právil..." Within the meter, the foot is a regularly recurring sequence of strong and weak syllables — in the iambic meter, for instance, the strong syllable following regularly the weak syllable. If, however, we introduce the principle of "replacement" and identify the foot with the actual elements of verse rhythm, the result is "mixed" verse, composed of various disyllabic and tetrasyllabic feet, the alternation of which in any one line or in a sequence of lines is not conditioned by any regular periodicity. Hence the familiar — and wholly erroneous — conclusion that the Russian iambic line can be "made up" of any disyllabic (or tetrasyllabic) feet — iambs, trochees, spondees, pyrrhics, paeons II and IV and others — arranged in any order, and that the so-called "iambic" meter exists only in "*school metrics*". The proof adduced in support of this opinion is already familiar to us: separate lines of poetry with various examples of "replacement" or "deviation" sharply divergent from the "normal" metrical type. But the principal error of these authors lies in their transferring the concept of "*foot*", the element of *meter*, to the actual rhythm of the line, and in their very system of notation, which is inspired by this transference. By means of such a notation, not only any verse line but even an excerpt of newspaper prose can be written down as a "mixed" meter composed of a "combination" of iambs, trochees, spondees and pyrrhics, following one after the other in an arbitrary order.

The term "rhythmic deviation" has also given rise to some misunderstanding. It is connected with the theory which regards rhythm as a deviation from meter, and promotes the erroneous notion of meter as the "norm" and rhythm as involving "exceptions", which are welcomed by theoreticians who see in them the expression of an original and creative personality. For this reason the term "rhythmic variation" is more exact and less dangerous.

Of course, one can employ such expressions as "pyrrhic in the second foot" or "omission of the stress" so long as these expressions are generally accepted and used purely as conventions. But it would be extremely undesirable to elevate a vague terminological convention to the status of a metrical theory explaining the interaction of meter and rhythm as the "replacement" of one group of feet by another group of feet. And in any case, one must avoid introducing into the terminology the concept of tetrasyllabic feet (paeons) in combination with the concept of disyllabic feet (iambs and trochees), since this arbitrarily destroys the sequence of alternately stressed and unstressed syllables characteristic of the binary meters.

14. SO-CALLED "SYLLABIC VERSE"

The identification of Russian syllabo-tonic verse with French "syllabic" is best refuted by comparing two samples. For our comparison we shall take the French twelve-syllable "Alexandrine line" and the Russian iambic hexameter, which has the same number of syllables.

When one examines the stresses of the iambic hexameter in Puškin's *Osen'* the metrical inertia of the stress on the even syllables is clearly revealed. In the first three stanzas (see above, § 9), containing 24 lines in all, we have the following distribution of stresses: syllable I-1, II-24, III-0, IV-16, V-0, VI-19, VII-1, VIII-23, IX-0, X-8, XI-0, XII-24. Thus the odd syllables carry no stress, except for one case of supplementary stressing on the first syllable and one case on the seventh (the syllable immediately following the caesura). Of the even syllables the last is always stressed (24); the first stress in each hemistich is extremely stable (24 and 23); the last stress before the caesura may be left out, but very rarely (19); there is somewhat more frequent omission of the penultimate stress in the first hemistich (16 stresses, however, are present, i.e., 2/3 of the total); only the penultimate stress of the whole line is discarded in a majority of the cases (16), but even in this position we find 8 stresses (1/3). Thus, the "iambic" metrical principle has left its unmistakable stamp on the poem as a whole.

Different results obtain if we turn to the French "Alexandrine":

Salut! bois, couronnés ‖ d'un reste de verdure,	(2, 3, 6; 8, 12)
Feuillages, jaunissants ‖ sur les gazons épars!	(2, 6; 10, 12)
Salut, derniers beaux jours! ‖ Le deuil de la nature	(2, 4, 6; 8, 12)
Convient à ma douleur ‖ et plait à mes regards.	(2, 6; 8, 12)
Je suis d'un pas rêveur ‖ le sentier solitaire.	(2, 4, 6; 9, 12)
J'aime à revoir encor, ‖ pour la dernière fois,	(1, 4, 6; 10, 12)
Ce soleil pâlissant ‖ dont la faible lumière	(3, 6; 9, 12)

Perce à peine à mes pieds || l'obscurité des bois...   (1, 3, 6; 9, 12)
Oui! dans ces jours d'automne, || où la nature expire   (1, 4, 6; 10, 12)
A ses regards voilés || je trouve plus d'attraits, —   (4, 6; 8, 12)
C'est l'adieu d'un ami, || c'est le dernier sourire   (3, 6; 10, 12)
Des lèvres que la mort || va fermer pour jamais.   (2, 6; 10, 12)

There are twelve lines in the poem. A comparison of the stresses with the syllables gives the following figures: I-3, II-6, III-4, IV-5, V-0, VI-12, VII-0, VIII-4, IX-3, X-5, XI-0, XII-12. By doubling these numbers one can easily compare them with those of the Russian sample.

The metrical pattern of so-called "syllabic" verse requires a constant stress at the end of the line and at the end of the first hemistich before the caesura (VI and XII-12). This requirement encourages the omission of the antecedent stresses (V and XI-0); classical French metrics recommended, for the sake of precise cadence and rhythmical euphony, the avoidance of stress on the penultimate syllable; however, this recommendation was not always followed.[16] The initial syllable in the lines above has an insignificant number of stresses (3), as does the first syllable of the second hemistich (0): a stress is permitted here only when the line begins with a monosyllabic, rather strong word, or with a disyllabic word whose second syllable is a "mute" e, which is elided before a vowel (cf. lines 6, 8, 9). Classical French versification traditionally proscribed such a beginning, especially after the caesura; but in this case also, one can speak only of a rule of rhythmic euphony, not of a fixed metrical scheme. There remain in the first hemistich syllables II, III and IV, and in the second hemistich syllables VII, IX, and X, and here the number of stresses fluctuates between 25 and 50%. Within the line it is rare to find two stresses standing side by side (cf. line 1) as this too was considered a cacophonous combination disrupting the cadence. Hence it is clear that syllables with the maximal number of stresses (II, III, IV — VIII, IX, X) can enter into two kinds of combinations with the syllables carrying an obligatory stress: in one the stresses are distributed on every other syllable (II, IV, VI and, correspondingly, VIII, X, XII), in the other they are repeated after each two syllables (III, VI and IX, XII). From the point of view of our syllabo-tonic meters we have in the first case "iambs" and in the second "anapests". Examples of anapests: whole line — "ce soleil pâlissant || dont la faible lumière..."; hemistich — "le sentier solitaire ... c'est l'adieu d'un ami ... va fermer pour jamais..." Examples of iambs: "salut, derniers beaux jours ... je suis d'un pas rêveur..." The stresses

---

[16]   On the question of the rhythm of French verse cf. particularly Becq de Fouquières and also Rob. de Souza, *Le rythme poétique* (Paris, 1892).

may fall on some, but not all, of the even syllables: in syllabo-tonic metrics we would regard such cases as iambs with pyrrhics or with a weakened stress on insignificant monosyllabic words. Cf. the whole lines "feuillages jaunissants ‖ sur les gazons épars" or "conviènt à ma douleur ‖ et plaît a mes regards" and the hemistichs "pour la dernière fois ... où la nature expire..." It would, however, be more correct to say that in French verse containing both iambs and anapests within one poem, i.e., recognizing no difference of principle between the two meters, we have *neither iambs nor anapests*, since we are basing the very concept of the foot not on the rhythm of a given line or lines, but on average figures obtained from a number of lines. Moreover, the general analysis shows that for French Alexandrines, the stresses on the second, third and fourth syllables of the first hemistich and on the eighth, ninth and tenth syllables of the second hemistich are treated, from the point of view of stress, completely on a par, so that no *difference in principle* exists between these syllables, as it does in Russian verse. There is no *inertia of accentuation* on, say, the even syllables such as exists in Russian iambics, an inertia which in Russian iambics makes it impossible to substitute amphibrachic or anapestic lines for iambs.[17] All that can be said concerning the Alexandrine is that the iambic type is encountered on the average more often than the anapestic; but even within one and the same Alexandrine line, an "iambic" hemistich may occur along with an "anapestic", e.g.: "Je suis d'un pas rêveur// le sentier solitaire", or "Des lèvres que la mort// va fermer pour jamais...". The only metrically regulated feature of the French Alexandrine line is thus the obligatory recurrence of the stress at the end of each hemistich, on syllables six and twelve; and along with this go, as we have seen, certain traditional requirements of rhythmical euphony and cadence. Only at the end of the line does the expectation of an *obligatory* stress establish rhythmical *inertia*. All other stresses belong to the area of rhythm and recur in various combinations. In this sense French verse is freer and more diverse than German or Russian, where the distribution of the strong

---

[17] B. V. Tomaševskij, *Russkoe stixosloženie*, p. 34, advances the concept of meter as the principle of *compatibility*. Among the early theoreticians of Russian verse, N. Nadeždin (*Versifikacija*, p. 518) expressed a similar thought: "Attention must be given to the musical similarity of feet, which serves as the basis for their compatibility in the line. The following are compatible: iamb and anapest, trochee with dactyl, dactyl with amphibrach, amphibrach with trochee and iamb. Furthermore, the pyrrhic is admissible with iambs and trochees, and the tribrach with anapests, dactyls and amphibrachs. Incompatible: iamb with trochee, anapest with dactyl... The chief rule for imparting melodic variety to the line: *learn to exploit the compatibility of feet in such a way that their variety does not impede the movement of the rhythm.*"

and weak syllables is determined by a definite rule: metrically, it is less precisely organized. If one were to apply the term "foot" to French verse it would be more appropriate to regard the entire line or hemistich as a large foot (in Alexandrine verse, for example, a foot of six syllables).[18] It is generally better, however, to avoid a term which pertains to another metrical system and which is actually not at all suitable to the French system, which is governed by different rules.

The Russian syllabic verse of Kantemir and his predecessors reveals the same characterictics which we observed in French verse. A count of the stresses in a sample of any length will show what is immediately perceived by the ear — the absence of an accentual inertia on any words except those at the end of the hemistich or line.

Take for example Satire I, *K umu svoemu*:

Raskóly i éresi ‖ naúki sut' déti;	(2, 5; 9, 12)
Ból'še vrët, komú dalós' ‖ ból'še razuméti,	(1, 3, 5, 7; 8, 12)
Prixódit v bezbóžie, ‖ któ nad knígoj táet.	(2, 5; 8, 10, 12)
Kritón s čëtkami v rukáx ‖ vorčít i vzdyxáet,	(2, 3, 7; 9, 12)
I prósit svjatá dušá ‖ s gór'kimi slezámi	(2, 5, 7; 8, 12)
Smotrét', skol' sémja naúk ‖ vrédno méždu námi:	(2, 4, 7; 8, 10, 12)
Déti náši, čtó pred tém ‖ tíxi i pokórny	(1, 3, 5, 7; 8, 12)
Práotčeskim šlí sledóm ‖ k bóžiej provórny	(2, 5, 7; 8, 12)
Slúžbe, s stráxom slúšaja, ‖ čto sámi ne ználi,	(1, 3, 5; 9, 12)
Tepér' k cérkvi sóblaznu, ‖ Bíbliju čést' stáli;	(2, 3, 5; 8, 11, 12)
Tolkújut, vsemú xotját ‖ znát' póvod, pričínu,	(2, 5, 7; 8, 9, 12)
Málo véry podajá ‖ svjaščénnomu čínu...	(1, 3, 7; 9, 12)

In the 13-syllable line the caesura stands after the seventh syllable; the obligatory stress is on the twelfth syllable. Before the caesura the stress falls either on the seventh or fifth syllable, in which latter case the sixth and seventh syllables are unstressed. This is, in fact, the way Kantemir himself formulates the rules of his verse in *Pis'mo k prijatelju o složenii stixov russkix* (Chap IV, §§ 25-30). A count of the stresses gives the following figures: I-4, II-8, III-6, IV-1, V-9, VI-0, VII-8, VIII-8, IX-5, X-2, XI-1, XII-12, XIII-0. The obligatory stress on the last syllable of the rhythmical sequence and the obligatory feminine ending explain the last two numbers. For the sake of rhythmical precision, the stress preceding the final stress is always absent (however, cf. line 10: "...čést' stáli"; the word *čest'* was probably regarded by the author as unstressed since it is monosyllabic). In the first hemistich we have two different types of ending: "Raskóly i éresi..." (stress on the fifth syllable with the

---

[18] The proposal to regard the line (or hemistich) in the French syllabic system as a large foot has been made by, e.g., J. Minor, pp. 47-48.

sixth and seventh unstressed) or "Bol'še vrët, komu dalos'..." (stress on the seventh syllable with the sixth unstressed for the sake of precise cadence); the sixth syllable, therefore, does not carry a single stress, while the fifth and seventh carry a high number of stresses (2/3-3/4). Syllables one to four, according to Kantemir's theory (§ 28) "can be long or short, however it chances". Actually the fourth syllable is stressed only in rare cases (cf. line 6) since the stress on the fifth syllable dominates. Syllables one, two and three, in combination with the two types of endings, provide the two basic rhythmical elements of the first hemistich. When the stress falls on syllables one, three, five and seven, we have verses of the trochaic type; cf. lines 2, 7, 9, 12 — e.g., "Ból'še vrët, komú dalós'..." When the stress falls on the second and fifth syllables, we have the amphibrachic type; cf. lines 1, 3 ("Raskóly i éresi..."). As with the French Alexandrine, one can not speak here either of binary or ternary meters, as is clear from, among other things, the presence of lines of a mixed type (II-V-VII); cf. lines 6, 8, 11 [Sic. Ž. means lines 5, 8, 11], e.g. "Praótčeskim šlí sledóm". The same thing applies to the second hemistich, which, as regards rhythmical configuration, is completely independent of the first hemistich. We have trochaic lines (VIII-X-XII); cf. lines 2, 3, 5, 6, 7, 8, 10, e.g. "Któ nad knígoj táet..." On the other hand there are lines of the amphibrachic type (IX-XII); cf. lines 1, 4, 9, 11, 12, e.g. "...svjaščennomu čínu". No single one of these rhythmical configurations is clearly dominant and consequently no accentual inertia is established either on the even syllables or on every third syllable. The trochaic cadence is, however, encountered more often than the others; as we know, Tred'jakovskij used it as the basis for his subsequent reform of Russian syllabic verse, when he introduced the principle of distributing the stresses on the basis of a division of the line into feet.

For the modern Russian reader brought up on the syllabo-tonic versification of the classical epoch or on the stress-counting of the dol'niki, Kantemir's syllabic verse appears lacking in rhythm: we attempt to assimilate it by relating it to familiar metrical schemes, by regarding it, for example, as trochaic with sharp "deviations" and "displacements" of the stress or as four-stress verse with varying numbers of unstressed syllables between stresses.[19] This modernization is in neither case justified by the rhythmical characteristics of the verse itself: in the first case we ignore the displacement of the stresses, in the second — the

[19]   The German syllabic verse of Hans Sachs is also regarded by some as iambic (with transposition of the accents), and by others as purely tonic in meter. Cf. J. Minor, pp. 333-346; H. Paul, pp. 88-89.

constant number of syllables. Kantemir's verse, however, was potentially capable of rhythmization, as witnessed by the subsequent development of Russian poetry. Especially in poems with shorter lines, where the number of rhythmical possibilities is limited, Kantemir himself recognizes these potentialities as rhythmical cadences of a special kind. For example, in an eight-syllable line which has an obligatory stress on the seventh syllable "care should be taken to make the third and seventh syllables long" (Chap. IV, § 51). If the poet, in doing this, avoids that clash of stresses on adjacent syllables which was considered rhythmically caco-phonous, the result is trochaic tetrameter. Cf. Kantemir's:

> Skól'ko bédnyj suetítsja
> Čelovék za málu slávu.
> Nóč' ne spít i dén' tomítsja,
> Čtob ne sél soséd po právu...

"This poem would be even more beautiful", writes Kantemir, "if the first, fourth and seventh syllables were kept long, and all the others short." (§ 52). This second rhythmical possibility produces verses of the dactylic type — as in Kantemir's:

> Tvári vladýko vsemóčnyj,
> Ésli moj glás tebe vnjáten
> Núždam doxód moim tóčnyj,
> Krátku xot' žížn', no bez pjáten...

By selecting from among the various rhythmical possibilities and varia-tions of cadence inherent in syllabic verse, Tred'jakovskij[20] arrives at his reform of the 13-syllable line in the first edition of his *Novyj i kratkii*

---

[20] B. V. Tomaševskij has pointed out that Tred'jakovskij, in the first edition of his *Novyj sposob* was not yet proposing a theoretically new system of versification based on the foot, but was only recommending the trochaic *cadence* as the most euphonic for the "heroic" (thirteen-syllable) line (*Problemy ritma*, p. 125). Actually, Tred'-jakovskij included within the concept of cadence "the smooth and pleasant sounding movement of the feet throughout the entire line to the very end" (p. 24, Def. VIII). Only disyllabic feet were to be admitted in heroic lines, viz., spondees, pyrrhics, trochees and iambs (p. 25, Rule I and corollary). "However, that line is in all ways better and more perfect which consists only or principally of trochees; and extremely bad is the line made up only or principally of iambs. Those lines which consist entirely or for the most part of spondees or pyrrhics are of middle value." As before, Tred'-jakovskij thought it possible to compose lines shorter than heroic without demanding a specific succession of accents. "Not all our lines need be measured into feet, only into syllables" (p. 61). Thus Tomaševskij is justified in asserting that, in the strictest sense, it was Lomonosov in his *Pis'mo* (1739), rather than Tred'jakovskij, who really laid the foundation of the new versification. In the second edition of his *Novyj sposob*, which for a long time overshadowed the first, Tred'jakovskij had already adopted Lomonosov's ideas on this subject.

sposob k složeniju rossijskix stixov (1735). Lomonosov's *Pis'mo* (1739) and the second edition of Tred'jakovskij's treatise are based on Latin and German models and are thus more consistent in their elaboration of the new principle of syllabo-tonic versification.

15. RUSSIAN VERSE AS COMPARED WITH GERMAN AND ROMANCE

The deviations from the metrical scheme in the Russian binary meters, investigated by A. Belyj and his followers, are also to be found in the syllabo-tonic verse of other peoples. Since the syllabo-tonic system, which developed as a peculiar attempt to reproduce the classical feet, imports into a national versification system its own alien rules prescribing a strict alternation of syllables and stresses, it invariably encounters resistance from the linguistic material, a resistance which will vary in accordance with the different phonetic characteristics of each language.

German iambs and trochees adhere very closely to the metrical scheme, and thereby produce upon Russian readers the impression of rhythmical monotony. Thus, Vostokov writes: "Our iambic verses, by means of an admixture of pyrrhics, enjoy much greater variety than the German, in which pure iambs are repeated unceasingly. It was perhaps this palpable monotony which hastened the introduction into German poetry of the classical meters." (*Opyt*, 28). In this last remark, Vostokov is repeating the opinion of Klopstock and his school, who championed the adoption by German poetry of the hexameter and "logaoedic" meters. Comparing German iambics with those of Milton, Klopstock sympathetically mentioned the greater variety of the latter. As a matter of fact, the rhythmical variety of German iambs is based on the varying *strength* of the stresses, which is not sufficiently felt by foreign readers.

A sample from Goethe's poem *Willkommen und Abschied* can serve to illustrate the apparent monotony of the German iambic:

> Der Mond von einem Wolkenhügel
> *Sah* kläglich aus dem Duft hervor;
> Die Winde schwangen leise Flügel
> Umsausten schauerlich mein Ohr;
> Die Nacht *schuf* tausend Ungeheuer,
> Doch frisch und fröhlich war mein Mut;
> In meinen Adern — welches Feuer!
> In meinem Herzen — welche Glut!

Compound German words (Wolkenhügel, Ungeheuer) are pronounced with two stresses: a stronger one (*Hauptton*), usually on the first component, and a weaker (*Nebenton*), on the second. Cf. in the same poem:

> Schon stand im Nebelkleid die Eiche
> Ein aufgetürmter Riese da...

The same sort of weaker, accessory stress is found on the major suffixes (schauer*lich*). Cf. in the same poem: "Wo Finster*nis* aus dem Gesträuche..." A slight stress is also placed on the auxiliary parts of speech — prepositions, conjunctions, articles — when they occur in a metrically stressed position between two unstressed syllables ("Sah kläglich *aus* dem Duft hervor...") Cf. also "Was hör ich draussen *vor* dem Thor... Ich singe *wie* der Vogel singt... Und *wie* er sitzt, und *wie* er lauscht..." and many others. As a rule German words (and word-groups) are monosyllabic or disyllabic, while polysyllabic words are — if one disregards the compound words with two stresses — extremely rare; for that reason one almost never finds in German poetry those "pyrrhics" which are so familiar to us (Cf., however: schmeichel*te*, flüchti*ge*, blühen*de*, zufrieden*en*... and so on). It must be pointed out that even where they occur German theoreticians are inclined to speak of a weak, secondary stress on the second syllable after the main one. "More than two completely unstressed syllables", writes J. Minor (*Neuhochdeutsche Metrik*, 79), "can occur between stresses only when the tempo of speech is very fast and deprived of all expressiveness. This follows from the relative intensity of any stress: one syllable will always be somewhat stronger than another and therefore more noticeable; when syllables are completely identical in strength, the decisive factor is a tendency toward the rhythmical alternation of stressed and unstressed syllables common to every language." Minor therefore seeks to establish the presence of a weak, secondary stress in such cases as: "So treten wir mit hohem Schritt auf Leichnam*en* umher... Die eignen grausam*en* Bigierden an... Ist das gefährlich furchtbar*e*..." and so on (p. 123).

Moreover, in German verse too it is possible to have supplementary stresses on metrically weak syllables (so-called "spondees"), especially in the first foot. Cf. in the example cited: "*Sah* kläglich... Die Nacht *schuf* tausend..." Cf. in the same poem, "*Dich* sah ich und die milde Freude... Und doch *welch* Glück geliebt zu werden!" The displacement of the stress from an even to an odd syllable is widespread in the first foot of the iambic. Cf., for instance, in Goethe's ballad *Der Fischer*:

> *Sah* nach dem Angel ruhevoll...
> *Kühl* bis ans Herz hinan...

> *Teilt* sich die Flut empor...
> *Labt* sich die liebe Sonne nicht...
> *Lockt* dich der tiefe Himmel nicht...
> *Netzt* ihm den nassen Fuss...

A disyllabic trochaic word can also stand at the beginning of a line. Cf. "*Nenne* mich nicht... *Weibchen*, oh sieh den Segen... *Preise* dein Glück... *Lacryma* Christi, frommer Nectar werde..." and others. Cf. also the displacement of stress after the caesura or a syntactic pause: "*Kennst* du mich nicht? || *sprach* sie mit einem Munde..." In other places in the line the shift of a stress is regarded as an abrupt rhythmical break, which is to be avoided. E.g. in the first version of *Willkommen and Abschied*: "Und fort, *wild* wie ein Held zur Schlacht!..." (in the later version corrected to: "Es war getan, fast eh' gedacht...").

The ryhthmic structure of the binary meters is in English poetry much freer and more varied — especially in the most frequently used meter, the iambic pentameter (drama and epic). It is true that the omission of stresses ("pyrrhics") is not characteristic of English meters: here one should speak, as in the Germanic languages in general, not so much of omission as of *weakening* of the metrical stress, although this weakening apparently goes further in English than in German. Cf. Milton's "Nor serv'd it *to* relax their serried files... Sole reigning holds the Tyrra*ny* of Heav'n... A dungeon horri*ble* on all sides round... His Minis*ters* of vengeance *and* pursuit... The Sojourn*ers* of Goshen, *who* beheld..." and many others.[21] A widespread phenomenon is the hypermetrical stressing of syllables in significant monosyllabic words: cf. in Gray's *Elegy*, "The lowing herd *winds* slowly o'er the lea..." Byron: "And Ardennes waves above them her *green* leaves..." Shelley: "*Spouse!* Sister! Angel! Pilot of the fate!..." Tennyson: "A star *shot*: "Lo!" said Gareth, a *foe* falls!..." and many others.

A famous line of Milton, which is in effect a list of nouns, has these hypermetrical stresses in the first three consecutive feet: "*Rocks*, *caves*, *lakes*, fens, *bogs*, dens and sha*des* of death!" (*Paradise Lost*, II, 261).

But specially characteristic of English iambs is the extensive use they

---

[21]   In the iambic meter there is apparently more weakening of the unstressed syllables in English pronunciation than in German; at any rate, English scholars speak in such cases of "pyrrhics" (cf. Mayor, Transactions, 1875-76, p. 433) or of "omitted stresses" (e.g. Robert Bridges, pp. 37-40), while German theoreticians see a weak secondary stress (Nebenton) (cf. Schipper, I, pp. 18-22). A. Ellis agrees for the most part with Mayor (cf. *Trans.*, 1875-76, p. 442 ff.). A contrary opinion is held by M. Liddell, p. 232, and P. Verrier, I, pp. 150-52, both of whom regard the weak stress as of considerable theoretical importance for English verse.

make of *displacement* of stress. Such displacement or shifting is admissible not only in the first foot of a line but also at any other place in the line, and not only on significant monosyllabic words, but also on disyllabic and trisyllabic words.[22]

First foot. Shakespeare: "*Doom'd* for a certain time to walk the night... *Giving* more light, than heat, extinct in both..." Milton: "*Infinite* wrath and infinite despair... *Regions* of sorrow, doleful shades, where peace..." Byron: "*Dewy* with Nature's teardrops as they pass..." Shelley: "*Pourest* such music, that it might assuage..." Tennyson: "*Suddenly* flashed on her a wild desire..."

Within the line. Shakespeare: "The eye *wink* at the hand, yet let that be... And yet dark night *strangles* the travelling lamp..." Milton: "Which, tasted, works *knowledge* of Good and Evil... As when two polar winds *blowing* adverse..." Shelley: "And wild *roses* and ivy serpentine... And from the waves *sound* like delight broke forth..." Tennyson: "Into the hall *stagger'd* his visage ribbed..." and others.

There are cases in which the shifting of stresses occurs twice in the same line — most frequently in the first and second feet. E.g., Milton: "*Mix'd* with *obdurate* pride and steadfast hate..." Shelley: "*Harmonising* with solitude..." Tennyson: "*Rolling back* upon Balin crushed the man..." Browning: "*Help* a *case* the Archbishop would not help..." But the same kind of shift can occur twice in other places in the line. Cf. Milton (third and fourth feet): "As a despite *done against* the most high..." (second and fourth): "In their *triple* Degrees, *Regions* to which..." Shelley (first and third): "*Rugged* and dark, *winding* among the springs..." Tennyson (first and fourth): "*Thicker* the drizzle grew, *deeper* the gloom..." In exceptional cases one finds as many as three stress shifts together (first, second and third feet). Cf. Shelley: "*Harmonising silence* without a sound..." Tennyson: "*Not to* tell her, *never* to let her know..." Browning: "*Matutinal, busy* with book so soon..."

Stress shift was very frequently used by Shakespeare during the period of his maturity, by the later Elizabethans, by Milton, as well as by the nineteenth century poets who returned to the metrical practices of Shakespeare and Milton, e.g., by Shelley, Tennyson and Browning. English Classicism of the eighteenth century (Pope and his school) opposed to this national tradition the demand for metrically correct alternation, permitting stress shift only in its mildest form: in the first

---

[22] In the English examples which follow the actual stresses are arranged with no regard for whether they fall on the place of a metrically strong or weak syllable.

foot of the iambic line. In this respect (as in many others), Byron follows the metrical practice of English classicism.

The ternary meters are used far less frequently in English and German poetry than in Russian, and in no case can they be considered on a par with the iambic and trochaic meters. A characteristic of ternary meters in the Germanic languages, especially English, is the frequent appearance of supplementary stresses on metrically weak syllables — in monosyllabic and disyllabic words which are lexically significant. This makes English anapests, especially those of inexperienced poets, seem heavy to our ear and somehow faltering in rhythm. Such a feeling is repeatedly experienced in reading the early verse of Byron. Cf. the elegy *Newstead Abbey*:

> Through thy battlements, Newsteads, the hollow *winds* whistle,
> *Thou*, the hall of my fathers, art gone to decay!
> In thy once *smiling* garden the hemlock and thistle
> Have choked up the rose, which late bloomed on the way...

A comparison of the binary with the ternary meters and of Russian versification with that of German and English once more clarifies the reason for the "deviations" marked above. The German word (more exactly, the word group unified by a stress, the *stress group*) tends to be disyllabic (Name, geben, der Tag, ich sprach) and is consequently most conveniently fitted into a binary meter, while the longer Russian words are more naturally suited to ternary meters. German poetry shows, therefore, a tendency to employ hypermetrical stresses in the ternary meters, while Russian shows the opposite tendency to obliterate stresses in the binary meters. English reveals the same tendencies as German, but in a more pronounced form, for most words of Germanic origin have in English lost their endings and been converted into monosyllables (cf. German *Name, geben,* but English *name, give*); the normal two-word group is in English usually composed of an auxiliary word (preposition, article) and of a "full" word (*a name, to give*). Consequently not only the ternary but even the binary meters show a tendency to admit a stress in metrically weak positions. Owing to the large number of monosyllabic words, the syntactic (phrase) accent acquires in English verse an especially significant role, allowing more variations within the metrical scheme than does the word stress of disyllabic and polysyllabic words. This probably explains the inherent *tendency of English to shift the stress*, although the development of this tendency is conditioned by poetic tradition, artistic taste of one period or another and the influence of widely acknowledged teachers. Among these influences one must take

note of the continuing importance of Italian models (as early as the time
of Chaucer, but especially in the days of Shakespeare and Milton).
The theoreticians of English verse have been inclined, at different times
and in different ways, to interpret the metrical structure of their native
verse either in terms of the classical tradition as iambic pentameter, or
in terms of modern Romance literatures as syllabic decasyllabic (corresponding to the Italian *endecasillabo*).

The example of English and German versification allows us once more
to consider in a general way the problem of the interrelationship between
the syllabo-tonic and syllabic systems. German and French versification
illustrate the extreme form of both: in German practice the metrical
alternation of stressed and unstressed syllables is realized with practically
no deviations from the scheme; French verse, on the other hand, with
a constant number of syllables per line and an obligatory stress on the
last syllable, permits the most varied number of stresses and their free-
est distribution. Russian and English verse occupy intermediate positions:
Russian verse departs from the scheme principally in the *number* of
stresses (omissions), English — in their *arrangement* ("displacement").
Within the so-called syllabic system, however, there exist varying degrees
of approximation to the syllabo-tonic system. French verse, as was
mentioned, admits the widest variation in the arrangement of stresses,
with exceptions for certain traditional (although not always observed)
demands of rhythmic euphony: e.g., the avoidance of a clash of stresses,
especially on the prefinal two syllables. Even these demands, by the way,
permit the use of several favorite *cadences*; for example, the iambic or
anapestic cadence in the Alexandrine. In Italian verse this use is far more
limited. For instance, in the decasyllabic line (and Italian endecasyllabic,
in which the feminine ending gives an eleventh syllable) the *iambic
cadence* clearly predominates. Consider the following sonnet by Dante
(vowels in parentheses are those which the rules of Italian metrics
ignore in the syllable count; cf. above, § 4):

> *Deh*, peregrini, che pensos(i) andate,
> *Forse* de cose, che non v'è presente,
> Venite voi da si lontana gente,
> *Com(e)* à la vista voi ne dimostrate?
> *Chè* non piangete, quando voi passate
> Per la su(a) mezza la città dolente,
> *Come quelle* persone, che neënte
> *Par* ch'intendesser la su(a) gravitate?
> Se voi restate per voler udire,
> *Certo* lo core nei sospir' mi dice,

Che lagrimando n'uscirete pui.
Ell(*a*) à perduta la *su*(*a*) Beatrice,
E le parole ch'uom di lei può dire
Hanno virtù di far *pianger*(*e*) altrui.

The iambic cadence runs throughout the entire poem with very insignificant deviations. Along with purely iambic lines ("venite voi da si lontana gente") there are others showing what we might regard as the *omission* of one or two stresses (e.g., "Che *la*grimando n'*u*scirete pui"). The shift of a stress to an odd syllable is encountered mainly at the beginning of a line and recurs here in the majority of the lines on monosyllabic as well as on disyllabic initial words (cf. "Certo lo core... Hanno virtù... Par ch'intendesser..." etc.). Within the line the most noticeable cases are the following: on the first and third syllables — "Come quelle persone...";￼ on the first and seventh — "Hanno virtù di far pianger altrui..." Aside from these, there are two less important instances on the seventh syllable: "...la su(a) Beatrice... la su(a) gravitate..." Such a rhythm approximates the normal type of English iambic pentameter, except for the frequent "omissions" of stress on even syllables, which is not customary in English verse. It is of course also true that the iambic cadence does not always emerge so clearly in the Italian decasyllabic line. Thus, one finds a more complicated rhythm in Petrarch's lines:

Occhi pianget(e), accompagnat(e) il core
Che di vostro fallir morte sostene.
Così sempre facciam(o); e nei convene
Lamentar piu l'altrui che'l nostr(o) errore...

Aside from the normal displacement of stress in the first line ("Occhi piangete...") the three following lines of this example show an almost "anapestic" opening ("Che di vostro fallir... Cosi sempre facciamo... Lamentar piu l'altrui..."). The rhythmical possibilities of the Italian decasyllabic line are thus generally much broader than those of the English iambic pentameter with their permissible displacements; however, as compared to French verse, Italian is the intermediate step closest to English.

The metrical structure of a poem is not determined by the stress pattern of isolated lines. Consequently, the iambic cadence of separate verses in an Italian poem does not produce the iambic structure of the poem as a whole; by the same token, even the sharpest deviations from the meter in an English line do not disrupt the iambic inertia of the whole poem. The English line "*Rolling back* upon Balin crushed the man" and the Italian "Come quelle persone che neente" are in stress distribution more or less identical. Nevertheless, the first is perceived in the context of the entire poem as a modified iambic line in which the first two stresses are retracted to the preceding odd syllables, while the second is a decasyllabic line with a weak iambic cadence in the second part. The adherence of English verse to the syllabo-tonic system and of Italian to the syllabic is determined *in general* not only by the character of the variations, but also by their frequency of occurrence. The more frequent the deviations and the greater their significance, the more difficult is the establishment of an iambic or trochaic inertia. Mechanical calculations alone, however, are not decisive. One can easily find a poem of Shelley which deviates much more from the iambic pattern than does the sonnet by Dante above. But the literary tradition is a powerful factor: in English poetry, where we have become accustomed to syllabo-tonic meters, each concrete poem is read, so to speak, against a syllabo-tonic background and even the most complicated rhythmical design is interpreted as a deviation from a simple metrical pattern. The specific charm of a romantic poem, let's say, by Shelley, with its wealth of deviations, resides principally in the fact that the norm (from which the poet deviates) is constantly in the background, as the point of departure. Whereas the same kind of stress distribution in an Italian poem will be a normal variation of the syllabic "decasyllable", which is less strict in this regard. But the appearance of a precise iambic cadence in the verse of Carducci would sound like a rhythmical novelty, while in English it would correspond to the normal type of iambic or dactylic meter. Of course, a more long-lasting and significant departure from the tradition must finally disrupt the balance of the existing system and lead to the formation of a new system.

When examined from the comparative-historical point of view, the syllabo-tonic and the so-called syllabic systems of versification turn out to be not only cognate, but united by transitional forms which can replace each other in the process of metrical evolution. The meters of the syllabo-tonic system are thus potentially inherent in syllabic verse as rhythmical "cadences" not yet canonized into a new system.

III. CONCERNING RUSSIAN PROSODY

16. THE CONCEPT OF STRESS

To the extent that recent works dealing with the theory of Russian verse follow A. Belyj in opposing the actual rhythm of specific lines to the abstract metrical scheme, they inevitably arrive at the question as to how various lines should be pronounced. In many cases there is no doubt whatsoever about the location of the stresses, while other cases give rise to disputes. The resolution of each separate problem may affect the results obtained by statistical calculations of "deviations", as well as the theoretical inferences about the nature of Russian verse. Therefore, it is necessary first of all to investigate the linguistic material itself, its natural phonetic characteristics, and the influence exerted upon this material by the metrical organization. The study of the phonetic characteristics of a given language as the material submitted to metrical organization belongs to the field of *prosody*. A scientific theory of verse must be based for its concrete conclusions on the *prosody* of the language in question. Unfortunately, works on Russian metrics, unlike similar investigations in German, English and French, have up to the present time scarcely dealt with questions of prosody.[1]

First of all, the very concept of stress demands revision from the point of view of modern phonetics.[2] School metrics bases the concept of the foot, by analogy with classical metrics, on the contrast of stressed and unstressed syllables. In an isolated word of more than one syllable there can be no doubt whatever about this contrast; in the word *vodá* the word

---

[1] The problems of prosody are discussed, for German verse, by J. Minor, pp. 64-110; H. Paul, pp. 91-93 (the question of the accentuation of monosyllabic words in particular on p. 92); Fr. Saran, p. 49 ff.; for English verse by J. Schipper, I, pp. 76-162; M. Liddell, pp. 227-234; P. Verrier, I, *passim* (pp. 49-50 for monosyllabic words of the functional variety).

[2] On stress cf. Ed. Sievers, *Grundzüge der Phonetik* (1901), pp. 228-254; Jespersen, *Lehrbuch der Phonetik* (1904), pp. 207-240.

accent is located on the second syllable. In a phraseological unit, however, the question is more complex. In many cases the impression of
stress is created by the interaction of a great many factors not always
operating in the same direction; it also turns out that the stress can be
stronger or weaker and that in this case the concept of relativity is involved, i.e., the intensity of the stress on a given syllable is perceived in its
relation to the intensity of the stress on another given syllable. Several
general remarks of a phonetic character are therefore necessary for the
further study of problems connected with Russian prosody.

Modern phonetics distinguishes *stress* from the *factors* creating it.
Owing to the presence of stress, we perceive one syllable as *stronger* or
heavier and another as *weaker* or *lighter* (*Silbengewicht*). The relative
weight (or *strength*) of the syllable in question can be determined by
various factors.[3]

A most important factor affecting stress in our languages is the *force
of exhalation* (of the expiratory flow of air) and the associated *tension of
the vocal chords*. Such stress is called *expiratory* or *dynamic*. The
acoustical correlate of these articulatory phenomena will be the impression of *loudness* produced by the syllable in question. There is, however,
reason to believe that the rhythmical impression, not only for the reader
of a line of verse but also for the listener, is determined not so much by
the alternation of sounds varying in loudness as it is by the exchange of
articulations with greater or less tension, that is, the perception of rhythm
is more closely connected with motor impressions (although received
through the medium of speech) than with purely acoustical sensations.[4]

Another factor of stress can be the length of the syllable. In certain
languages — in, for example, Greek, Latin and German — length does
not depend on stress; that is to say, a stressed syllable can be short and an
unstressed long. In Russian, as Vostokov pointed out, "there is no
lengthening independent of exhalation", i.e., length depends on stress.

---

[3]   A discussion of stress and its factors will be found in Fr. Saran, § 12, p. 93 ff.
[4]   Fr. Saran, who limits himself in his study of verse to the analysis of *acoustical*
phenomena (*Standpunkt des Hörenden*), asserts that for the listener who has no means
of immediately observing the strength of pronunciation (*Stärke*) the dynamic factor is
replaced by its acoustical correlate, loudness (*Lautheit*) (p. 94). Cf., however, the
statements of Landry, pp. 80-81; "rhythmical sound, especially when accompanied by
melody, is perceived by us as having some relationship to voice and is reproduced in
internal speech (*reproduit intérieurement*). As a matter of fact, the larynx is in this
regard a very active organ, sensitive to the most insignificant external stimuli... In this
way rhythmical sound — that of music, for example, or of a speech — is perceived by
the hearer not only as sound, but at the same time, and unconsciously, as motor
rhythm, thanks to the movements reproduced by his own body..."

(cf. *Opyt*, pp. 21-22). According to the experimental observations of Prof. L. V. Ščerba, the stressed vowel in Russian pronunciation lasts, other things being equal, approximately $1\frac{1}{2}$ times as long as the unstressed.[5] Moreover, the stressed vowel can be prolonged without causing any essential deformation of the word while the unstressed vowel cannot. Ed. Sievers regards this capacity for prolongation as the feature which basically distinguishes the long vowel from the short.[6]

Connected with the expiratory accent and length — in some languages at least — is the precision or *clarity* with which a vowel is uttered. In Russian pronunciation, for instance, unstressed vowels undergo *reduction*, i.e., show a tendency to become an obscure front or back vowel (in Russian phonetic transcription written ь or ъ). The vowels least subject to reduction are those immediately preceding the stress and those in a final open syllable just after the stress. In German the majority of unstressed vowels are reduced to the obscure whispered vowel indicated in normal orthography by *e* (in phonetic transcription — ə), e.g., Nam*e*, Gebirg*e*, and so on. The same origin is to be ascribed to French "silent *e*" (*e* muet), which in the majority of cases is no longer pronounced after the stress in the colloquial language, but is artificially preserved, at least within the line, by the archaizing poetic pronunciation.[7] The other unstressed vowels are maintained with complete clarity in French pronunciation. In the same way, all vowels in Italian are spoken with the same distinctness.

An important factor affecting stress is *musical accent*, i.e., a *rise in pitch* of the voice. In certain languages (e.g., in Ancient Greek) the raising or lowering of the voice pitch constitutes the basic feature of word-accent. In the majority of modern languages musical accent plays an independent role only in the sentence as a whole: within the word it usually coincides with the expiratory accent so that the syllable which is dynamically stronger is usually melodically higher (or lower, in certain languages).

Finally, in some languages one can speak of the semantic weight of certain syllables as a factor of stress. Thus, in the Germanic languages the accent generally falls on the first root syllable of the word — e.g., Name, Garten, sterben, etc. In compound words with major derivative suffixes the element which is semantically weaker receives the secondary stress (Váterlànd, Brúderschàft, etc.). In such cases semantic relationships

---

[5] Cf. L. V. Ščerba, *Russkie glasnye* (1912), p. 148.
[6] Ed. Sievers *Grundzüge der Phonetik*, pp. 257, 261 ff.
[7] Cf. *Rifma*, notes 7 and 83.

are taken as one of the factors determining the *weight* of the syllables. In Russian the semantic weight is significant only within larger syntactic units; this is the so-called *logical* stress (e.g., Èto *moj* drug, a ne *tvoj*. [That is *my* friend, not *yours*.]).

The phonetic factors of accent normally operate in unison and are subordinated to the influence of the predominant factor — the expiratory accent. There are, however, cases when each of them operates independently. For instance, in the group *Drug-moj*! the word *moj* is *deprived* of stress, since it is joined to the preceding word like a particle, but the vowel *o* does not undergo any qualitative reduction (cf. *Drúg-moj*! and *drúžboj*, where the final vowel is reduced to ə — [drúžbəj]). The semantic independence of the pronoun makes possible the preservation of clarity in the pronunciation of the vowel. Therefore in the line "Drug-*moj*, drug dalëkij..." the second syllable, metrically unstressed and bearing no dynamic stress, is nevertheless clearly pronounced and carries more weight than the usual vowel in post-stress position. In exactly the same way certain unstressed conjunctions maintain their qualitative identity, e.g., *no* in "*No* ty ot gor'kogo lobzan'ja..." In just the same way the melodic accent is in some less frequent cases separated from the dynamic. Thus, the melodic rise of the voice marks the interrogative pronoun and adverb in the immediate vicinity of the stress. E.g., "Uvjal... ¡*Gde* žarkoe volnen'e?... ¡*Gde* mnete vešnie cvety?... ¡*Kto* budet tam? — svoja sem'ja." In demonstrative adverbs, signifying an object at some distance from the speaker, there is in any case a predominant musical accent (a *demonstrative* intonation); e.g.: "¡*Tam* nekogda guljal i ja... ¡*Von* begaet dvorovyj mal'čik..." and others.

Around every strong syllable there is a cluster of one or more weaker syllables. In an isolated word this clustering is determined principally by the semantic unity of the *word*. In a sentence the boundaries of the so-called stress-groups (*rečevye takty*) certainly do not coincide in every case with the boundaries of words.[8] Furthermore, the phraseological stress (*Satzaccent*) comes into play here. Strong syllables are differentiated among themselves according to their prominence and are subordinated to other, stronger syllables. Around a strong *phraseological stress* clusters a more or less extensive *phraseological group*, usually also defined by the syntactic interrelationship of its elements. Thus every

---

[8] On the boundaries of the verbal stress groups cf. Sievers' views below, § 26, and in his *Grundzüge* pp. 232-240. For Russian pronunciation cf. certain observations by B. Černyšev in "Zametki o delenii slov v russkom proiznošenii", *Izv. otd. russk. jaz. slov.*, vol. XVI (1911), 2.

sufficiently extended verbal utterance (sentence) is divided into several mutually dependent phraseological groups, united by stresses of varying intensity. Let us take the following example:

Ja – povstrečalsja – s = nim || kogda – my = šli | po = ulice – Gogolja.
ᴦI   met   with him || when we were walking | along Gogol Street.]

As regards both stress and syntax, this sentence falls into two parts (separated by ||). In the first part the strongest stress is on the word *povstrečalsja*. The words *ja* and *s = nim* are joined to this base word to form a unified phraseological group. Both monosyllabic words, however, have independent stresses: *s = nim* — the stronger stress (the utterance functions semantically as the indirect object); *ja* — the weaker stress (the personal pronoun as subject attached to the verb). In the second part there are two phraseological groups: *kogda — my = šli | po = ulice — Gogolja*. The main stress of the first group is on the word *šli*, which is semantically the most significant; the conjunction *kogda* (auxiliary part of speech) has a weak stress, and the pronoun *my* is completely unstressed since it is immediately joined to the stress of its verb (in the combination *ja — povstrečalsja* the pronoun is separated from the stress by two unstressed syllables and is therefore relatively stronger).[9] In the second group the word *Gógolja* has the strongest stress (*úlica — Gógolja* forms a unified semantic complex with a phraseological stress on the second element; cf. *úlica — Glínki, úlica — Žukóvskogo*). Nevertheless, the word *úlica* also has a rather strong stress, not only because of its semantic weight, but also because of the mechanical conditions of its pronunciation (there are two unstressed syllables between the stresses). The preposition *po* has no independent stress and is linked as a *proclitic* to its noun. As compared to the word *my*, its stress is weaker (in their syntactic functions prepositions correspond to case endings) and its vowel undergoes qualitative reduction. Of the two phraseological groups forming the second part of the sentence, the second group (...*Gógolja*) apparently has a somewhat stronger phraseological accent in normal pronunciation than the first (*šli*), since the point of the utterance is not that the meeting took place when we were *walking* (šli) rather than *riding* (éxali), but that we were walking along *Gogol Street* rather than

---

⁹ F. Korš formulates the following "general rhythmical law": "The final stress, no matter how weak it may be by itself, acquires strength in direct proportion to the number of unstressed syllables which precede it." (*O russkom narodnom stixosloženii*, p. 22). "The same holds also in reverse, counting from the final stressed syllable toward the front of the word" (p. 23). For German, cf. § 15 above (J. Minor, p. 79).

Žukóvskij Street.[10] Thus we might observe several degrees of stress within this sentence, marking them with numbers, e.g., 1, 2, 3, etc. Then the strongest stresses fall on the words *povstrečálsja* and *Gógolja* (1), somewhat weaker — *šli* (2), still weaker — *po* = *úlice* (3), still weaker — *s* = *nim* (4), weakest — *ja* (5) and *kogdá* (5). The number of degrees must change, in view of the fact that stress is determined by the relationship of one syllable to others, but, as we shall see later, in studying verse it is expedient to set up at least *two* degrees of stress for the stressed syllables (strong and weak stress) and *two* degrees for the unstressed (completely unstressed and very slightly stressed). In any case, the practice of describing the actual rhythm of verse by means of the traditional foot, based on the elementary opposition "stressed" vs. "unstressed", leads to numerous misunderstandings.

17. DISPUTED QUESTIONS OF RUSSIAN STRESS

In the work of A. Belyj some of the examples of rhythmical deviation have been so labeled as a result of a misunderstanding. Thus, in the analysis of Puškin's poem "Ne pój, krasávica, pri mné..." (pp. 400-401) we are given the following examples of an iamb being replaced by a *spondee*: on the first foot — "Ty pésen Grúzii pečál'noj... Ja prízrak mílyj, rokovój..."; on the second foot — "Egó ja vnov' voobražáju..." In all three cases the personal pronoun (ja, ty) is the subject and, in the vicinity of the accent, is devoid of stress. Compare an analogous example from Baratynskij — "Ni žit' im, ni pisát' eščë ne nadoélo..." — the first two feet of which Belyj regards as *spondees*. N. V. Nedobrovo reads the line "Kto b ne oter ix u pečali..." with a trochee in the first and third feet (in reality otér-ix forms one stress-group, since the pronoun is weakened and subordinate to the verb-stress). In the line "Mysl' izrečënnaja est' lož'" he not only sees a trochee in the first foot but also a *spondee* in the fourth (while as a matter of fact the auxiliary copula verb is weakened next to the stress of the subject). The lines "S temnokudrjávoj golovój" and "V jarko blestjaščej pyšnoj zale" serve in his book as examples of a disyllabic trochaic word creating a trochaic beginning in an iambic line (though in fact one must take into account the special accentual treatment

---

[10] On the problem of phrase stresses cf. L. V. Ščerba, *Opyt lingvističeskogo tolkovanija stixotvorenija* (*Russkaja Reč'*, 1923). According to Ščerba's observations, the normal phrase accent, if it does not serve to emphasize the sense of what is being said, occurs in Russian at the end of a phrase group and attracts no special attention to itself (p. 24).

of compound words). But the greatest number of such readings are to be found in V. Brjusov's book *Nauka o stixe* (especially in the first edition). Perusal of this book could easily lead to the erroneous conclusion that Russian binary meters show replacement of iambs by trochees and spondees, and of trochees by spondees and iambs, in all feet of the line, under all possible conditions, and with striking frequency. The whole difficulty, however, is simply in the improper arrangement of stresses in Brjusov's textbook, which furnishes every monosyllabic word, even slightly stressed ones, with a stress. *In iambic*, for instance: "Začem ja mimoletnoj vstreči..." (trochee in the second foot); "V nej strastnyj žar; ej dušno, durno..." (spondee in the first and third feet); "A bez togo vam raj ne raj..." (spondee in the third foot); *in trochaic*: "Viš' nelegkaja ix nosit..." (spondee in the third foot);" "Prazdnovat' moj prazdnik svetlyj..." (iamb in the second foot); "Kto tvoj nežnyj Seladon?..." (spondee in the first foot); "Čto tam bylo, čto tam stalo?..." (spondee in the first and third feet) and many others.[11] Even in the work of B. V. Tomaševskij, who devotes several pages to the problem of stress both in *Russkoe stixosloženie* and in his earlier book *Ritmika cetyrëxstopnogo jamba*, one encounters here and there stresses which, at least, give rise to some misgivings. Thus, in the examples of a stress on a metrically weak syllable (from *Evgenij Onegin*): "U káždogo *svoj* úm i tólk... Kto v dvádcat' lét *byl* fránt i xvát... Mečtý, mečtý, *gde* váša sládost'?... I, méždu tém, dušá v *nej* nýla... (pp. 177-180)". In *Russkoe stixosloženie*: "*Tam* górdo bléščet Rím čužój..." (p. 29) "*Tam* górdo ja dušóju vosparjú..." (32) "*Tak* nékogda obdúmyval s roptán'em..." (32) The following line is quoted with some hesitation "Ty byl, ty est', ty budeš' vvek..." (33). But in his examples of ternary meters with *unmetrical stress on the first syllable* the following line is introduced without any reservation: "*Mne* snílsja mučítel'nyj són..." (37).

V. Čudovskij, on the other hand, in his article *Neskol'ko myslej k vozmožnomu učeniju o stixe* (*Apollon*, 1915, no. 8-9) proposes to consider all words not expressing independent *"concepts"*, but simply *"relationships"* or *modalities"*, as unstressed. Into this category fall all words with a weak stress — both monosyllabic and disyllabic, both those occupying metrically weak positions in the line and those falling under the metrical accent. The absence of a stress is shown by writing the words together (p. 77):

---

[11] Cf. R. Jakobson, *Brjusovskaja stixologija*, p. 227-228. Under the influence of this article Brjusov, in the second edition of *Nauka o stixe*, excluded the greater part of the above examples, with two exceptions (A bez togo *vam* raj ne raj... Viš', nelëgkaja *ix* nosit...).

Mojdjadja samyx čestnyx pravil
Kogdanevšutku zanemog
Onuvažat' sebja zastavil
Ilučše vydumat' nemog
Egoprimer drugim nauka
Nobožemoj kakaja skuka... etc.

Finally, there are many cases in which the authors themselves are un-
certain about the stress. Čudovskij presents a great many such doubtful
cases (pp. 77-82). E.g.: "Bezmolvno budu *ja* zevat' ... *mog* iz"jasnjat'sja
i pisal... *kak my* ni bilis' otličit' ... *ja byl* ozloblen, on ugrjum... Zatem,
čto ne vsegda že mog..." and others. It is possible, for instance, to have
the following readings: "Mog-iz"jasn**ja**t'sja i pis**al**..." or "Mog iz"jasnjat'sja i pis**al**;" "Kak-my-ni-bilis' otličit'..." or "Kak-my ni-bilis' otličit'"
or, finally, "K**a**k my-ni-bilis' otličit'..." and so on.

B. V. Tomaševskij had the same kind of doubts in his work on *Evgenij
Onegin*. For example, the line "Byvalo on eščë v posteli ..." according to
Tomaševskij, "can be pronounced in two ways: either by stressing all the
feet or by considering *on* and *eščë* as unstressed, which would cause this
line to resemble the phrase "Vlečen'em nepreodolimym" (p. 146).

As is clear from all the examples cited above, the doubtful cases in
Russian prosody belong to a specific category of weakly stressed words —
monosyllabic, for the most part, and more rarely disyllabic — which
occupy something like an intermediate position between significant words
("concepts") and purely functional words (like prepositions and conjunctions): here belong, for the most part, pronouns and certain adverbs
(pronominal), auxiliary verbs, and a few others. These difficulties arise
principally in the study of binary meters, while the ternary meters, with
their immobile stresses, show far greater accentual inertia and precision;
the latter, furthermore, permit the greatest liberty and variety in the
positioning of supplementary stresses on metrically weak syllables.

It is interesting to note that the Russian theoreticians of the eighteenth
and early nineteenth centuries had already given some consideration
to the dubious cases of Russian prosody mentioned above. Tred'jakovskij
set the monosyllabic words apart in a special category as *"general"* (i.e.
metrically ambiguous). Cf. *Sposob k složeniju stixov rossijskix*, Chap. 1,
§§ 13-15: "There is not one word which it would be possible to utter
without stressing it once on some one syllable; i.e., there is not one word
which would not contain a long syllable. And as there is a vast multitude
of monosyllabic words, it follows that they, too, cannot be spoken
without a stress... In view of this, all monosyllabic words are long

by their very nature. However, although this is beyond any doubt, they are all considered *general* in the usage of our poets for the purposes of composing feet, i.e. they are either short or long according to what is needed. This license is so necessary that without it one could hardly compose a single line without a multitude of difficulties." Tred'jakovskij repeats this theory in the prefaces to *Tilemaxida* and *Argenida*[12] and he carries it out in his own verse with his characteristic pedantry. For him any monosyllabic word, even a preposition or a conjunction, could be used to carry the stress or could, on the contrary, be considered unstressed, even when it expressed a concept of considerable import, e.g., as a noun or a verb. Cf. "Petux vzbeg na navoz, a ryt' načav tot vskore..."

Lomonosov, in replying to Tred'jakovskij, establishes three categories of monosyllabic words: absolutely stressed, absolutely unstressed and variable. "In my opinion", he writes in his *Pis'mo*, "some of our monosyllabic words are always long and others always short, e.g., the conjunctions *že, da, i*; and others are sometimes short and sometimes long, e.g., na more, po godu, na volju, po gore." In the latter category, however, Lomonosov puts not so much the metrically ambiguous words as those combinations which allow variable stressing in ordinary speech (na-móre or ná-more).

Sumarokov's observations in his article *O stoposloženii* are much more varied. In opposition to Tred'jakovskij he, like Lomonosov, declares that *prepositions* and *conjunctions* are absolutely unstressed. "Prepositions and conjunctions are particles, not words or expressions, and they do not have roots. In the vicinity of monosyllabic words and expressions they never have full force; so I wish that those who are not sufficiently educated to know the rules of proper versification would at least not use prepositions and conjunctions as long words, for it is this ignorance which makes their lines of so-called poetry repulsive to the ear" (p. 70). Sumarokov's observations on logical stress are also interesting. "The syllable

---

[12]　Tred'jakovskij, *Coll. Works*, ed. A. Smirdin, Vol. II, *Tilemaxida. Pred"iz"jasnenie ob iroičeskoj piime*, p. LXIX. The polemic with Sumarokov on the question of monosyllabic words is in the preface to the *Argenida*: "However, a certain clever person has caused some difficulty about this most simple matter. He asserts that our monosyllabic words are some of them long, others short, and others general, that is, both long and short." In his rejoinder Tred'jakovskij points out, as in his other articles, that all words including monosyllabic, have a stress, and that monosyllabic words are therefore "long" by their very nature and "are regarded as general only under a sort of restricted license". Besides, the division of monosyllabic words into three categories presents enormous difficulties. "In my opinion, whichever system is simplest is the best: there is already enough difficulty in poetry just to seek out the thoughts" (p. LXX ff.).

bearing the sense is the longer of two longs" (68). He illustrates his point with the two following examples: "Bog mudr, a ja bezumen" and "Mudr *bog*, a ne *ja*." In the first example, Sumarakov points out, "the syllable forming the name of God is shorter, but in the second it is longer" (68). But of especial interest is Sumarokov's polemic with Lomonosov in regard to the pronoun. For Sumarokov the pronoun always carries stress and he therefore regards as impermissible the positioning of pronouns on metrically weak syllables. "Mr. Lomonosov, by taking away the strength of the pronoun, has not infrequently marred his own versification" (68). He cites many examples taken from Lomonosov's odes and from his epistle to Šuvalov. E.g., the interrogative pronoun: "*čtó* vsex umy k sebe vlečët?" Sumarokov points out: "*Čto* is both a pronoun and a conjunction: here a pronoun was required, but the versification turned it into a conjunction, and the line was ruined" (72). Other examples of pronouns which add extra stresses to the line "Na verox *ix* vozvraščajus'..." "Steklo *im* roždeno..." "*on* proizvest' xotja..." (73). Thus, in his treatment of unstressed syllables, Sumarokov is, compared with Lomonosov, the strictest of purists. He notes even such insignificant cases of hypermetrical stress on the first syllable as when a weak conjunction is followed by an unstressed syllable (cf. below, § 18): "ɪ tjagotu zemli..." "Even though conjunctions are short", he writes, "this is not the case in pyrrhics; and here there is a dactyl and a trochee, not an iamb" (74). Thus, in his evaluation of the accentual properties of pronouns, Sumarokov is close to certain modern theoreticians (e.g., V. Brjusov), though with the *essential* difference that he regarded "deviation" from the meter as a defect, and not as a virtue (53).

Vostokov, in his observations on the Russian "spondee" in *Opyt o russkom stixe* (1812-17), limits himself to pointing out that when two stresses fall side by side one of them is usually suppressed. "But when two stresses occur next to each other — e.g., gdé ón, podí próč, skazàt' vám — then one or the other is concealed and gives way to the other — e.g., *gdè-on* or *gde-ón, podi-próč, skazát'-vam*". "But if neither of the two stresses can yield, which most often happens in combinations of polysyllabic words, e.g., postirát' rúki, iskát' slávy, or of monosyllabic words which retain their stress on account of their importance and expressiveness, e.g., gróm grjánul, áz réx bózi estè, then one must not fail to allow an interval or interruption (*pause*) in the voice to come between the clashing stresses..." (21-22). Vostokov thus comes to deny the existence of balanced spondees in Russian verse (cf. below § 32). He regards monosyllabic words as those most apt to lose their stress, and from this point of view he divides them into two categories according to their semantic importance, without making, however, the effort to classify them more precisely in terms of grammatical criteria.

The problem of monosyllabic words receives its most extensive treatment in D. Samsonov's *Kratkoe rassuždenie* (*Vestnik Evropy*, 1817, vol. 94, p. 221). The monosyllabic words Samsonov divides into *absolutely unstressed* ("low") and *ambiguous* ("general"); within the latter category he is very soon obliged to set up a special group which, by reason of their semantic importance, can not lose the stress even in a metrically weak position; he too, however, is unable to draw a more exact line between the ambiguous ("general") and the absolutely unstressed words. He writes: "Monosyllabic words are either low or general, i.e., such as can be high or low according to circumstances. Conjunctions and prepositions are always low, even in those cases where the latter receive a stress transferred from a neighboring word, e.g., zá morem, pó suxu." Here follows a note: "Prepositions remain low also in those cases when, for the sake of euphony, monosyllables become disyllabic or even trisyllabic, e.g., nado mnóju, predo mnóju." Further: "All other monosyllabic words are general. Thus, in the verse of Deržavin "Grom na grom v vyšine, gul na gul v glubine..." the words *grom* and *gul*, according to the movement of the line, are low in the first instance and high in the second. One must however make certain distinctions in this matter. Monosyllabic words which attract especial attention to themselves, or which are very sonorous, i.e., contain many consonants, are almost always used, at least by good poets, as high syllables. "Ja *car'*, ja *rab*, ja *červ'*, ja *bog*" writes Deržavin in the well known ode. The words *car'*, *rab*, *červ'*, and *bog* are in high position, and not without reason. In the first place, the thought is principally expressed through them, and in the second place, they are more sonorous than *ja*. In the line "Bog *rek*, da budet svet" the forceful word is *rek*."

And so even the early theoreticians of Russian versification devoted themselves to the most essential and disputed question of Russian prosody — the accentuation of monosyllabic words — although no very exact definition was found for that category of words which, for the most part, can be considered metrically ambiguous (monosyllabic "general" words). In what follows we shall try to put this question in a more systematic form, both for the binary and ternary meters.

18. AMBIGUOUS MONOSYLLABIC WORDS

We distinguish three groups of monosyllabic words: (1) obligatorily stressed words, (2) absolutely unstressed words, and (3) metrically ambiguous words.

In the first category belong all words with full material meaning (word-concepts or, as Lomonosov called them, "significant" words): 1) nouns, 2) adjectives, 3) verbs (except the auxiliary), 4) adverbs (except pronominal). When they occur in a metrically weak position in the line, these words retain their stress, creating a rhythmical stress which is outside the regular pattern. It is incorrect, however, to view such cases as the replacement of an iamb (or a trochee) by a *spondee*, since the syllable bearing the hypermetrical stress is still weaker than the following (or preceding) syllable, i.e., the relationship between stresses characteristic of the iambic rhythm is preserved. Cf. "Dux pylkij i dovol'no strannyj... *Cel'* žizni našej dlja nego... Pod nej *sneg* utrennyj xrustit..." G. Šengeli (*Traktat*, p. 35) associates this subordination of the preceding stress to the following one with the "logical" (i.e., syntactic) relationship between the corresponding words: at all events, a syntactic pause between two stresses noticeably disturbs the iambic rhythm, isolating the metrically weak monosyllable and thus increasing the weight of its stress. Cf. Šengeli's examples for the normal subordination occurring when there is no break in the syntax: "Groza. *Dožd'* xlynul. Luč..."; with the syntactic break: "Pošël *dožd'*. Svetlyj luč..." Such isolation occurs when a list of objects is given, e.g., Puškin's "Slova — *bor*, burja, voron, el'... Skučna mne ottepel': *von'*, grjaz'; vesnoj ja bolen..." Deržavin's "Poljak, *Turk*, Pers, *Pruss*, Xin i Švedy..." The same holds true when there is emphatic repetition: "*Tam, tam* pod seniju kulis..." A change of rhythm is perceived only if — in addition to the presence of a hypermetrical stress — there is also failure to stress a syllable in a metrically strong position (displacement of stresses, replacement of an iamb by a "trochee"). In this case also, however, there is a dominant tendency to subordinate hypermetrical stresses to the nearest following normal stress. Thus in the first foot of an iambic line: "*Boj* barabannyj... *P'ët* obol'stitel'nyj obman..." As exceptions to the general rule of hypermetrical stressing one must mention those cases where, even in everyday speech, a normally stressed word is deprived of stress; e.g., in phrases where the individual words are inseparable, such as "byt'-možet, daj-bog" and so on. Cf., for example, Puškin's "Byt' možet na bedu moju... Itak, daj-bog im dolgi dni... I zapiščit ona (bog-moj!)..."

The category of absolutely unstressed words comprises, besides dependent particles (-že, -li, -by), monosyllabic prepositions and conjunctions which play an exclusively auxiliary (formal) role in the sentence. They attach to the preceding or following word as absolute proclitics or enclitics. Cf. "...ko-mne, ...so-mnoj, ...za-vami, ...o-tom, ...mež-nix; ty-i-ja; ne-ty, a-ja; ...no-ty ne-možeš'..." etc. In a line of verse, these always remain unstressed both in metrically strong and metrically weak positions. But, as we shall see later, there are certain special conditions under which even these auxiliary words are perceived as more stressed than the unstressed syllables of a polysyllabic word. This applies in particular to the more important conjunctions derived from pronouns or pronominal adverbs (e.g., čto, čem, gde, kak and certain others) and to prepositions which have not lost all connection with the corresponding nominal or adverbial forms (e.g., vkrug, vdol', sverx, etc.) (see below for further details). Of course one must also make an exception here for those cases in which, even in ordinary speech, the stress is transferred to the preposition from a following noun (enclisis) e.g., na-dom, na-pole, po-lesu, za-zimu, etc. Cf. Puškin's "Tri doma na-večer zovut... Prosnětsja za-polden' i snova... Solila na-zimu griby... So sna saditsja v vannu so-l'dom..." and so on.

In the category of ambiguous words we have pronouns and pronominal adverbs (and conjunctions), monosyllabic numerals, auxiliary verbs and interjections, i.e., words occupying a sort of intermediate position between significant and auxiliary. They are not wholly enclitic or proclitic, always exert some resistance to vowel reduction, and possess syntactically the independence of significant words.[13] Their ambiguous character from the point of view of stress can be seen even in everyday speech. Cf., for example, the possessive pronoun: moj (tvoj, svoj, etc.). In the phrase moj-drug or drug-moj the word *moj*, immediately linked to the stressed syllable of the accompanying noun, is perceived alongside it as unstressed, though it is distinguished from the usual unstressed syllable (especially one in post-stress position) by the fact that its vowel remains unchanged in quality. The same is true of the phrase moj-milyj drug, where there is another adjective between the pronoun and the noun. The situation is different in the phrases "moj tovarišč... moj ljubimyj

---

[13] Metropolitan Evgenij Bolxovitinov, an opponent of Lomonosov's system, in his letter to Deržavin (1815), also accused Lomonosov and Tred'jakovskij of having "made our monosyllabic words, which are long by nature, into short ones". For example: "Lomonosov regards as iambic the line 'On bog, on bog, tvoj byl Rossija.' But these are spondees, not iambs. And amongst the trochees he includes 'gospodi, kto obi-taet'... But that is dactylic, not trochaic!" (*Moskvitjanin* 1842, I, pp. 173-174).

drug... èto moj ljubimyj drug..." or "mal'čik moj... ljubimec moj".
There the word *moj*, separated from the nearest stress by one or more
unstressed syllables, is perceived as a stressed syllable, although its stress
is weaker than that of the neighboring significant word (noun or adjective).[14] The same may be said of the personal pronouns: *ja, ty, on.*
Cf. šla-ja (de-stressed) — xodila ja (with a very weak stress); ja šël po
gorodu (de-stressed) — ja ušël iz goroda (with a very weak stress) — noč'ju
ja ušël iz goroda (ditto). And the personal pronoun, like the possessive,
is distinguished from the usual unstressed syllable by lack of vowel
reduction. It should be noted that the suppression of stress is more
strongly felt in enclisis, i.e., when the pronoun *follows* the dominant
word (e.g., drug-moj, šël-ja).

Not all ambiguous words are reduced to the same degree. Alongside
forms with a lighter stress (the personal pronoun in the nominative, the
possessive pronoun) there exist forms with a somewhat heavier stress.
Cf., for instance, the oblique cases of the personal pronoun (functioning
as an object): Daj-*mne* obedat'... *Mne*-nado uxodit'... Protjani-*ej* ruku...
Ej-xočetsja videt' tebja... A somewhat heavier stress is carried, for
example, by the demonstrative adverbs, in which the greater dynamic
force is accompanied by a characteristic rise in intonation (*demonstrative
intonation*): ¡*Tak*-veselo nam s toboj... ¡*Tam*-v'ëtsja žavoronok. These
relatively more heavily stressed forms lose their stress, in the vicinity of
another stress, to a far lesser degree than the weaker forms; moreover,
separated from a stress by one or more unstressed syllables, they possess
much greater weight than the corresponding "lighter" forms. Cf. **Ej**
xotelos' tebja videt'... **Ta**m zav'etsja xmel'. In both positions, however,
the words of this category are much weaker than monosyllabic nouns or
verbs.

Thus, in the immediate vicinity of a stress,. monosyllabic ambiguous
words lose their stress (not always to the same degree); in the vicinity
of an unstressed syllable they retain a more or less noticeable stress, but
it has less force than that of an obligatorily stressed word.

We must mention, as an exception to this rule, those cases when the
ambiguous word is subjected to a *logical* or *emphatic* stress. E.g. Èto
moj drug, a ne *tvoj*... Èto *ja* šël noč'ju iz goroda... *ty* vspomnil obo
mne v ètot trudnyj čas... [*you* remembered me in that difficult hour]
(i.e., you *alone, you* in particular). When such words occur in a metrically weak position in a line, the logical stress gives them a certain degree
of hypermetrical stress. Cf. "I ja ljubila vas, i čto že? *čto* v serdce vašem

---

[14] Cf. Korš's rule in footnote 9 on p. 92.

ja našla?... *tam, tam* pod seniju kuplis... *vy*, ravnodušnye sčastlivcy, *vy* školy Levšina ptency, *vy*, derevenskie Priamy i *vy*, čuvstvitel'nye damy..." Those ambiguous words which are especially subject to logical stress are the demonstrative pronouns and adverbs, the interrogatives and the second person pronoun (in emphatic use).

These characteristics of the ambiguous words are to be seen with unusual clarity in verse. For Russian verse — especially for the binary meters — it is one of the most essential prosodic laws. It was noted as far back as Tred'jakovskij, although he incorrectly applied it to all monosyllabic words — regarded as "general" in his system — regardless of what grammatical category they belonged to. Russian prosody, based on phonetic principles, should once more make use of this modified concept of the "ambiguous" (or "general") monosyllabic word (*syllaba anceps*).

Let us return to the examples cited above. The personal and possessive pronouns (ja, on, moj...) can be used in various ways in verse depending on their position in the metrical scheme. In a metrically weak position they are unstressed, losing their stress because of the neighboring stress either preceding or following. E.g., in *Evgenij Onegin* (most of the examples are from there): "Moj-djadja samyx čestnyx pravil... Ja-pomnju more pred grozoju... On-znal dovol'no po latyne... Ljublju eë, moj-drug Èl'vina... Drug-moj, drug dalëkij... (Fet) Ljublju-ja bešennuju mladost'... Pridi, pridi ja-tvoj suprug... Imel-on sčastlivij talant... čto znal-on tverže vsex nauk... Kak tomno byl-on molčaliv... Otveta net. On-vnov' poslan'e..." When these words carry the rhyme, where the metrical stress is obligatory, they also carry a stress. Cf. "Zamena sčast'ju, bože moj! (:pokoj)... Domoj odet'sja edet on (:vyšel von)... užasno nedovolen on (:storon)..." etc. When they occur in metrically strong positions in binary meters they carry a weaker-than-normal stress, which is more or less pronounced depending on the style of recitation. Cf. "No bože *moj* kakaja skuka... Onegin dobryj *moj* prijatel'... Kuda ž poskačet *moj* prokaznik?... Bezmolvno budu *ja* zevat'... Balety dolgo *ja* terpel... Byvalo *on* eščë v posteli... Už temno. V sanki *on* saditsja... K Talon pomčalsja: *on* uveren..." Weaker-than-normal stresses of this kind may for the sake of convenience be termed "half-stresses".

Of the greatest importance for prosody are cases where the stress is suppressed. As has been mentioned, an ambiguous word can lose its stress under the influence of a preceding or following stress. But the de-stressed word need not be in any way syntactically subordinate to the neighboring metrically stressed word to which it is linked. Cf., for example: "No v čëm on-istinnyj byl genij... On-tri časa po krajnej mere... Ja-vas xoču predosterč'... Ja-negoj naslaždus' na vole... Moj-modnyj dom i večer..." Since it is extremely rare for two stresses to be omitted in adjacent feet in the binary meters ("i klanjalsja neprinuž-dënno...") an ambiguous word located in a metrically weak position always has a stress just next to it and therefore is always more or less de-stressed unless it carries logical stress.[15] Only when the ambiguous word is syntactically linked not to a stress but to an unstressed word, especially where there is a rather significant syntactic pause between the stress and the monosyllabic word in question, is there a somewhat more noticeable accentuation. Cf. "I deva gor, *moj*-ideal... Davno l' dlja vas *ja*-zabyval... Už otvorjal *svoj*-vasisdas... Zanjav *vaš*-ljubopytnyj vzor..." This hypermetrical stressing becomes much more noticeable, of course, for the "heavier" words (e.g. oblique cases of pronouns). Cf. "No i Didlo *mne*-nadoel... I voobšče *ix*-preziral..." etc.[16]

The only position in which a monosyllable in a metrically weak position can be easily found in the vicinity of an absolutely unstressed word is at the beginning of an iambic verse or hemistich when there is no stress on the following (metrically strong) syllable. Then we perceive the ambiguous word at the beginning of the line as a slight hypermetrical stress on the first syllable (in other words: as the shift of the stress from the second to the first syllable). But these slight hypermetrical stresses must be distinguished from those cases in which the first syllable is a significant word with its own independent strong stress (e.g. "*Boj* bara-bannyj...") Cf. "*Moj* bestolkovyj, učenik... *Ja* ne želal s takim mučen'-em... *On* uvažat' sebja zastavil... On po-francuzski soveršenno... On zastrelit'sja, slava bogu..." In examining examples of hypermetrical stressing on the first syllable such cases as these must be grouped in a special category.

To the category of ambiguous words, aside from those mentioned above, belong all other personal and possessive pronouns. Cf. examples of de-stressing in a metrically weak position: "Ty-negu žizni uznaëš'... Ty-p'ëš' volšebnyj jad želanij... Byla-ty vljublena togda... My-vse učilis' ponemnogu... My-lučše pospešim na bal... Vy-takže, mamen'ki, pos-

---

[15] One of such rare cases is the line of Tjutčev "V zavetnuju *ix* citadel'...", where the ambiguous word *ix*, surrounded on both sides, thanks to the omission of the stresses on the fourth and sixth syllables, by a group of unstressed syllables, would have in another context a fairly strong stress, usable perhaps in an amphibrach, but in iambic surroundings should be weakened if possible. (Cf. § 12 above).

[16] In such cases also, however, it is possible for the ambiguous word to be linked to the adjacent stress without regard for syntax; e.g., *I voobšče-ix preziral...*

trože... Kogda b vy-znali, kak užasno... Tvoj-čudnyj vzor menja tomil... Kogo tvoj-stix bogotvoril... Svoj-vek blestjaščij i mjatežnyj... Cenzure dolg-svoj zaplaču... U každogo svoj-um i tolk... Kak na lugax vaš-lëgkij sled... Komu porok-naš ne beda... Da zdravstvuet Ai, naš-drug... Ljublju ix-nožki, — tol'ko vrjad... Ix-obraz tajnyj soxranil...''

Examples of a slight hypermetrical stress on the first foot (the second being unstressed): "*Ty* posvjatil eë napev... *My* ne slyxali pro ljubov'... *Vy* ne ostavite menja... *Tvoj* iskusitel' rokovoj...'' etc.

More important are the oblique cases of the personal pronouns in the metrically weak position, which is understandable when one considers their semantic weight (direct or indirect objects). When they are just next to a stress, however, they also lose their stress. Cf. *mne*: "Mne-pamjatno drugoe vremja... Mne-snilis', i duša moja... I zasluži-mne slavy dan'... Čto Tanja? Čto s toboj?-Mne-skučno...'' *Ej, nej*: "Ej-šepčut: Dunja, primečaj... Ej-skučen byl i zvonkij smex... Gde skučnyj muž, ej-cenu znal... V nej-strastnyj žar, ej dušno, durno...'' *Nam, nas*: "Javljal-nam svoego geroja... Supružestvo nam-budet mukoj... No ot druzej, spasi-nas, bože!...'' *Vam, vas*: "Čego-ž-vam bol'še... Vam slovo molvit', i potom... Puskaj sožžët-vas božij gnev... V vas-iskru nežnosti zametja...'' *Im, ix*: "Im-kvas, kak vozdux, byl potreben... Itak, daj bog-im dolgi dni... Ja vsë-ix pomnju... Ix-posle muža oživila... Ja povedu-ix pod venec...'' Since the stress on the oblique cases of the personal pronoun is somewhat stronger, it appears more prominent on the first syllable of an iambic line in the vicinity of an unstressed syllable. Cf.: "S *nim* podružilsja ja v to vremja... *Nam* prosveščen'e ne pristalo... *Im* ovladelo ponemnogu... *Mne* neprijaznennoj stixii... *Ix* ne zovët ego rožok...'' and so on. Cf. also after a significant pause within the line "Predvižu vsë: vas oskorbit...''

The demonstrative adverbs and pronouns, by their very nature, demand greater accentual prominence and are subject to a logical or emphatic stress. The demonstrative pronoun *tot* (*ta, to, te, toj,*... etc.) is weaker than the other forms. Cf. "V tot-god osennjaja pogoda... On pel te-dal'nie strany... S nim podružilsja ja v to-vremja... Užel' ta-samaja Tat'jana... V toj-kučke, vidiš', vperedi... "Cf. also the substantivized forms: "To-vvyssem suždeno sovete, to-volja neba — ja tvoja...'' But with emphatic stressing: "V *tom* sovesti, v *tom* smysla net...'' The archaic *sej* (*sim, six,*... etc.) stands out more prominently for us today — stylistically and therefore also with regards to stress — than was probably the case during the age of Puškin. Cf. "Sej-angel, sej nadmennyj bes... Sej-lëgkoj žizniju, druz'ja... V sem-slučae sovsem ne prav...''

Considerably heavier — with regard to stress — is the demonstrative adverb of place; for some forms (*tam, tak, von*) there is a characteristic rise in voice pitch. Cf. *tam*: "Tam-nekogda guljal i ja... Tam-drug nevinnyx naslaždenij blagoslovit' by nebo mog... Tam-karla s xvostikom..." *Tut*: "Tut-verno kljatvy vy pročtěte... Tut-ostov čopornyj i gordyj..." *Zdes'*: "Zdes'-barin sižival odin..." The dynamic and melodic accent is clearly perceptible when there is a special emphasis or logical stressing: "*Tam* budet bal, *tam* detskij prazdnik... *Tam* skuka, *tam* obman i bred... *Tam, tam* pod seniju kulis..." But even in these cases the stress on the following word still dominates. The demonstrative adverb *tak* rates high from the point of view of stress. It is weaker when it is in the company of adjectives or adverbs: e.g., "Ego tak-milo iskažali... Tak-točno ravnodušnyj gost'..." It is considerably stronger when it appears with a verb (in the meaning "thus"): "Tak-dumal molodoj povesa... Tak-zajčik v ozimi trepeščet..." It is strongest of all when it is syntactically isolated, e.g., "Tak, zdravaja ona vostoržestvuet..." (*Boris Godunov*). With emphasis: "K tomu ž oni *tak* neporočny, *tak* veličavy, tak umny, *tak* blagočestija polny..." etc. The weakest of all, so far as stress is concerned, is the demonstrative adverb *vot* (*von*), which often has the meaning of a simple demonstrative particle. Cf. "Vot-utro; vstali vse davno... I v mysljax molvila: vot-on... Von-begaet dvorovyj mal'čik..." Of course, for all the words mentioned, the rule still holds that they furnish a supplementary stress at the beginning of an iambic line when the stress on the second syllable is omitted, and this stress is more or less prominent depending on the significance of the word itself. Cf.: "*Tam* Ozerov nevol'ny dani... *Tut* nepremenno vy najděte... Zdes' opisat' ego narjad... *Tak* unosilis' my mečtoj... *Tak* ja bespečen vospeval..." Weaker: "*To* nesomnennyj znak ej byl... *Sej* Grandison byl slavnyj frant..."

The relative and interrogative pronouns and adverbs (*kto, čto, čej, gde, kak*) have varying degrees of stress depending on their significance and syntactic function. These words are most apt to be de-stressed when they are reduced to the level of simple conjunctions. When this happens, the conjunction *kak* undergoes qualitative reduction (kək). Cf. "Gde, - možet byt', rodilis' vy ... Gde-mod vospitannik primernyj... Čto-on umën i očen' mil ... Čto - novyj načalsja balet... Kak - dandy londonskij odet... Letit, kak - pux ot ust Èola..." As relative pronouns and adverbs, the same words lose their stress easily, although they retain considerable semantic independence. Cf. *Kto* (= tot, kto...): "Kto - čuvstvoval, togo, trevožit... Blažen, kto-s neju sočetal... Blažen, kto-videl

ix volnen'ja..." or *čto* (= to, čto...; to, čego...); "Vsego, čto-znal eščë
Evgenij... Čto-znal on tverže vsek nauk... I to, čto-my nazvali frant..."
The oblique cases of the same words (the weightier forms): "V čëm-vse
uvereny davno... S čem-molča soglašalsja on..." *Čej*: "O ty, č'ja-pamjat'
soxranila... Č'ë serdce opyt ostudil..." The word *kak*, used in the sense
of an exclamation, is heavier: "Kak-grustno mne tvoë javlen'e!... Kak-
tvërdo v rol' svoju vošla!... Kak-vzor ego byl bystr i nežen!..." So is
kak in those cases where it means *how, in what way*: "Ne mog ponjat'
kak-važnyj Grimm mog čistit' nogti pered nim..."

The interrogative pronouns and adverbs show somewhat greater
resistance to de-stressing than do the other forms; in combination with
stress, their principal means of achieving prominence is a heightened
pitch of the voice. Cf. "Gde-mnëte vešnie cvety?... Uvjal. Gde-žarkoe
volnen'e?... Kto-budet tam? — Svoja sem'ja... Kto-nas zabotlivo leleet?...
Kto-ty? Moj angel li xranitel'...? Kem-sorvan byl? Kakoj rukoju... (Cv.)
Čto-možet byt' na svete xuže?... Čto-bylo sledstviem svidan'ja?... Čem
nyne javitsja? Mel'motom?... Č'ej-kazni? Starec nepreklonnyj! Č'ja doč'
v ob"jatijax ego? (*Poltava*)... Č'ej vzor, volnuja vdoxnoven'e...?" Cf. also
certain special cases of accentual prominence, e.g., when the interrogative pronoun replaces an entire sentence. "*Čto*? Priglašen'ja? V samom
dele... *Čto* ž? Tajnu prelest' naxodila... *Kak*? Iz gluši stepnyx selenij...?"
In the same way: "*Tak*, bylo vremja: s Kočubeem..." (*Poltava*). Once
again, of course, the first foot of an iambic line, when followed by an
unstressed syllable, is a special case: depending on the semantic value
and the syntactic function of the pronouns in question, the supplementary
stress will be of greater or less importance. Cf. "*Kto* oxlaždal ljubov'
razlukoj..." (relative); or "*Kto* klevety pro nas ne seet...?" (interrogative). "*Čto* zanimalo celyj den'..." (relative) or "*Čto* Godunov? Vo
vlasti li Borisa?" (*Boris Godunov*) (interrogative). "*Č'ja* blagosklonnaja
ruka..." (relative); "*Č'ja* ne kružitsja golova...?" (interrogative). "*Kak*
gosurdarstvo bogateet..." (relative); or "*Kak* nedogadliva ty, njanja!"
(exclamatory), and so on.

Of the other pronouns, the word *ves'* (vsja, vse, vsë) belongs to the
category of the heavier ambiguous words. Cf. "Vsja-žizn' moja byla
zalogom... Vse-jarusy okinul vzorom... Vsem-serdcem junošu ljubja...
Vsju-povest' o tvoej sud'be... S det'mi vsex vozrastov..." The same
applies to the more independent and significant substantivized forms:
vse (vse ljudi), *vsë*. Cf. "Vse-vstali. On k dverjam idet... Vse-družbu
prekratili s nim... Vsex-prežde vas ostavil on... Vsë-tixo. — Svetit ej
luna..." The pronoun *ves'* (vsë) is very liable to receive emphatic stress.

Cf. "Vsë, čem dlja prixoti obil'noj torguet London ščepitil'noj... vsë ukrašalo kabinet..." The word *vsë* used as an adverb is weaker: "Vsë-dumat', dumat' ob odnom... Vsë-te-že slušat' vozražen'ja..." With supplementary stress on the first syllable: "*Vsë* dlja mečtatel'nicy junoj..." Cf. also the pronoun *sam*: "Za nej sam-Getman svatov šlët..." With hypermetrical stress: "*Sam* o sebe vezde tverdja..."

One should also mention the very weak monosyllabic adverbs: *už, liš', čut'*. E.g. "Liš'-lodka, veslami maxaja... Čut'-otrok Ol'goju plenënnyj... Už-temno. V sanki on saditsja... Teatr už-polon. Loži bleščut..."

Ambiguous words in other grammatical categories are, for instance, the monosyllabic cardinal numerals (*dva, tri, pjat', sto*, etc.). Cf. "Dva--dnja emu kazalis' novy... Dve-nožki. Grustnyj, oxladelyj... Tri-doma na večer zovut... Daval tri-bala ežegodno... Prošlo sto-let, i junyj grad..." The monosyllabic forms of the auxiliary verb are also weak (*byl, byt', est'*): "No ja, ljubja, byl-glup i nem... Sej Grandison byl-slavnyj frant... Gotov-byl žertvovat' soboj... Byt'-čuvstva melkogo rabom... Mysl' izrečënnaja est' lož'..." (Tjutčev). The verb *byt'* in the meaning "to exist" (verbum substantivum) carries more weight. The forms especially employed in this meaning are *est'* (= exists) and *net* (= does not exist): "Vernej net-mesta dlaj priznanij... Est'-mesto: sleva ot selen'ja... Est'-nekij čas v noči vsemirnogo molčan'ja..." (Tjutčev). Other verbs which undergo the same kind of weakening in the vicinity of an accent are those called semi-auxiliary, i.e., those which have to a greater or lesser degree lost any material meaning and serve largely to add certain nuances to the action described by the base verb to which they are joined: e.g., *mog, stal*. Cf. "Mog-dumat' tol'ko ob odnom... Stal-ždat', čto kto-nibud drugoj..." They gain stress weight when followed by an unstressed syllable: "*Mog* iz"jasnjat'sja i pisal... *Stal* oživljat'sja..."

Finally, this category also includes the majority of the monosyllabic interjections — if they are not separated by a syntactic pause from the neighboring stress. Cf.: "O-vy, počtënnye suprugi... O-Brenta! net, uvižu vas... Ax, — dolgo ja zabyt' ne mog... Ax, — nožki, nožki! Gde vy nyne...? Ax, — milyj, kak poxorošeli..." etc. Punctuation marks (commas, exclamation points after interjections) only rarely indicate syntactic isolation. Example of an isolated interjection: "U! Kak teper' okružena kreščenskim xolodom ona..."

When two monosyllabic ambiguous words happen to occur side by side the stress is retained by the one which is also more important in prose. The personal pronoun as subject is ordinarily weaker than the others: as an enclitic, it tends to be de-stressed very easily. Cf. Kto-ja?

(rhyming with: geroja), gde-ty? (:odety), vse-my (:nemy), mne-ty (:odety), and so on. In the same way, however, a personal pronoun preceding another one is de-stressed, e.g., "my-vsę, ty-mnę, ty-gdę?" etc. Verse lines which show examples of such indisputable cases are, e.g., "My-vse učilis' ponemnogu... Ne mog-on jamba ot xoreja... Kak tomno byl-on molčaliv... Ja-vsë-ix pomnju... Čto-tam už ždët ego Kaverin..." and many others. In other cases, on the contrary, both monosyllabic words have approximately the same weight; when there is this sort of "accentual equilibrium" ("schwebende Betonung"), the intonation of whoever recites the poem determines whether the approximate equilibrium of both syllables will be maintained (to form a special kind of accentual "spondee") or whether one of them will be given more prominence, in which case the stress on the even syllable of an iambic line will correspond to the rhythmical inertia and that on the odd syllable, disrupting the metrical movement, will be conducive to semantic foregrounding. Cf. "*Kak on* umel zabyt' sebja... *Tam naš* Katenin voskresil... Vot moj Onegin na svobode... *Kak ja* zavidoval volnam... *Čto ž moj* Onegin ?... *Čto ja* mogu ešče skazat'?... *Vot kak* ubil on vosem' let... *On mne* znakom, *on mne* rodnoj... *Gde ja* stradal, *gde ja* ljubil..." To be sure, such accentual equilibrium can be developed with complete freedom only at the beginning of a line or in the middle after a relatively strong pause.

As has already been pointed out, all monosyllabic ambiguous words which occur in a metrically strong position carry stress, but it is ordinarily weaker than that of neighboring words (semi-stress). For example: "Nu čto ž, Onegin? *Ty* zevaes'... Tak, esli pravdu *vam* skazat'... No zvon bregeta *im* donosit... Uslyšu *vaš* poslednij glas... Deržite prjamo *svoj* lornet... Kto žil i myslil, *tot* ne možet... Rebënok *byl* rezov, no mil... Kak tomno *byl* on molčaliv..." etc. The stress on the heavier words is stronger: "Tak veličavy, *tak* umny... Čto *tam* už ždët ego Kaverin... I *čem* živët i počemu... C mužčinami so *vsex* storon... On *tri* časa, po krajnej mere... Ne *mog* ponjat', kak važnyj Grimm..." On the pronominal conjunctions the stress is very weak: "V pustyne, *gde* odin Evgenij... On veril, *čto* duša rodnaja... On veril, *čto* druz'ja gotovy... I molčaliva, *kak* Svetlana... Vezde byl prinjat, *kak* ženix... Čistoserdečnej, *čem* inoj... I *čtob* eë rassejat' gore... To govorlivoj, *to* nemoj... Tat'jana *to* vzdoxnët, to oxnet..." Cf. also certain especially weak adverbial forms (*už, liš', čut'*), e.g., "Vsë bylo tixo, *liš'* nočnye... Muzyka *už* gremet' ustala... Pogasšyj pepel *už* ne vspyxnet... S suprugom *čut'* ne razvelas'..."

The ternary measures exhibit the same basic conditions for the accentuation of monosyllabic ambiguous words. In a metrically weak position these words are de-stressed in varying degrees under the influence of the neighboring stress, either preceding or following. Here also, one can distinguish two groups, weak and strong, those that lose their stress and those that show greater resistance to loss of stress. In the poetry of Fet, for example, the following lines belong to the weaker group: "Drug-moj, ostan'sja so mnoj... Nežnyj lik-tvoj vstaet predo mnoj... Kogda-ja blestjaščij tvoj-lokon celuju... Tebja-ja v širokij svoj-plašč zavernu... Ždu-ja, trevogoj ob"jat... I emu-ja pro tajnu šepču... Ja-serdcem i razumom čišče... Ty-smotriš' mne-v-oči; ty-pravda — moj-trepet... Začem-vy sred' dnja i v časy polunoči... Začem govoriš'-ty pro devu inuju... Kak-mne pečal' prevozmoč'!... Bliže nel'zja-nam i byt'..." The following belong to the stronger group: "Poët i k svetu vsë-prosits-ja... Ja vsju-noč-im rasskazyvat' rad... Stanu slušat' te-detskie grezy... Kotorogo serdcu tak-žal'... I žarko dyšu-tak na miluju grud'... Vse vokrug i pestro-tak i šumno... Ždu-tut na samom puti... Tam-kto to manit za soboju... Za ramoj dve-svetlyx golovki... I naših dvux-tenej gromada..." A certain amount of hypermetrical stressing is noticeable in those cases in which the monosyllabic word is accentually and syntactical-ly linked not to the stress but to a neighboring unstressed syllable, especially when a considerable syntactic pause intervenes between it and the stress. Cf. "Ja prošeptal *vse*-četyre stixa... Mne *tak*-otradno s toboj... No *mne*-ponjatnej eščë govorit... Svež i dušist *tvoj*-roskošnyj venok... Kudri tvoj *tak*-obil'ny i pyšny... Skažu *toj*-zvezde... Serdce moë *vsë*-po-prežnemu nežno... My seli-s-nej *drug* protiv druga... Duša otkrovenno-tak s žizn'ju miritsja... Znat' vas ne uslyšat'-*mne* dvaždy..." and so on.

In the ternary meters, the first syllable of an anapest, separated as it is from the metrical stress by an unstressed syllable, occupies a special position. Here, as in the first foot of an iamb next to an unstressed syllable, the presence of a monosyllabic word always gives rise to a more or less prominent hypermetrical stress. Cf. "*Vsë* vokrug i pestro tak i šumno... *Vsë* blednej stanovilas' ona... *Ej* pro tajnu svoju govorju... *Mne* dyxanie skažet, gde ty... *Mne* sdaëtsja, čto krug blagovonnyj..." And even in weaker combinations: "*Ja* tebe ničego ne skažu... *Ty* ulybku moju unesla... *Gde* ronjaet cvety blagovonnyj mindal'..." and so on.

When monosyllabic ambiguous words occur in a metrically strong position in the ternary meters they carry a stronger stress than in the binaries, since the distance separating them from the nearest stress is greater. Cf. Nekrasov's lines: "Golod mučitel'nyj *my* utolili... Daj-ka jablonku *ja* za tebja posažu..." and others. In the first syllable of a dactyl, however, one clearly feels a weakening of the stress. Cf. Fet's *"Ja* prošeptal vse četyre stixa... *Ty* obeščala pritti... *Ja* rasskažu, čto tebja bespredel'no ljublju... *Čto* op'janennomu Muza prošepčet sama..."

19. DISYLLABIC AMBIGUOUS WORDS

The category of metrically ambiguous words includes not only mono-syllabic words but also disyllabic words belonging to the same gramma-tical categories and performing the same auxiliary functions within the syntactic unit: the word stress of such words is subordinated in the sentence to the dominant stress on more important neighboring words, except when the ambiguous words have a logical or emphatic stress. In actuality we have a great many disyllabic forms which resemble the monosyllabic words in their grammatical and syntactic function. Among the personal pronouns we have, alongside the monosyllabic *my* the disyl-labic *oni*, alongside the oblique cases *mne, ej, ix, im* the disyllabic *menja, mnoju, imi, nami,* etc. Among the possessive pronouns, we have alongside the monosyllabic *moj, naš, ix* the disyllabic *moja, moi, moix, naši, eë* and many others. Among the demonstrative pronouns: along with the word *tot* (*ta, to, te*) the disyllabic *ètot* (*èta, èto, ètim,* etc.), along with the oblique cases *tem, tex* the disyllabic cases *togo, temi,* etc.; in the demon-strative adverbs *tuda, togda.* Among the interrogative and relative pronouns and adverbs one can mention here, e.g., the oblique cases *kogo, čego, komu, čemu,* the adverbs (conjunctions) *kogda, kuda,* and many others. Among the verbal forms — the disyllabic forms of the auxiliary verb: *byla, budet* and so on. Notice also the extremely large group of disyllabic prepositions and conjunctions which have a very weak but nevertheless very precise word accent, e.g., *meždu, pered, posle, sredi, krugom,* etc., and *xotja, esli, čtoby* and so on.

In the binary meters these words are used only in such a way that their word stresses coincide with the metrical stresses. In spite of this the stress in question is always noticeably weaker than its neighbors: the term "semi-stress" can be extended to apply to this group also. Cf. at the beginning of *Evgenij Onegin*: *"Kogda* ne v šutku zanemog... *Ego* primer drugim nauka... *Emu* poduški popravljat' ... Naslednik vsex *svoix* rodnyx... Dolgami žil *ego* otec... Potom Monsieur *eë* smenil... Učil *ego* vsemu šutja..." and many others. Notice also the trisyllabic forms: *"Kakoe* nizkoe kovarstvo...! S geroem *moego* romana..." and others.

Such weakening of the metrical stress can be of essential importance for the rhythm of a poem, as we shall see later.

In the binary meters a special place is occupied by certain very weakly stressed conjunctions and prepositions, e.g., *ili, čtoby, čerez, pered, meždu, protiv* and several others. While in prose they are syntactically dependent and are completely subordinate to the stress of the following word, in verse they have a weak stress, sometimes on the first, sometimes on the second syllable, depending on the placement of the metrical accent. Cf., with the stress on the *second* syllable: "*Ili* kakoj-nibud' izdatel'... *Ili* zadumčivyj vampir... *Čtoby* nasmešlivyj čitatel'... *Čtoby* prošlo lanit pylan'e... Pered pomerkšimi domami... Pered suprugom dveri groba... Perebralas' *čerez* ručej ... *Čerez* Livonskie ja proezžal polja (Tjutčev)... Meždu Oneginym i mnoj... Meždu ljudej blagorazumnyx... Protiv užasnyx potrjasenij..." (*Mednyj vsadnik*). The same words with the stress on the first syllable: "A Buanarotti? I*li* èto skazka?... (*Mocart i Sal'eri*) Smel čistit' nogti pered nim... I pered sinimi rjadami... (*Poltava*). Za vorotami. Čerez den'... (*Mednyj vsadnik*). Grozy ne čuja meždu tem... (*Poltava*). Rvalasja k morju protiv buri... (M.vs.)" and others.[17] The poets of the eighteenth and early nineteenth centuries show more examples of forms with shifted stress (on the second syllable), but in the second half of the nineteenth century these become rarer, yielding to forms with the normal prose stress.

In the ternary meters, when the metrically ambiguous disyllabic words occur in the two-syllable interval between metrical stresses they undergo more or less severe destressing under the influence of the preceding or following stress. This was noted by D. Samsonov, who wrote in his *Kratkoe rassuždenie*: "However, in verses consisting of trisyllabic feet or of mixed feet, the disyllabic word can sometimes lose its stress when its stressed syllable is thrown up against another more sonorous syllable..." (229). The degree to which disyllabic words undergo destressing depends in great measure on whether they are proclitic or enclitic. The greatest weakening of the stress occurs when the word is attracted as an enclitic to the preceding accent — especially if the word stress of the disyllabic word is one syllable removed from the foregoing metrical stress (schematically:... $\perp$ | $-\perp$ || $\perp$ ...). Cf. for instance Nekrasov's lines: "Razdajutsja šagi-*moi* zvonko... Vižu ten'-*ego*, sel na stupeni... I pošli-*oni*, solncem

[17] On the stress shift in disyllabic conjunctions, cf. B. Tomaševskij, *Ritmika četyrëx-stopnogo jamba*, p. 174; *Russkoe stixosloženie*, p. 69; G. Šengeli, *Traktat*, pp. 39-40. Historically, the conjunction *ili* [or] occupies a special position, since it has "in living modern Russian the stress on the first syllable, in the literary Slavonic style on the second" (*Russkoe stixosloženie*, p. 69).

palimy... Puskaj beregut-*ego* svjato... Ja zastavlju stradat'-*tebja* vnov'... Ja sovetuju gnat'-*eë* proč'... I pugat'-*menja* budet mogila... On i teper'-*eščë* tupo molčit... On tak-*eščë* mal, a kogda podrastët... Ne tak-*uže* jarko svetilis'..." The accentuation is slightly heavier when the stress of the ambiguous word is immediately linked to the preceding metrical stress (schematically:... $\perp$ | $\stackrel{\perp}{-}$ || $\perp$ ...). Nekrasov's lines furnish examples once more: "Trud-*ètot* Vanja byl strašno gromaden... I žizn'-*naša* mirno letela... On vzmaxnul-*imi* sil'no i plavno... Ničego-*tol'ko* russkogo net... Izreki-*tol'ko* slovo proščenija..." From Fet: "Teply-*byli* nežnye ruki, svetly-*byli* zvezdy očej..." The accentual weighting is considerably heavier when the word is proclitic. Here also, when the word stress of the disyllabic word is one syllable removed from the metrical stress on the following word, there is a slight lessening of stress (schematically: ... $\perp$ || $\stackrel{\perp}{-}$ | $\perp$ ...). Cf., for example, Nekrasov's: "A v obyčnye dni *ètot*-pyšnyj pod"ezd... Čto tebe *èta*-skorb' vopijuščaja...? Čto ne veritsja mne v *ètu*-poru..." and Fet's "Sletel v *ètot*-mig, ne zemnoj, ne slučajnyj... Skazat'sja dušoj *bylo*-možno..." and others. The stress on the proclitic disyllabic word is heaviest when it is immediately linked to the metrical stress of the following word (schematically: $\perp$ || $- \stackrel{\perp}{} $ | $\stackrel{\perp}{}$). Theoreticians of Russian verse have repeatedly argued against this method of placing a hypermetrical stress on syllables in ternary meters.[18] But it is nevertheless constantly to be seen in the ambiguous words. Cf. Nekrasov's: "Ne vidna *eë*-bednost' nagaja... Gde ležit *moja*-bednaja mat'... Poza-budet na mig *svoi*-muki... Slyšu šum *ego*-zvonkix kopyt... Ja tebe *moju*-pesnju poslednjuju... V podarok žene *ego*-vykoval ded... Ljubja, *menja*-mučil moj bednyj otec..." and Fet's "Prixodi *moja*-milaja kroška... Unosi *moë*-serdce v zvenjaščuju dal'..." and so on.

[18] G. Šengeli cites a negative example (from an anonymous translation of Byron): "Pust' tot, kto razbil *moju* cep' *tvoej* šei..." Brjusov, in his discussion of the weighting of metrically unaccented syllables in the ternary meters with additional stresses (*Osnovy stixosloženija*, pp. 80-94) greatly complicated his classical terminology, which was different for each meter; as a consequence, an essentially identical phenomenon in the dactylic, amphibrachic and anapestic meters is everywhere called by a different name. For example, the absence of a monosyllabic word in the first unstressed position in the line will in the first case amount to the replacement of the dactyl by an *antibacchiac* with a "caesura" (i.e. word division) after the arsis ($\perp$ | $\stackrel{\perp}{}$ | $-$); in the second case, to the replacement of the amphibrach by a *bacchiac* with caesura ($- \perp$ | $\stackrel{\perp}{}$); and in the third case, to the replacement of the anapest by an *amphimacer* with caesura after the arsis (... $\perp$ || $\stackrel{\perp}{}$ | $- \stackrel{\perp}{}$). G. Šengeli simplifies the terminology somewhat by using that of the anapestic scheme for all the ternary meters (pp. 63-80). Neither writer, however, pays sufficient attention to the most essential questions: 1. the varying strength of the supplementary stress on words of varying semantic value (absolutely stressed words and ambiguous words); 2. the direction of accentual and syntactic links (proclisis and enclisis). Cf., however, G. Šengeli, p. 71.

As the above examples make clear, one encounters in such metrically weak positions the personal pronouns (in all cases), the possessive and demonstrative pronouns, the auxiliary verb, and several adverbs (*tol'ko, ešče*). Other disyllabic words of this category — e.g., the demonstrative adverbs (*tuda, togda*), the relative and interrogative pronouns, the numerals, and certain others — carry a considerably heavier stress in whatever position they occur and are therefore encountered only in very rare instances. Cf. Nekrasov's "Vse, čego ne vidal *stol'ko*-let..." and Fet's "Ne vysmotret' vam, *čego*-nęt i čto bylo... No ču! *kto*-to-rezko udaril v timpan..."

As for the disyllabic prepositions and conjunctions, they are always unstressed when they occur in any metrically weak position. Fet: "O, *esli*-noč' unesët tebja v mir ètot strannyj... Ètoj tropoj *čerez*-sad... To kulik prostonal *ili*-syč..." and so on.

In this instance also the first foot of an anapest constitutes a special case. Here a disyllabic ambiguous word with a stress on the first syllable furnishes a perceptible extra stress, although it is weaker than would be that of an independent word under the same circumstances. Cf. Nekrasov's "*Esli* vęter osennij buntuet... *Tol'ko* snom i vozmožno pomoč'... V *ètu* ulicu roskoši, mody..." Fet: "*Tol'ko* stanet smerkat'sja nemnožko... *Budu* ždat' ne drognët li zvonok... V ètom plačuščem zvuke slity... Esli zimnee utro lučami gorit... *Posle* skučnogo tjažkogo dnja..." and so on.

If in ternary meters the metrical accent falls on a metrically ambiguous disyllabic word that word is unequivocally stressed; there is considerably less weakening here than in the binary meters since the distance from the closest metrical stress is greater. Cf. for instance Nekrasov's "Sovest' pesnju svoju zapevaet... Ja segodnja ne *budu* tomitsja... Budet vremja *ešče* sosčitat'sja... Čto obxodjat *oni* xladnokrovno... Ja kručinu *moju* mnogoletnjuju..." Fet: "*Tvoej* nedoverčivoj reči... I poduška *eë* gorjača... U *menja* zakipajut v grudi... Serdce *moë vsë* po-prežnemu nežno..." and so on. The weakening of such a stress in the first foot of a dactyl, however, has considerable rhythmical importance. Cf. Fet's "*Ètoj* tropoj čerez sad... *Ètot* pravdivyj rumjanec lanit..." and Nekrasov's "*Tol'ko* razvit' vospitan'em, uvy! *Ètu* golovku ne dumali vy..." and so on.

20. THE "INTENSE" SYLLABLE THEORY (TEORIJA INTENS). COMPOUND WORDS

While in metrics the stress is important principally as the *relationship* between stronger and weaker syllables, in prosody the relative strength of the so-called "unstressed" syllables in a polysyllabic word can be of essential importance. It is generally believed that according to the laws governing the reduction of vowels the strongest of the unstressed syllables is the one immediately preceding the stress, while the weakest are the syllable standing next but one before the stress and the syllable immediately after the stress. Thus, in words which begin with an anapest (– – $\perp$) such as *golova* [gъlav**a**], *zolotoj* [zъlatoj], *paroxodom* [pърахodъm], the laws of reduction indicate that the first syllable is the weakest of all, the second is somewhat stronger, and the third is stressed.[19]

However, F. Korš has pointed out[20] that in Russian pronunciation the first and last syllables, if they are separated by at least one syllable from the stress, carry a secondary (i.e. weak) stress, e.g. *pjatídesjatì*, *vzleléjanỳj*, *pèrepisát'*. And according to the observations made by Korš, the farther the first or last syllable is from the principal stress, the stronger is its stress, e.g., *pjatídesjatì*, *vyígryvalì* and similar words have stronger secondary stresses than *výnestì*. In words having many syllables in prestress or poststress position, the secondary stresses, if possible, are distributed on every other syllable between the initial (or final) syllable and the stress, e.g. sleduju*š*čim*ì*, preizbytočestvuju*š*čim*ì*. In the most recent work on Russian metrics similar observations are found in the investigations of B. V. Tomaševskij, and G. Šengeli in his *Traktat o russkom stixe* used this theory as the basis for his systematic study of the rhythms of binary and ternary meters. Šengeli calls these secondary stresses "intense" syllables and suggests that they, in contrast to the main

---

[19] According to O. Brok, for example, (*Očerk fiziologii slavjanskoj reči*, § 245, p. 225), the syllable immediately preceding the stress "is quantitatively more prominent, but it has also apparently more force of expiration than the other unstressed syllables..." My own observations of the slovenly and accelerated colloquial speech of (for the most part) the younger generation in Leningrad have, however, led me to believe that in a word with anapestic onset the weakest syllable is the one just before the stress, where in rapid speech it frequently approaches phonetic zero or a completely "irrational" syllabic equivalent, while the initial syllable, even under reduction, manages to conserve a certain amount of independence and strength. Cf. xor(o)šó! [xaršo, xъršo]; ob(ja)zátel'no [abzat'ьl'nъ]; nap(i)sát', [napsat', nъpsat'] poč(i)táem! [pъčtajm]; čto-k(a)sáetsja [čtъksajcъ, štъksajcъ]. It is interesting to note that in the words *objazatel'no*, *kipjačennaja*, *napisat'* the consonants *b* and *p* also lose their palatalization. These most recent phenomena have, of course, no relation to the old Moscow literary language, but, in their extreme form, they do disclose a general *tendency* in the spread of accentual characteristics whereby the first syllable, although it is reduced in quality, is nevertheless dynamically stronger than the second. On the word *xorošo* cf. Turgenev's observations in *Vešnie vody*, Chap. XXXV: "Mar'ja Nikolaevna intentionally pronounced *xorošo* in exactly the petit bourgeois manner — *xeršòo*."

[20] F. Korš, *O russkom narodnom stixosloženii*, p. 23.

stress, are produced only by a heightened tension of the glottis, without any increase in the force of expiration.[21]

The word accentuation which is of greatest practical importance for Russian prosody is that of words with an anapestic beginning or a dactylic termination (e.g. gόlova, zόloto); according to Šengeli's theory, such words have slight secondary stresses at one syllable remove from the main stress. Korš has pointed out the significance which these stresses have for the explanation of "disruptions" of meter in the binary meters. He cites the following example: "Vzlelejan*y*j v te*ni* dubravnoj." In an iambic or trochaic line, when a metrical stress is omitted, there are three unstressed syllables between the two nearest stresses, as follows: $\acute- - - - \acute-$. It most frequently happens that these three syllables are so distributed among adjacent words that two of the unstressed syllables are linked to one of the stresses and the other one to the other stress; type I: $\acute- - |$ $- - \acute-$, type II: $\acute- - - | - \acute-$. In the first instance the word beginning with an anapest has a secondary stress on a metrically accented syllable, e.g. "Kogda ne v šutku *za*nemog." In the second, the metrical accent falls on the final syllable of the word with a dactylic ending, e.g., "I lučše vydum*at*' ne mog..." Cf. also "Em*u* poduški *po*pravljat'... Presledov*at*' ljubov', i vdrug... Rastёt, volnuetsj*a*, kipit... Privyčki mirnoj st*a*riny..." and many others. In the trochee: "Trojka borzaj*a* bežit... Probiraetsja lun*a*... *ne*vidimkoj*u* luna..." and many others. The secondary stresses are more noticeable when the word in question begins or ends with a vowel, since in these positions the vowel is less likely to be reduced and is, by the same token, given a certain prominence. Cf. "Nevol'noj laski *o*židat'... Stoit Istomin*a*..." or, in trochaic meter, "*o*sveščaet sneg letučij..." There is considerably less doubt about the presence of a certain accentual weighting on monosyllabic *prepositions*, *conjunctions* and even *particles* located in metrically strong positions: these auxiliary words, even though they ordinarily have no independent stress, are nevertheless made to stand out when juxtaposed to the unstressed syllables of nearby polysyllabic words. Cf. "Vzdyxat' i dumat' *pro* sebja... Monsieur prognali *so* dvora... Kosnut'sja *do* vsego slegka... Ne mog on jamba *ot* xoreja... Obyčaj — despot *mež* ljudej... Ja pomnju more *pred* grozoju... Votšče li byl on *sred*' pirov... Na scene skačut *i* šumjat... Vo dni veselij *i* želanij... Dlja zvukov žizni *ne* ščadit'... Stydliv i derzok, *a* poroj..." and many others. According to Šengeli's calcula-

<hr/>

[21] G. Šengeli, pp. 31-33; B. Tomaševskij *Problemy ritma*, p. 129-30; *Russkoe stixosloženie*, p. 72. Cf. R. Jakobson, *Stixologija Brjusova*, p. 229. Cf. F. Korš, *Razbor v oprosa o podlinnosti Rusalki*, pp. 726-29.

tions, 80-90% of all "pyrrhics" have an "intense" syllable — the initial syllable of an anapestic word or the final syllable of a dactyl.

In the remaining cases (10-20%) all three unstressed syllables are completely attracted to the preceding or following word; type III: $\underline{\prime}---\mid\underline{\prime}$; type IV: $\underline{\prime}\mid---\underline{\prime}$. An example of the former: "Tixa ukrainskaja noč'"; and of the latter: "Duša vosplamenilas' v něm..." In an isolated word having three unstressed syllables at the beginning or end the secondary stress, according to Korš, would fall on the first or last syllable, e.g. *vos*plamenilas'... ukrainskaj*a*. In a phraseological unit, however, the weak secondary stress is completely subordinated to the strong main stress of the immediately adjacent word. When this situation occurs in verse, at any rate, the secondary stress will fall on a metrically strong syllable, i.e., in the middle of three unstressed syllables standing between the heavy accents: "Duša vospl*a*menilas' v něm...". Korš, taking note of this phenomenon, explains it by the fact that, in words having a large number of unstressed syllables before the primary stress, "a secondary stress is often heard on the *second syllable* from the beginning". His examples are: pèrepisát' and perèpisát', pèrenočevát' and perènočevát', ìzborozdít' and izbòrozdít', and so on. It may be that in prosaic speech also this transposition of the "intense" syllable is dependent upon the arrangement of stresses on adjacent words, so that the secondary stress, subordinated to the main stress of the adjoining word, is shifted one syllable. Cf. "Duša vospl*a*menilas' *i* zagorelas'..." Unfortunately, therè have been no really reliable experimental observations of this feature.[22]

At the beginning of an iambic line, when the metrical accent is omitted on the second syllable, the strongest of the three unstressed syllables is apparently still the first one. Cf. "*p*ereskazat' mne nedosug... *n*eotrazimoe ničem..." This stregthening is somewhat more perceptible when the word begins with a vowel and thus offers more resistance to qualitative reduction. E.g. "ozarena lučem Diany... očarovatel'nyx aktris..." It is still more perceptible in those cases when the initial position is occupied by a monosyllabic preposition or conjunction, i.e., by an auxiliary part of speech which has no independent stress of its own but is nevertheless stronger than the adjacent absolutely unstressed syllable. Cf. "*Bez* predislov'ja v tot že čas... *Iz* Èneidy dva stixa... *Bliz* neokončennyx stixov... *Ne* otxodja ni šagu proč'... *I* promotalsja nakonec... *I*

---

[22]   G. Šengeli explains the unusually low incidence of such verses as "Tixa ukrainskaja noč'..." by the necessity for a certain amount of effort "to move the natural "intense" syllable to the place prescribed by the scheme." (p. 61).

vozbuždat' ulybku dam... *Il'* preduznav izdaleka..." If the line begins
with two monosyllabic auxiliary words standing side by side, the first
"foot" has *accentual equilibrium*, in which case the strengthening of the
metrically strong or of the preceding unstressed syllable depends on the
style of recitation. Cf. "*i dlja* vručenija pis'ma... *i o* bylom vospominat'
i dlja nogtej i dlja zubov... *no i* Didlo mne nadoel..." and certain others.

The "intense" syllable theory is beset with difficulties in general not
only because of the insufficient phonetic research that has been done on
the question of Russian accentuation but also, in particular, because of
the insignificant role played in Russian pronunciation (as compared, for
example, to German or even English) by the secondary stresses themselves.
Since these have no connection with the meaning of the various morphological elements (as in German) they therefore depend exclusively on
the mechanical conditions of the utterance and consequently do not even
enter our consciousness in the great majority of cases. The function of
secondary stresses in compound words is altogether different; here they
easily acquire their own significance, and in poetic language, under the
influence of the accent, they often acquire considerable prominence.

As compared to German, with its obligatory secondary stress (Nebenton) on the less important component of a compound word (Váterlànd),
Russian shows a tendency to unite both components firmly together
under one stress. Therefore it is a general rule of the Russian language
to admit the free use of compound words in verse under the same conditions as those governing simple words, i.e., the principal word stress
coincides with the metrical stress, regardless of any possible distribution
of the marginal stresses. Cf. e.g., in iambic and trochaic lines, with the
metrical accent on the *root vowel* of the secondary (usually the first)
element: "Tíxij, tomnyj, bl*a*govonnyj..." (Tjutčev); "Vse zvuki žizni
bl*a*godatnoj..." (Tjutčev); "Vozžgu kuren'ja bl*a*govonny..." (Deržavin).
But cf. with the metrical accent on the *linking vowel*: "Blag*o*uxanija,
cveta i golosa..." (M. ....); "Blag*o*ux*a*juščie slëzy..." (M. ....
...); "Blag*o*tvorïtelju prjamomu..." (Deržavin); Na lože roz bl*a*gouxan-
nom..." (Deržavin)'; I bud'te stol' blag*o*polučny..." (Deržavin). Cf.
further examples where the metrical accent is on the root: Tjutčev's "I
na kamen' s*a*mocvetnyj... *o*gnedyšaščij i burnyj... I b*e*lokrylye viden'ja...
Kakoj-to m*i*rotv*o*rnyj genij..." and further examples of metrical accent
on the *linking vowel*: Tjutčev's: "Grom*o*kipjaščij kubok s neba... Est'
v oseni perv*o*nač*a*l'noj... Perv*o*nač*a*l'nyx dnej zvezda... Čuvstva mgloj
s*a*mozabven'ja... Krugl*o*obraznyj svetlyj xram... Ne dlja nego goste-
priïmnyj... S novorožděnnoju ix ten'ju..." etc.

The extent to which an "intense" syllable is more prominent on the first weak component of a compound word than in a simple monosyllabic word depends on the degree of isolation of these components. It is difficult to establish a general rule for such isolation: the components are more isolated in compounds regarded as neologisms of the poetic language, especially if they are constructed on the model of a morphological type which is still productive or is represented in the language by numerous analogous formations. As examples, consider the adjectives *zlatotkannyj* (cf. srebrotkannyj, zlatocvetnyj), *belokrylyj* (cf. legkokrylyj, belokudryj), *ognecvetnyj, bystrotečnyj, širokolistvennyj*, and many others. The secondary stress is most clearly to be seen in compound words like *temno-sinij, bešeno-igrivyj* and so on. Here the graphic device of indicating isolation by means of writing the components as separate words linked by a hyphen is used rather inconsistently and varies with different authors. Compound words of this kind are not infrequently made up *ad hoc* and belong to the individual vocabulary of a given author; in general, they are more or less border-line phenomena between compound words and syntactic groups. Cf. Tjutcev's "To gluxo-žalobnyj, to šumnyj... Iz pyšno-zolotogo dnja... Tak milo-blagodatno... Pyšno-strujnaja vesna..."; Deržavin's "Na temnogolubom èfire... Iz serebrorozovyx svetlic... Iz černoognenna vissona... Šumjašči krasnoželty list'ja... Po želtosmuglym licam dolu... Na srebrolunnom gosudarstve..." It should be mentioned that words in this category also freely permit the metrical accent to fall on the *linking vowel*, in which case there occurs an accentual shift as in the disyllabic prepositions and conjunctions (čerez, meždu, etc.): the secondary stress is transferred to the metrically accented syllable. Examples from Tjutčev: "Kak sladko dyšit sad temno-zelënyj... S bledno-zelenoj grivoj... Dymno-legko, mglisto-lilejno... Nad volnoj temno-lazurnoj..." From Baratynskij: "V jarko-blestjaščem pyšnom zale... S očami temno-golubymi, s temno-kudrjavoj golovoj" (cf. above, p. 90). From Deržavin: "Perom moim slavno-školjarnym..." There are a very great many examples of ambiguous accentuation in compound words beginning with the numeral *polu-*. Cf. the following examples from Tjutčev (with the accent on the root vowel): "Kak grustno polusonnoj ten'ju... No ne togda, kak s neba polunoči... Kogda on tixoj polumgloju..."; (with accent on the linking vowel): Poluprozračnoju kak dym... Na ètom son polumogil'nyj..." From Puškin (accent on root): "Čto ž moj Onegin. Polusonnyj..."; (on the linking vowel): Polu-milord, polu-nevežda..." and so on. In our contemporary pronunciation, as Nedobrovo makes clear in his remarks on Baratynskij (*Ritm i metr*, p. 20), the shift of stress to the first syllable often replaces trans-accentuation.[23]

21. PROSODY AND METRICS

A more detailed study of the problems of Russian prosody must be left to special investigations. However, certain conclusions of fundamental importance for the theory of Russian metrics can be drawn from the basic questions that we have touched upon here.

First of all, it has clearly become imperative to discard the widespread terminology which introduces spondees and pyrrhics into Russian iambic and trochaic feet as "replacements". There is a difference in principle between the so-called "spondees" and "pyrrhics" in iambic verse and those in trochaic.[24] The "spondee" occurring in an iambic line is in the majority of cases essentially nothing more than an iamb with a somewhat more prominent first syllable, but the obligatory relationship between the two syllables — the first being in principle unstressed and the other stressed — is still maintained (cf. "pod nej *sneg*-utrennyj xrustit..."). A pyrrhic in an iambic verse, according to the "intense" syllable theory, has a slight secondary stress on the second syllable instead of an independent stress; in trochaic verse, on the contrary, the pyrrhic has a second syllable which is lighter than the first (which is an "intense" syllable in place of a full stress). In both cases, however, the customary sequence of light and heavy, or of heavy and light syllables is preserved. Thus, the cases of so-called "omitted stress" or "supplementary stress" are in actual fact to be considered as cases in which certain syllables are made more or less prominent, but in no sense are they disruptions of the basic metrical pattern, of the rhythmical inertia. Consequently, the difference between syllables which are stressed and those which are unstressed in principle — which we perceive chiefly as the artistic inertia of rhythm or as the correspondence of an actual line to an ideal pattern in our minds — is in the great majority of cases also realized in actual pronunciation. And where it is not so realized (e.g. when the stress is shifted from a metrically strong to a metrically weak syllable) we perceive such a displacement as a disruption of the rhythmical inertia, as a peculiar kind of break in the rhythm, i.e., as an exception which confirms the existence of the rule. This is so especially in the first foot of an iambic (or anapestic) line.

[23] On trans-accentuation of compounds, cf. R. Jakobson, p. 229; B. Tomaševskij, *Russkoe stixosloženie*, p. 69.
[24] Cf. R. Jakobson, p. 229.

The establishment of a category of metrically ambiguous monosyllabic words destroys once and for all the illusion which serves as the basis for V. Brjusov's textbook, namely, the illusion that any foot in either binary or ternary meters could with the greatest of ease be replaced by any other foot of the most widely diverse variety. Some of these "replacements" are simply imaginary, others can be reduced to various kinds of weighting on metrically weak syllables or lightening of metrically strong syllables, which for the most part do not disrupt the fundamental rhythmical movement.

In general, the division of syllables into two neatly contrasting groups — stressed and unstressed — does not correspond to the rhythmical complexity in the actual sound of a line of poetry. In order to achieve any adequate notation for this complexity, one must at the very least introduce two intermediate categories — a weak stress ("semi-stress") and a somewhat stronger-than-normal unstressed syllable (involving various degrees of "weighting"). To the category of weak stresses we have assigned those cases which, in a binary meter, exhibit an ambiguous word (monosyllabic or disyllabic) in a metrically strong position. All such cases must be treated as separate from unconditionally stressed, strong syllables. Often they lend a very characteristic emphasis to the general rhythmical tendency of certain poetic types, e.g., lightening of the stress on the first syllable of the dactyl, or the tendency to omit the stress on the third foot of the iambic tetrameter, on the first and third feet of the trochaic tetrameter, on the second and fourth feet in the iambic hexameter. Submitting in such cases to the general rhythmical tendency, we willingly weaken such stresses in our reading. Cf. in Puškin's iambic hexameter: "Poslednie listy || s nagix *svoix* vetvej... Žurča, *ešče* bežit || za mel'nicu ručej... No prud *uže* zastyl; || sosed moj pospešaet... Ljublju *eë* snega; || v prisutstvii luny..." and so on. And vice versa, in a more stable position (e.g. in the second foot of iambic tetrameter) we are inclined to increase the stress in accordance with the general movement of the line. E.g., "Brožu li *ja* vdol' **ulic** šumnyx".

On the other hand, unstressed syllables can also differ in strength. A metrically ambiguous monosyllabic word in unstressed position is regarded as "unstressed". But the very absence of the qualitative reduction customary in an unstressed syllable (*moj* **drug**...) (even more — a rise in intonation: ¡ *Gde* mnëte vešnie cvety?) weights the syllable, just as the semantic importance of the monosyllabic word in question also furnishes a certain degree of stress. Along with the lighter cases of such stressing (the nominative of the personal pronoun, the possessive and relative pronouns) we mentioned the cases of heavier weighting (oblique cases of the personal pronouns, demonstrative adverbs, interrogative pronouns and adverbs, and others) and, finally, the heaviest of all — the independent monosyllabic word with full material meaning (nouns, verbs, etc.). In our calculations it is necessary to distinguish at least this latter category (the unconditionally stressed words) from the first two (the lighter and heavier ambiguous words). The same thing applies to the hypermetrical emphasis on the first syllable of an iambic line in which the stress on the second syllable is omitted and to the same phenomenon on the first syllable of an anapest: here also one must distinguish at least two categories — unconditionally stressed words and metrically ambiguous words. Least essential of all is the counting of the so-called "intense" syllables: they are automatically distributed through a polysyllabic word as a result of the metrical pattern, and in actual pronunciation they are not only difficult to catch but are apparently subject to considerable individual fluctuations.

It may seem that to establish the category of "ambiguous" words is nothing more than to introduce into the rhythmic analysis of Russian verse a new convention not altogether justified by anything in particular. To be sure, the boundaries separating these categories are rather fluid and, consequently, somewhat arbitrary, but the system proposed here does differentiate essential nuances which could not be distinguished in the traditional system. One can make this difference very obvious by illustrating it with figures. The traditional system recognized only stressed and unstressed syllables, which we might represent as 0 and 1. Against this we can set up a number of intermediate steps: 0, 1/4, 1/2, 3/4, 1. Thus traditional logaoedic metrics regards the weighting of a metrically weak syllable in the binary meters as a "spondee" (1-1). For Brjusov, the following combinations are all spondees of this sort: (1) "*Šved, russkij...* (2) *Den'* celyj... (3) *Ej* nado ... (4) *Moj* drug..." For us only the first case (*Šved,* russkij...) shows stresses that are more or less equivalent (1-1). In the second case (*Den'* celyj) an unconditionally stressed word is subordinated to the adjacent, syntactically dominant stress (let us say 3/4-1). In the third instance (*Ej* nado) we have a heavy ambiguous word (1/2-1). In the fourth (*Moj'* drug) the stress is extremely light (1/4-1). It is possible to introduce still further distinctions, e.g., "*Tam* vstretil..." could be represented as 1/2-1 and the somewhat weaker "*Ej* nado" as 3/8-1. The same thing refers to a "trochee" in the first foot: for traditional metrics "reversed" stress can only result in a trochee (i.e., 1-0). But we must make such distinctions as, e.g., "*Boj* barabannyj... (1-0);

Ej otvečali... (1/2-0); *Ja* otvečal... (1/4-0); *I* otvečal... (1/8-0)" and so on. For traditional metrics the "omission" of a stress is the "replacement" of an iamb or trochee by a "pyrrhic" (i.e., 0-0); but we, together with Korš and Šengeli, assume that the metrically accented syllable is "intense" (let us say 0-1/8), e.g., *za*nemog, vydum*a*t'. This "intensity" can be greater with a preposition or conjunction, e.g., "Takoj prekrasnoj ı bezgrešnoj..." (say 0-1/4). "Full" stresses can in their turn also be of varying strength, and the metrically ambiguous words carry a weaker-than-normal stress (e.g., 0-1/2, 0-3/4). These figures are of course also artificial, but they do help us to differentiate the more complex rhythmical distinctions, and to illustrate the basic principle of *stress as relative.*[25]

---

[25] For a numerical designation of the relative strength of stresses cf. § 25 below, especially fn. 18.

IV. STRUCTURAL MODIFIERS OF VERSE

22. METRICAL MODIFIERS. THE ENDING

The metrical structure of a line is determined by its conformity to one system of versification or another (syllabo-tonic, purely tonic, etc.) and, within the limits of this system, to one metrical type or another: iambic, trochaic, and so forth. Within one and the same type, lines vary according to the number of feet or (for syllabic verse) the number of syllables, or the number of stress groups (for purely tonic verse). In this way the metrical pattern of the iambic tetrameter, of the purely tonic four-stress line, or of the syllabic decasyllable determines the basic rule of metrical structure in the line and the distribution therein of the syllables and stresses. Within the limits of the basic metrical schema, — within, say, the iambic tetrameter or the dactylic pentameter — it is possible to have substantial metrical variations: they occur as changes in the beginning or end of the line, which can, to a certain degree, be independent of the basic metrical scheme, and also as variations in the placement of the metrical break (or caesura) in the line. The beginning (*anacrusis*), the ending (*clausula*) and the obligatory break (*caesura*) are thus modifiers of the meter or the metrical determinants of verse. Their function can be explained with greatest precision by the example of syllabo-tonic versification, whence its concepts and terms can be transferred to purely tonic poetry.

In syllabo-tonic verse the number of syllables within the line is, as we have seen, constant. This rule, however, does not extend to the unstressed syllables following after the last stressed syllable; their number usually changes according to special rules.

Cf. in *trochaic*:

> Mčátsja túči, v'jútsja túči   (8 syllables: 7 + 1)
> Nevidímkoju luná   (7 syllables: 7 + 0)

Or in *iambic*:

Moj djádja sámyx čéstnyx právil   (9 syllables: 8 + 1)
Kogdá ne v šútku zanemóg   (8 syllables: 8 + 0)

The group of syllables *beginning* with the last stressed one in the line is called the ending or *clausula*. One distinguishes monosyllabic or *masculine* endings, when the line ends with a stress (...nevidimkoju luna... kogdá ne v šútku zanemog); disyllabic or *feminine* endings, when one unstressed syllable follows the stress (...mčatsja tuči, v'jutsja tuči... moj djadja samyx čestnyx pravil.); trisyllabic or *dactylic* endings, where two unstressed syllables follows the stress (...my p'ëm v ljubvi otravu sladkuju... v armjake s otkrytym vorotom.). Tetrasyllabic endings (*hyperdactylic*) are met with very rarely: in the first place, the language itself does not possess a large number of such words, and the rhymes almost always involve suffixes; and in the second place, such an ending in binary or ternary meters constitutes a rhythmical interruption that is too noticeable and obtrusive. Cf. Del'vig's *Žavoronok*:

Ljubljú ja zadúmyvat'sja
Vnimája sviréli,
No slášče mne vslúšivat'sja
V vozdúšnye tréli
Vesénnego žávoronka...

The pentasyllabic ending is still less frequent; in binary meters it submits to the general tendency to spread secondary stresses over every other syllable. Cf. Brjusov's:

Xólod, dúšu tájno skovyv*a*juščij
Xólod, dúšu očarovyv*a*juščij...

The alternation of various kinds of endings is one of the most important factors in the make-up of the stanza and is best studied in connection with the stanza (cf. § 1 above).[1] For the general theory of verse it is sufficient to point out that endings of various kinds can be freely used with lines of diverse metrical structure. For each meter, therefore, there are at least three metrical modifications depending on the character of the ending. For example, in *iambic*:

Glagól vremën, métalla zvón...   (masculine)
Dlja beregóv otčízny dál'noj...   (feminine)
Po večerám nad restoránami...   (dactylic)

Or *anapestic*:

Znamenítyj Smol'gól'mskij barón... (masculine)
Nadryváetsja sérdce ot múki...   (feminine)
Ukrašájut tebjá dobrodételi...   (dactylic)

[1] Cf. *Rifma*, p. 24 ff.

If we include the end of the line in our count of the feet, then the line, depending on the structure of the ending, may be said to be either *full* or *truncated* (*catalectic*). Thus, when a trochaic line has a feminine ending the line is full (*acatalectic*), since it accommodates a full number of the specified trochaic feet, with the last one constituting the ending; when the ending is masculine the line is, as it were, cut short by one unstressed syllable, the absence of which deprives the last foot of its full complement. Cf. in the trochaic tetrameter:

> Mčátsja túči, v'jútsja túči... (full)
> Nevidímkoju luná... (catalectic)

On the contrary, in iambic measures a line which has a full number of iambic feet and a masculine ending is acatalectic; such a line with a feminine ending has, so to speak, an *additional* unstressed syllable (*hypercatalectic*). Cf.:

> Moj djádja sámyx čéstnyx právil... (hypercatalectic)
> Kogdá ne v šútku zanemóg... (acatalectic)

The concept of *catalexis* applies in all the syllabo-tonic meters. For instance, the acatalectic (non-truncated) dactylic line has a dactylic ending, the amphibrachic has a feminine ending, the anapest — a masculine ending; a feminine or masculine ending in the dactylic line reduces it by one or two syllables, making it catalectic; the feminine and dactylic endings in the anapest extend it by one or two syllables, rendering it hypercatalectic (expanded), etc.

Catalexis, which is completely normal for us, draws attention to itself only in those systems of versification where it is not customary. Thus, Tred'jakovskij, trained in the traditions of feminine endings found in Polish and Ukrainian verse, objected to a mixture of feminine and masculine endings, since this prevented all lines from having an equal number of syllables.[2] In the same way, English theorists, accustomed to the masculine endings which predominate in English poetry, regard the hypermetric feminine endings in Shakespeare's blank verse as "deviations" from the metrical norm.[3] There thus arises the theoretical problem of justifying catalexis in syllabic verse, where it disrupts the principle of syllable counting.

The most widespread theory, developed under the influence of classical

---

[2] For Tred'jakovskij on the alternation of endings, cf. *Rifma*, p. 31.
[3] G. Saintsbury, for example, in his *Historical Manual*, p. 175, regards feminine endings as deviations ("...the more doubtful and dangerous *redundant* syllable...").

metrics, explains truncation by likening it to a musical *pause*. Beginning with the comparison of the foot and the musical bar, Westphal[4] sees in the catalectic ending a certain pause corresponding in length to one (or two) syllables. Cf.:

Mčátsja túči, v'jútsja túči...   (full line)
Nevidímkoju luná ∧   (line with pause)

But according to Westphal the pause can also replace a stressed syllable. For example, when an iambic tetrameter with a masculine ending and an iambic trimeter with a feminine ending (hypercatalectic) are combined, the difference in number of syllables is accounted for by a pause in the second line replacing an accented syllable:

Na póle bránnom tišiná...   (8 syllables, *full* line)
Ogní meždu šatrámi ∧   (7 syllables with a *pause* instead of a stressed syllable)

In general, a hypercatalectic ending in such a system is always accounted for by the truncation of a stressed syllable, which raises some very awkward difficulties. Thus even an ordinary iambic tetrameter can be transformed by such attempts at levelling into a pentameter: with one pause, when it has a feminine ending, or with two pauses (replacing a truncated *foot*) when the ending is masculine. E.g.:

Moj djadja samyx čestnyx pravil ∧   (unstressed syllable cut off) [*sic*]
Kogda ne v šutku zanemog ∧ ∧   (stressed and unstressed syllables cut off) [*sic*. Žirmunskij surely means a "stressed syllable" in the first line and "unstressed and stressed syllables" in the second].

Finally, in complex stanzaic forms, when long and short lines are combined, the inequality of the rhythmic units is also levelled by the pause, which corresponds to a whole foot (measure) or to two feet, and so on.

The practical difficulties in the theory of pauses have already been seen clearly enough in the examples of hypercatalectic verse. In actuality, the view of our familiar iambic tetrameter as a pentameter line with a pause is a serious distortion of our perception of this verse, and is motivated solely by the desire to substantiate an abstract theory positing the syllabic equality of adjacent lines. Aside from these particular diffi-

---

[4]   R. Westphal, *Theorie der neuhochdeutschen Metrik* (1870); on the iambic tetrameter, cf. p. 176 ff.

culties, Westphal's theory also arouses general theoretical objections. Westphal begins by identifying the foot and the bar, verse meter and musical rhythm. Historically, to be sure, this identification is valid for the early stages in the development of poetic art, which is known to have been initially connected with music and the dance: many stanzaic forms, from this point of view, hark back to different forms of song, and catalexis might be explained historically by the use of the pause, just as other peculiarities of stanzaic composition are conditioned by the early connection of word and music in song. In contemporary verse, however, which is independent of any connection with music, musical theory no longer has any application. As was pointed out above, verbal rhythm, having lost its original dependence on musical rhythm, develops in the direction of greater compositional freedom, including temporal relationships. While in music, especially in the simplest song or dance melody, the rhythmic-melodic group must be constant, (melodic construction such as the $(4+4) + (4+4)$ measure), in poetry it is perfectly admissible to have a regular alternation of identically constructed lines containing a varying number of stresses without the least tendency towards syllabic equality. Cf. the lines of Bal'mont $(5+3+5+2)$:

> Ja v ètot mír prišël, čtob vídet' sólnce
> I sínij krugozór,
> Ja v ètot mír prišël, čtob vídet' sólnce
> I výsi gór.

In the same way it is possible to have at the end of each rhythmical line a special rhythmical movement, a group of final syllables ("clausula") built on a specific pattern, signalling the line boundary. From the point of view of speech rhythm there cannot be any motivation for the demand that adjacent lines contain the same number of syllables, and therefore the attempt to equalize lines by positing a metrical pause is based on a false analogy with the rhythmical laws of music.

In music, on the other hand, where each sound has a specific temporal duration that is strictly proportional to the duration of adjacent sounds and unites with them to form a larger unit of constant duration, namely, the measure, the uncompleted *empty time* (pause) can justly be regarded as a temporal element proportional to the other elements of the given group. In tonic versification, as has been shown, there is no such proportionality of temporal length between separate syllables or even separate lines, and consequently it is impossible to reckon the pause as a part of the meter, as a temporal interval equal to one or several syllables. And in fact when stops exist between words and syntactic groups they depend on semantic considerations, not on the demands of the meter, and they follow the requirements of expressiveness in recitation.

Aside from these theoretical considerations, the lessons of immediate experience can be regarded as decisive: at the end of a "truncated" line we really do not go through a pause of a specified length which we might perceive as a "substitute" for an omitted syllable. When we attempt to test this fact by reading verse aloud the chief difficulty arises from the fact that lines, periods, stanzas, etc., as rhythmical units of various kinds, do really terminate in an *ideal pause*, which permits one to perceive a given rhythmical sequence as a unit, complete in itself. Different means are employed to realize this ideal pause and to achieve the feeling of closure that goes along with it in actual pronunciation: it is far from true to say that the verse boundary is always silence (i.e., pause in the exact sense of the term); more often we observe a slowing down at the end of the line, e.g., the lengthening of the stressed syllable or a special kind of intonational clausula, and so on.[5] Catalexis, of course, has no influence on this ideal pause. Its significance is proportional to the size of the rhythmical unit for which it serves as the signal of closure: the pause after a rhythmical period is greater than that at the end of a line, and the pause terminating a stanza is still stronger:

> Kóni snóva poneslísja; |
> Kolokól'čik dín', din', dín'... ||
> Vížu: dúxi sobralísja... |
> Sred' beléjuščix ravnín. |||

In this example the end of the period and of the stanza is marked by a shorter, more catalectic line. The interrelationship, however, is not changed by transposing the lines: the ideal boundary of a period will always be perceived as stronger than that of a simple line. Cf.:

> Kolokól'čik dín', din', dín'... |
> Kóni snóva poneslísja. ||
> Sred' beléjuščix ravnín |
> Vížu: dúxi sobralísja... |||

It should be added that in actual pronunciation the relationship between the ideal boundaries of metrical units can vary quite widely: in different styles of recitation the ideal metrical divisions can be emphasized or, on the contrary, the greatest attention can be paid to the semantic and syntactic groupings and associations. Again, all this is independent of catalexis.

---

[5] On the question of the line boundary and the "pause" cf. especially P. Verrier, I, p. 146, 177; **B.** Tomaševskij, *Russkoe stixosloženie*, p. 77.

Thus "catalexis", borrowed from classical metrics and applied to the syllabo-tonic versification familiar to us today, must be treated as simply a convenient term. There is in actual fact no "truncation": there is an alternation of lines having various endings — masculine, feminine and dactylic.

23. ANACRUSIS

The term *anacrusis* was unknown to the classical theoreticians of verse: it was introduced into discussions of classical metrics by modern scholars and thence transferred to syllabo-tonic versification.[6] Anacrusis is used to designate a group of syllables preceding the first metrical stress of the line. It corresponds to the "up-beat" in music. In the contemporary notational system of music the counting of bars begins with the down-beat: consequently, the portion of the melody preceding the down-beat is placed before the beginning of the bar. E.g.:

$$3/4 \quad \text{♩} \mid \text{♩♩♩} \mid \text{♩♩♩} \mid \ldots$$

Our metrical terms, inherited from the ancients, go back to a musical system which knew nothing of the modern bar as a device for marking the beat. Therefore, in metrics we count the feet, the units of periodicity, beginning not with the first stress but from the first syllable in the line. Thus the difference is established between the trochaic ($\perp - \mid \perp - \mid \perp - \ldots$) and the iambic ($- \perp \mid - \perp \mid - \perp \mid \ldots$), although from the point of view of contemporary musical notation the iambic meter should be regarded as trochaic with a constant "up-beat" (anacrusis). The same distinction may be made in the ternary meters: thus the dactylic begins with a stress, the amphibrachic has a constant anacrusis of one syllable, and the anapestic has one of two syllables. It is interesting to note that in German and English metrics, where the number of unstressed syllables before the first stress usually varies (1, 2), the term "amphibrach" is not used at all: a distinction is made between the dactyl (beginning with a stress) and the anapest (with one or two unstressed syllables before the stress); in some cases the broad term dactyl alone is used for all ternary meters.[7]

---

[6] Cf. Masqueray, *Traité de métrique grecque*, p. 152.

[7] Cf. A. Heusler, *Über germanischen Versbau*, p. 31. "In contemporary anapestic verse the monosyllabic onset (Auftakt) alternates freely with the disyllabic; at the same time the *absence* of an unstressed beginning is felt as a violation of the established pattern..." J. Minor, p. 280, uses the term "anapestic verse" exclusively; J. Schipper, I, p. 400 ff., speaks of an "iambo-anapestic" meter. The concept of the "amphibrachic"

The introduction into metrics of the concept of anacrusis is important because it enables one to see, on the one hand, how the different binary meters are in principle related and, on the other, how the ternary meters are similarly related, even though this fact has been obscured by traditional terminology. Cf. in the *binary meters*:

without anacrusis: | ⊥ – | ⊥ – ...   (trochaic)
With one-syllable anacrusis: – | ⊥ – | ⊥ – ... (iambic)

and in the *Ternary meters*:

without anacrusis: | ⊥ – – | ⊥ – – | ⊥ – – ...   (dactylic)
with one-syllable anacrusis: – | ⊥ – – | ⊥ – – | ⊥ – – ... (amphibrachic)
with two-syllable anacrusis: – – | ⊥ – – | ⊥ – – | ⊥ – – ... (anapestic)

Prompted by these considerations, certain investigators (e.g., in Russia, B. V. Tomaševskij) believe that it is theoretically more correct to indicate in the metrical scheme the pre-stress portion of the line as an anacrusis and to discard the traditional division of the line into iambic and trochaic feet.[8] We have already said that the foot is a part of the metrical scheme, an ideal unit of repetition, and not an element in the actual sound of the verse, in its concrete rhythm: the actual line consists of words, not of feet. If one begins by accepting the "foot" as a conventional concept, it is a matter of complete indifference whether one considers the first stress in the line or the first syllable as the beginning of such a group ("stress period", in Tomaševskij's term). In actuality, a new system which begins the count of "stress periods" with the first stress is just as conventional as the former system; it reflects our system of musical notation just as the old terminology reflects the classical system. The traditional terminology, however, aside from its familiarity, has other substantial advantages: in our syllabo-tonic versification lines with constant anacrusis, e.g. the iambic, have been so isolated from lines without anacrusis, e.g. the trochaic, as to constitute a completely independent meter. We not only generally fail to see the kinship of the iambic and trochaic meters but even perceive them as opposed to each other — a fact which is

---

as a special meter was introduced anew into English metrics by Robert Bridges (under the name of "britannic", p. 97) and W. Skeat (in the preface to his Chaucer, p .LXXXIII). On the term "dactyl", which was established in German metrics in connection with the ternary meters of the medieval poets, cf. H. Paul, pp. 81-82; for the poets of the seventeenth century, ibid., pp. 95-96.

[8] B. Tomaševskij, p. 46 ff. Among foreign theoreticians, P. Verrier, I, p. 98 ff., is especially given to the use of anacrusis. Cf. also A. Heusler *Über germanischen Versbau*, pp. 30-32 ("*freier*" and "*gebundener*" *Auftakt*).

reflected in the widely accepted, though dubious, terminology distinguishing these meters as *descending* and *ascending*. Cf. e.g. the lines of Puškin: "Mčátsja tuči, v'jútsja túči..." (*Besy*) and "Dlja beregóv otčízny dál'noj..." and Fet's "Mésjac zérkal'nyj plyvět po lázurnoj pustýne..." and "Istrepálisja sósen moxnátye vétvi ot búri..."[9] In the *history* of syllabo-tonic metrics, of course, the concept of anacrusis assumes greater significance inasmuch as we find poetic periods and styles for which the binary (and ternary) meters had not yet made a distinction between lines with constant anacrusis and those without anacrusis. We shall therefore speak of anacrusis only in those cases when the number of unstressed syllables before the accent is a variable quantity (the so-called "variable anacrusis"). In purely tonic verse, where there is no counting of syllables, such variations are altogether natural; but they are also encountered in syllabo-tonic verse — chiefly in those historical periods marked by a struggle between the syllabic principle and the purely tonic principle.[10]

We distinguish two types of anacrusis. In one anacrusis enters into

---

[9]   B. Tomaševskij denies that there is any difference in principle between "rising" and "falling" meters; e.g., in both iambic and trochaic alike he sees transitions both from an unstressed to a stressed (rise) and from a stressed to an unstressed (fall). Cf. *Problemy ritma*, p. 125, and *Russkoe stixosloženie*, p. 45 ff. However, the psychological experiments of Wundt and Meumann show that there is a difference — at least for abstract rhythm — in the grouping of syllables in rising and falling meters; with a rising rhythm we hear a pause just *after the stress* (giving the succession: unstressed, stressed, pause), but with falling rhythm the pause falls after the *unstressed* syllable (stressed, unstressed, pause). Cf. Wundt, *Grundzüge der physiologischen Psychologie*, 1905[5], Bd. III, p. 55 ff; Meumann, p. 304. Wundt even thinks it is possible to speak, as did the classical theoreticians, of the different "ethic type" (*Ethos*) of the rising and falling meters (the iambic is a "stimulating" metrical type, the trochaic a "tranquillizing", p. 166). In an actual line of verse, of course, the positioning of the word boundaries can establish a rhythmical grouping which does not coincide with the metrical grouping: Moj djadja | samyx | čestnyx | pravil...

[10]   B. Tomaševskij sees a disyllabic anacrusis in the trochaic and a trisyllabic one in the dactylic meter (p. 47). He does so on the basis of the fact that the first stress in these meters is often left out or displaced from the initial syllable to its neighbor. As a matter of fact, however, even for the first foot of the dactylic and trochaic meters there exists a difference between the syllable that is *stressed in principle* and that which is *unstressed in principle*. Here also, any displacement of the stress is felt as a deviation from the norm, i.e., as a deformation of the metrical scheme. Cf. Kol'cov: Ja sam-drug s toboju, | *Sluga* i xozjain... Or Lermontov: *Okruž*i sčastiem sčast'ja dostojnuju, | Daj ej soputnikov, polnyx vnimanija... Tomaševskij's theory is based on a confusion of the concepts of meter and rhythm. Thus, in the iambic tetrameter the sixth foot is *stressed in principle* (has a metrical accent), even though there are poems in which the stress is missing on the sixth foot in the majority of the lines. One should mention the existence of dactylic poems which preserve the heavy stress on the first syllable (cf. Fet: "Mesjac zerkal'nyj plyvět po lazurnoj pustyne..."). This widespread rhythmical type should, according to the theory held by Tomaševskij, be set aside as an independent metrical form, the *dactyl without anacrusis*.

the composition of a stanza according to a definite rule of arrangement. Cf. Bogdanovič's *Ody duxovnye*, V[11] (two-syllable anacrusis in the odd lines, one-syllable in the even):

> ‿‿ *Ne strašis'*, dobrodétel', naprásno
> ‿ Ljudéj ot neprávdy unját',
> ‿‿ V nix poróki plodjátsja vsečásno
> ‿ Nel'zjá ix ničém ispravl'ját'

In the other type the sequence of lines with and without anacrusis is not regulated. Cf. S. Tučkov's sonnet *Pobediteli bogatstva* (*Besedujuščij graždanin* III, 10) where the first line has a one-syllable anacrusis and the others an initial stress:

> ‿ *Igrájte*, potóki na mjágkix lugáx,
> Ptíčki, vesëlyj vznosíte vy glás,
> Pójte, pastúški, na krásnyx bregáx
> Prjámo stokrátno vy sčástlivej nas...

In Russian poetry anacrusis is used only in the ternary meters, which, because of the stability of the metrical accent, are similar to the purely tonic *dol'niki*. The Germans and English also use this device most frequently in ternary meters: as was mentioned above, English and German verse makes no distinction, even theoretically, between "amphibrachs" and "anapests"; and in the seventeenth and early eighteenth centuries the term "dactyl" was customarily used in Germany to refer to all ternary meters. Cf., for German, Goethe's "anapests" from *Pandora*:

> ‿‿ Alle blinken die Sterne mit zitterndem Schein,
> ‿‿ Alle laden zu Freuden der Liebe mich ein,
> ‿ Zu suchen, zu wandeln den duftigen Gang
> ‿ Wo gestern die Liebste mir wandelt' und sang...

For English, cf. Byron's elegy:

> ‿‿ Shades of heroes, farewell! your descendant, departing
> ‿‿ From the seat of his ancestors, bids you adieu!
> ‿ Abroad, or at home, your remembrance imparting
> ‿ New courage, he'll think upon glory and you...

In English poetry, however, one also encounters this variable opening of the line in the binary meters. Consider, for example, Shakespeare's iambic pentameter, which in other ways too retained many forms of

---

[11] In a Bogdanovič poem (*Lira*, 1773, 2nd edition) the ode has as its subtitle the words "In *dactylic* verse". This name is linked to the German tradition of the seventeenth and early eighteenth century. Cf. footnote 7, on p. 129.

license characteristic of the national tonic verse, including the trochaic opening of the line. Cf. *Measure for Measure*, Act V, Sc. I:

> ◡ Take him hence; to the rack with him! We'll touse you
> Joint by joint, but we will know the purpose...

Or in Byron's *Parisina*:

> ◡ ...Those lids — o'er which the violet vein
> Wandering, leaves a tender stain,
> Shining through the smoothest white
> ◡ That e'er did softest kiss invite...

In Russia we encounter the first experiments with anacrusis in the verse of Sumarokov, along with his other experiments in mixed meters, "logaoedic" verse and so on (cf. § 33). Cf. his *Preloženie psalmov* (from the 28th Psalm), where, among a number of lines with one-syllable anacrusis (amphibrachic), he introduces an isolated group of three verses without anacrusis (dactylic):

> O, čáda, podvlástnye lóžnym bogám,
> Uzríte vladýki vselénnyja čest',
> Počúvstvujte óblast' egó mnogomóčnu,
> I slýšite slávnoe ímja egó:
> Uzríte tvorcá i padíte pred ním:
> Uslýšite výšnego glás nad vodámi:
>   Glás sej gremít na velíkix vodáx,
>   Glás sej po vséj razdaëtsja vselénnoj,
>   Glás sej presílen, sej glás velelépen,
> Livánskie kédry sej glás istorgáet...

Experiments of this sort are encountered in Deržavin's work. The poem *Lástočka* is of special interest as an attempt to imitate folk meter: in the original version it approaches the type of the *dol'niki*, but in the final version it has anacrusis in the second stanza while keeping to the normal amphibrachic [sic! Žirmunskij must mean dactylic] form in the remaining portions:

> Ó, domovítaja lástočka!
> Ó, milosízaja ptíčka!
> Grúd' krasobéla, kasátočka,
> Létnjaja góst'ja, pevíčka!
>   ◡ Ty část o po króvljam ščebéčeš'
>   ◡ Nad gnëzdyškom sídja, poëš';
>   ◡ Krylýškami dvížes', trepéščeš'
>   ◡ ◡ Kolokól'čikom v górlyške b'ëš'
>   ◡ Ty část o po vózduxu v'ëš'sja... etc.

Cf. also the choruses of the cantata *Ljubitel'ju xudožestv* (*1791*):

> Čёrnye mráki,
> Zlýe prizráki
> ◡ *Užásnyx* strastéj,
> ◡ *Begíte* iz gráda.
> ◡ *Sokrójtes'* v dnó áda
> ◡ *Ot nášix* vy dnéj... etc.

At the end of the eighteenth century one can also point out isolated attempts of this same kind (Bogdanovič, Kamenev's ballad *Gromval*, and several others). Independently of these experiments, the poets of the Puškin era again made attempts in this direction: in Lermontov's early poetry we can observe many examples of anacrusis prompted by the influence of the English ternary meters and by other efforts to liberate poetry from the syllabic principle.[12] Consider, for instance, the following excerpt, where anacrusis is utilized with regularity, the first line having a one-syllable "up-beat" and the second a two-syllable "up-beat":

> ◡ Začém ja ne ptíca, ne vóron stepnój,
> ◡◡ Proletévšij sejčás nado mnój?
> ◡ Začém ne mogú v nebesáx ja parít'
> ◡◡ I odnú liš' svobódu ljubít'?

In Lermontov's later poetry, cf. *Rusálka*, where anacrusis is used irregularly:

> ◡ Rusálka plylá po reké golubój,
> ◡◡ Ozarjáema pólnoj lunój,
> ◡◡ I starálas' oná doplesnút' do luný
> ◡◡ Serebrístuju pénu volný.
> ◡◡ I šumjá i krutjás', kolebála reká
> ◡◡ Otražёnnye v nej oblaká;
> ◡ I péla rusálka, i zvúk eё slóv
> ◡◡ Doletál do krutýx beregóv...

In the further development of the Russian lyric we find anacrusis in those Romantic poets who are generally inclined to experiment with the syllabic nature of the line, i.e. tend toward a freer accentual structure. Cf., for example, the following verses, with regular alternation, from Fet:

> V péne nesёtsja potók,
> ◡ Lad'jú obgonjájut burúny, —
> Kórmčij gljadít na vostók
> ◡ I búdit drožáščie strúny...

---

[12] On anacrusis in Lermontov, cf. B. Èjxenbaum, *Melodika stixa*, p. 93; *Lermontov*, 1924, p. 37.

Or, from another poem:

⌣ ⌣ Tol'ko v míre i ést', čto tenístyj
Drémljuščix klënov šatër!
⌣ ⌣ Tol'ko v míre i ést', čto lučístyj,
Détski-zadúmčivyj vzor!...

In the following, one line differs from the rest:

⌣ Niktó mne ne skážet: — "Kudá ty
⌣ Poéxal, kudá zagadál?"
⌣ ⌣ Ševelís' že, vesló, ševelísja!
⌣ A béreg vo mráke propál...

But most recently this device is to be seen especially often in the poetry of Bal'mont, marking the break in the direction of *dol'niki* which was taking place at the same time in the work of his younger contemporaries.

In Bal'mont anacrusis is always used with regular alternation:

⌣ Ja žít' ne xočú nastojáščim,
⌣ ⌣ Ja ljubljú bespokójnye sný,
⌣ Pod sólnečnym bléskom paljáščim
⌣ ⌣ I pod vlážnym mercán'em luný...

Or:

⌣ Moí pesnopén'ja — žurčán'e ključéj,
⌣ ⌣ Čto zvučát vsë zvončéj i zvončéj.
⌣ V nix žénstvenno-strástnye šópoty strúj,
⌣ ⌣ I devíčeskij v nix pocelúj...

Or, with the more complex compositional arrangement of the anacrusis:

⌣ ⌣ Esli médlenno pádaja
⌣ ⌣ Kapli žgúčej smolý
⌣ Mučítelej-démonov ráduja,
⌣ ⌣ Ottenjájut čudóviščnost' mglý,
⌣ ⌣ Mne vsegdá predstavljáetsja
⌣ ⌣ Budto vnóv' ja živú,
⌣ I sérdce moë razryváetsja,
⌣ ⌣ No vpervýe — mne vsë najavú...

Thus, anacrusis is ordinarily met with wherever there is a struggle between strict syllabism and free tonic verse. As a violation of the syllabic principle at the beginning of the line, beyond the limits of the meter, so to speak, it is always less perceptible than irregularities in the number of syllables between stresses, and it will therefore appear as the first symptom of the emancipation of verse from strict syllabism, or, alternatively, as the last stronghold of free tonic versification when strict syllable-counting is gaining the upper hand. Thus in the medieval German lyric of the minnesingers, during the time when the Romance principle of syllable counting within the line was spreading, the beginning of the line remained free for a long time and could arbitrarily be either iambic or trochaic (cf. § 29). The same applies to medieval English poetry up to the time of Chaucer, who still admitted such license (and even, as we saw, in modern times, e.g., in Shakespeare). On the other hand, during the rebirth of the purely tonic system, the first attempts at introducing the ballad measures (in Germany and England) begin the metrical reform with the device of anacrusis (cf. §§ 29-30), and we saw the same thing in the Russian poets of the nineteenth century whose experiments were motivated by the desire to liberate Russian verse from the syllabic principle.

24. THE CAESURA

The caesura is a metrically obligatory cut at a specified place in the line. It is a *metrical* break, i.e., a division in the rhythmical movement, prescribed beforehand as a general rule of the verse structure, as an element in the metrical scheme. The caesura cuts the line into two hemistichs — i.e. it transforms a higher order metrical unit into smaller metrical groups (of the same or different dimensions), which are united and at the same time opposed to each other. The metrical significance of the caesura can best be illustrated by the example of the classical hexameter: here the metrical break occurs most often in the third foot after the long or after the first short syllable, more rarely in the fourth foot after the long. Owing to this placement of the caesura, which never coincides with the boundary of a dactylic foot, it exerts an influence on the general character of the meter: before the caesura it is descending (long-short-short, etc.) but afterwards it is obligatorily ascending (short-long-short, etc.). This two-way flow of the meter — descending at the beginning of the line and ascending after the caesura — is of great importance for the *metrical* structure of the classical hexameter:

> Dóč' dorogája, prosnís'! ‖ Ty svoími očámi uvídiš'
> Tó, k čemu sérdce tvoë ‖ stol'ko lét už tak strástno stremílos':
> Znaj, Odisséj vozvratílsja! ‖ On zdés' posle dólgix skitánij...

When, in a departure from the classical pattern, the caesura occupies a different position, the character of the meter is destroyed: cf. Modest Gofman, *Gimny i ody*, p. 39:

> ...V róščax velíkogo bóga ‖ véter proxládoju véjal...
> ...V výs' ustremljájas' toržéstvenno. ‖ Mólča, kak búdto vo xráme...

Thus the caesura is not an accidental halt in the line depending on a syntactic or declamatory pause, or on the boundaries of words or syntactic groups, and it certainly does not always coincide with such natural pauses in speaking. In the linguistic material of the verse the presence of a caesura is signalled by various devices. (1) Obligatory for the caesura is a word boundary. (2) In certain systems of versification, the caesura is marked by an obligatory pre-caesural stress. (3) The caesura, like the end of the line, coincides with the boundary of an independent syntactic group, sentence, etc. (4) At the caesura, as at the beginning or end of the line, an extra measure of variation is permissible (we may find either caesural anacrusis or a clausula with various types of catalexis). (5) Finally, at the end of the hemistich, just as at the end of the line, there can be harmonizing groups (rhymes), either occasionally or regularly (so-called internal, caesural rhymes). Depending on these devices the caesura can be stronger or weaker, i.e., the hemistichs can be to a greater or lesser degree independent of each other. Such independence is furthered by increasing the length of the rhythmical line.

Of these various devices for dividing the verbal material the only obligatory one is in all cases the word-boundary. Does this word boundary within the line correspond to any pause in pronunciation? This question is answered in the case of the caesura just as it is answered for the end of the line. The metrical cut dividing the line into hemistichs constitutes an *ideal* pause, i.e., an interruption in our perception of the verse form, which results from breaking a more extensive rhythmical group into two independent sections equally subordinate to a larger unit. In the actual phonetic realization of the line this pause is indicated sometimes by *silence*, more often by *retardation* in uttering the last part of the hemistich, or by a special *intonational cadence*; and it is sometimes not indicated by anything at all. In any case, a great deal depends on the style of recitation, just as is the case at the end of the line; and here the style is even more decisive than at the end of the line since the caesural pause is always less prominent than the pause at the end of the line.

An obligatory stress before the caesura is characteristic of the so-called syllabic system, where, thanks to this, the role of the caesura takes on special importance. For example, the French Alexandrine (twelve-syllable) line has an obligatory stress on the sixth syllable and a caesura just after it. Cf. the lines of Alfred de Musset:

...Lorsque le pélican, ‖ lassé d'un long voyage,
Dans les brouillards du soir ‖ retourne à ses roseaux,

Ses petits affamés ‖ courent sur le rivage
En le voyant au loin ‖ s'abattre sur les **eaux**...

The metrical reform which eliminates the caesura in syllabic verse actually creates a wholly new meter. The French Romantics (Victor Hugo and his school) did not, as is generally said, abolish the caesura; what they did was to maintain the word-division on the sixth syllable while greatly reducing its significance through a regrouping of the syntactic elements. Thus was created the "Romantic trimeter", in which one is hardly aware of the presence of a caesura since the caesural accent is overshadowed by two others — usually after the fourth and eighth syllables. Cf. the line of V. Hugo:

...Marcher à jeun, ‖ marcher ⋮ vaincu, ‖ marcher malade...
...Vivre casqué, ‖ suer ⋮ l'été, ‖ geler l'hiver
...Il vit un oeil ‖ tout grand ⋮ dans les ténèbres...

In the most recent period, the French Symbolists do away with the word division after the sixth syllable.[13]

...D'oublier ton pauvre a- ⋮ mour-propre et ton essence... (Verlaine)
...Brouille l'espoir que vo- ⋮ tre voix révéla... (Verlaine)
...Tu files à ton rou- ⋮ et le triste écheveau... (A. Regnier)

In Russian verse the caesura requires the word boundary, but the stress is not obligatory in all meters. In the iambic hexameter, where the caesura falls after the third foot, this question was the occasion of a spirited debate between Tred'jakovskij and Sumarokov. Tred'jakovskij, who would not permit the replacement of an iamb by a pyrrhic in the third foot, proceeded from the French Alexandrine line — in general, from the old tradition of syllabic verse — and relied also on the Germans. Sumarokov challenged this reliance on German evidence by pointing out that Russian, in contrast to German, has a multitude of long words, although even in the German poets he found examples of the iambic hexameter with a weakened caesural stress (cf. "Ist Varus wenigst*ens* ‖ noch nicht gewisser Sieger..." and others). "And for that reason", he writes, "I end the first hemistich with something other than iambs more frequently than do the Germans: I think, however, that others among our writers of tragedies do not avoid this, and there is really no reason to avoid it. And it seems to me that whoever gives himself pains over this is taking

---

[13] Cf. Tobler, pp. 118-119. On the question of the caesura and syntactic breaks cf. Fr. Saran, p. 214; B. Tomaševskij, *Četyrëxstopnyj jamb*, p. 147 ff; *Russkoe stixosloženie*, p. 20 ff.

needless trouble and wasting his efforts in trying to find pure iambs to mark the caesura..."[14]

History has revealed the correctness of Sumarokov's position: the Russian iambic hexameter has a caesura after the third foot and freely permits the omission of the stress on the sixth syllable. Examples from Puškin have been mentioned earlier:

> ...I stráždut *ózimi* || ot béšenoj zabávy,
> I búdit láj sobák || usnúvšie dubrávy...

or:

> Kogdá pod *sóbolem* || sogréta i svežá,
> Oná vam rúku žmët, || pylája i drožá...

In the majority of cases the caesural break is also a rather clear syntactic division. But cf. an example of weak caesura concealed by the syntactic grouping:

> Sijála nóč'. || Lunój ⋮ byl pólon sád. || Ležáli
> Lučí u nášix nóg || v gostínoj bez ognéj...

An iambic hexameter with caesura is used only in imitations of the classical iambic trimeter. In the German and Russian imitations it became standard practice — following the example of the classical authors who allowed a long as well as a short to serve as the final (twelfth) syllable — to omit the accent on the twelfth syllable, and owing to this the iambic trimeter of the Russian and German poets is confused with an iambic pentameter having a dactylic ending. Cf. Goethe's iambic trimeter (Faust, II):

> Bewundert viel und viel gescholten, *Helena*,
> Vom Strande komm' ich, wo wir erst gelandet sind,
> Noch immer trunken von des Gewoges *regsamen*
> Geschaukel, das vom phrygischen Blachgefild uns her
> Auf stäubig-hohem Rücken, durch Poseidon's Gunst
> Und Euros Kraft, in vaterländische Buchten trug...

Cf. the translation of N. Xolodkovskij:

> Xvalój odníx, xulój drugíx *proslávlena*
> Javljájus' já, Eléna, prjámo s *bérega*,
> Gde výšli mý na súšu, i tepér' eščë
> Morskój živóju zýb'ju *op'janënnaja*...

There were complaints at the end of the eighteenth and beginning of the

---

[14] Tred'jakovskij, *Novyj sposob* (1735), rule III (p. 26), and Chap. II, § 16 (p. 138); Sumarokov, *Otvet na kritiku*, X, 96-97.

nineteenth century about the monotonous character of the iambic hexameter, and experimental attempts were made to shift the place of the regular caesura. D. Samsonov, the champion of the iambic meter, suggested a reform intended to accomplish this (*Nečto o dolgix i korotkix slogax, o russkix geksametrax i jambax, Vestnik Evropy*, 1818, pp. 270-7). As early as Sumarokov, however, the attempts to shift the caesura show interesting results. Cf. *Pesni* (CXLIV):

> Prostí, mojá ljubéznaja, ‖ moj svét, prostí,
> Mne skázano na závtree ‖ v poxód ittí,
>   Ne védomo mne tó, ‖ uvížus' li s tobój,
>   I ty, xotjá v poslédnij ráz, ‖ pobúd' so mnój...
> Kogda umrú, umrú ja tám ‖ s ruž'ëm v rukáx,
> Razjá i zaščiščájasja, ‖ ne znáv, čto stráx;
>   Uslýšiš' ty, čto já ‖ ne róbok v póle býl,
>   Dralsjá s takój gorjáčnost'ju, ‖ s kakój ljubíl...

The caesura is not obligatory in the Russian iambic pentameter. The classical tradition, supported by the French ten-syllable line, required a caesura after the fourth syllable (the so-called "second foot caesura"). As early as the eighteenth century, however, one can find deviations from this tradition, and in the nineteenth century Vostokov comes forward (in *Opyty*, pp. 35-37) as the theoretical champion of "the mobile break", which lent "greater variety and movement" to the line. The new type of the iambic pentameter is backed by the authority of English and German models, and also by the Italian ten-syllable line ("endeca-sillabo"). However, the obligatory caesura was still observed by Puškin in the early stages of his development. This can be seen in *Gavriiliada* and in *Boris Godunov*. Of course the caesura is everywhere weak, since it is not supported by a precise syntactic division, and following the general rule, allows the stress to be omitted from the fourth syllable. Cf.:

> Eščë odnó ‖ poslédnee skazán'e —
> I *létopis'* ‖ okónčena mojá,
> Ispólnen dólg, ‖ zavéščannyj ot Bóga
> *Mne gréšnomu.* ‖ Nedárom mnógix lét
> *Svidételem* ‖ Gospód' menjá postávil
> I *knížnomu* ‖ iskússtvu vrazumíl...

In the second period of his poetic development, after 1830, Puškin turns to a free iambic line without the caesura. In the "small tragedies", for example, cf. *Skupoj Rycar'*:

> Čtó ne podvlástno mné?... Kak nékij démon
> Otséle právit' mírom já mogú;

Liš' zaxoču — vozdvígnutsja čertógi;
V velikolépnye moí sadý
Sbegútsja nímfy rézvoju tolpóju...

In *Domik v Kolomne*, as is well known, Puškin gives preference to the caesural iambic although he himself uses the line without the caesura:

Priznát'sja vam, ⫶ ja v pjatistópnoj stróčke
Ljubljú *cezúru* na vtorój stopé.
Ináče stíx ⫶ to v jáme, to na kóčke,
I xot' ležú ⫶ tepér' na kanapé,
Vsë, *kážetsja mne*, búdto v trjáskom bége,
Po mërzloj *pášne* mčús' ja na telége...

In spite of the fact that there is no constant metrical caesura in this type of iambic pentameter, the line is almost always divided into two hemistichs by the mobile syntactic pause, which is occasionally also called a caesura on the analogy with the obligatory metrical break. With such a *syntactic caesura* the variable elements of the rhythm, such as the disposition of word boundaries and the grouping of words, serve as a kind of substitute for the missing signal of a regular metrical division, though they are naturally less distinct. Similar phenomena are to be seen in the non-caesural iambic pentameter of the English and German poets. Cf. Shakespeare's *Macbeth*:

Is this a dagger ⫶ which I see before me,
The handle toward my hand? ⫶ Come, let me clutch thee!
I have thee not, ⫶ and yet I see thee still.
Art thou not, ⫶ fatal vision, ⫶ sensible
To feeling as to sight? ⫶ Or art thou but
A dagger of the mind, ⫶ a false creation,
Proceeding ⫶ from the heat-oppressed brain?...

Or Goethe's *Iphigenia*:

...Red' oder schweig ich, ⫶ immer kannst du wissen,
Was mir im Herzen ist ⫶ und immer bleibt.
Löst die Erinnerung ⫶ des gleichen Schicksals
Nicht ein verschlossnes Herz ⫶ zum Mitleid auf?
Wie mehr denn mein's! ⫶ In ihnen seh' ich mich!...

In binary meters having a larger number of feet than those just mentioned, the caesura is obligatory. Such meters tend to break up into hemistichs which are isolated as independent lines. Cf. Brjusov's *V sklepe*:

Tý v grobníce rasprostërta |
            v mírtovom vencé. ||
Já celúju lúnnyj ótblesk |
            na tvoëm licé. ||

> Skvoz' rešétčatye ókna |
>> víden krúg luný. ||
> V jásnom nébe, kak nad námi, |
>> tájna tišiný... ||

For an interesting example of an extended line which preserves a homo
geneous unity of its parts cf. Brjusov's *Kon' Bled*: (trochaic heptametei
with no caesura):

> Úlica bylá — kak búrja. Tólpy proxodíli,
> Slóvno ix preslédoval neotvratímyj Rók.
> Mčális' omnibúsy, kéby i avtomobíli.
> Býl neisčerpáem járostnyj ljudskój potók...

In ternary meters, there is usually a caesura for tetrameters and lines
longer than tetrameters. Owing to the immobile stress before the caesura,
such lines tend to be rather monotonous. Cf. Puškin's (amphibrachic
with feminine ending at the caesura):

> Gljažú, kak bezúmnyj, || na čërnuju šál',
> I xládnuju dúšu || terzáet pečál'.
> Kogdá legkovéren || i mólod ja býl,
> Mladúju grečánku || ja strástno ljubíl...

Or Lermontov's (dactylic, with dactylic ending at the caesura):

> Já, máter' bóžija, || nýne s molítvoju
> Pred tvoim óbrazom, || járkim sijániem,
> Ne o spasénii, || ne pered bítvoju,
> Ne s blagodárnost'ju || il' s pokajániem...

Or Nekrasov's (anapest with masculine ending at the caesura):

> Ne guljál s kistenëm || ja v dremúčem lesú,
> Ne ležál ja vo rvú || v neprogljádnuju nóč'.
> Ja svoj vék zagubíl || za devícu-krasú,
> Za devícu-krasú, || za dvorjánskuju dóč'...

B. Tomaševskij shows (*Russkoe stixosloženie*, p. 56) that it is possible to
have a stable stress before the caesura in the binary meters also. He cites
the example of Polonskij's trochaic hexameter in *Kuznečik-muzykant*.
Here the caesura has a feminine ending:

> Ne sverčká naxála, || čto treščít u péček,
> Ja pojú: gerój moj — || molodój kuznéčik...

Nekrasov uses the same sort of "tonic" feminine caesura in the trochaic
pentameter. Cf. *Katerina*:

Vjánet, propadáet ‖ krasotá mojá!
Ot lixógo múža ‖ nét v domú žit'já.
P'jányj vsë kolótit, ‖ trézvyj vsë vorčít.
Sám, čto ni popálo, ‖ íz domu taščít!...

The caesura is especially strong in those cases when, as compared to the norm of the metrical scheme in question, there is an extra syllable or a syllable missing at the caesura (in the terminology of Brjusov: *hypermetria* and *lipometria* at the caesura). Depending on the part of the line in which the deviation occurs — at the end of the first hemistich or at the beginning of the second — we speak of a catalectic (or hypercatalectic) ending in the first hemistich or of anacrusis in the second hemistich. These instances of catalexis at the caesura show that the hemistich, like the whole line itself, constitutes an independent rhythmical unit allowing extra-metrical cadences at the beginning and end — either additions or truncations. In classical metrics, catalexis is explained as the replacement of a syllable by a pause equivalent to it. An example of such a catalectic line is the classical pentameter — reduced by two short syllables at the caesura and at the end. Whatever its origin,[15] it was perceived by the Romans as a dactylic hexameter with a caesura after the third foot and with catalexis in the third and sixth, as in the following scheme:

$$- \cup \cup \ - \cup \cup \ - \wedge \wedge \ \| \ - \cup \cup \ - \cup \cup \ - \wedge \wedge$$

In the tonic version of this line the catalexis of the unstressed syllables is kept at the caesura and the ending, as follows:

$$\acute{\ } - - \acute{\ } - - \acute{\ } \ \| \ \acute{\ } - - \acute{\ } - - \acute{\ }$$

In the so-called "elegiac couplets" a hexameter line is paired with a pentameter — a non-truncated line with a truncated line. Cf. Puškin's:

Úrnu s vodój uroník │ ob utës eë déva razbíla.
Déva pečál'no sidít, ‖ prázdnyj deržá čerepók.
Čúdo! Ne sjáknet vodá, │ izlivájas' iz úrny razbítoj;
Déva nad véčnoj struëj ‖ véčno-pečál'na sidít.

We cannot speak of a pause in the catalexis of tonic verse; the caesura in such cases is especially distinct because of the interruption in the syllable-count. Besides this, the metrical division in hemistichs is very often reinforced by syntactic parallelism. There are two kinds of catalectic caesura. In the first kind, catalexis occurs in separate lines which are not sub-

---

[15] The pentameter, as the name itself shows, was at first considered a five-foot meter in which the middle foot (two longs) was split by a caesura, as follows: $- \cup \cup \ \vdots \ - \ \| \ - \ \vdots$ $\cup \cup \ - \ \vdots \ \cup \cup \ -$ Cf. B. Kazanskij, *Učenie ob arsise i tezise*, p. 369.

ordinated to any regular order in the stanzaic composition. Cf. Brjusov's:

> Járostnye ptícy ∧ ‖ s ógnennymi pér'jami
> Proneslís' nad bélymi ‖ rájskimi preddvér'jami.
> Ógnennye ótbleski ‖ vspýxnuli na mrámore,
> I umčális' stránnicy, ‖ uletéli zá more...

In the second type (which constitutes the majority) the catalexis in the caesura is maintained systematically throughout the entire poem or recurs with regularity, e.g., in every even line. Thus in Bal'mont's verses (the even lines have a hypercatalectic caesura):

> Ja mečtóju lovíl ｜ uxodjáščie téni,
> Uxodjáščie téni ‖ pogasávšego dnjá.
> Ja na bášnju vsxodíl, ｜ i drožáli stupéni
> I drožáli stupéni ‖ pod nogój u menjá...

The use of catalexis in the caesura is evidence of a revolt against the syllabic principle of versification. The first such experiments in the Russian lyric are to be seen at the end of the eighteenth century in the work of Karamzin. Cf. his *K D...* (1788), a dactylic poem with the odd lines showing catalexis at the caesura:

> Mnógie bárdy, ‖ líru nastróiv,
> Smélo igrájut, pojút.
> Zvúki ix lír, ‖ glásy ix pésnej
> Mčátsja po róščam, lugám...

Cf. also *Kladbišče* (1792), ("Strašno v mogile, ‖ xladnoj i tëmnoj..."). Somewhat later Deržavin begins to use this device — like Karamzin, in dactylic lines — but with no distinct compositional arrangement. Cf. his *Oda na vzjatie Varšavy* (1794):

> Čërnaja túča, ‖ ∧ mráčnye krýla
> S cépi sorváv, ∧ ‖ ves' vózdux pokrýla;
> Víxr' polunóčnyj, ‖ letít bogatýr'!
> T'má ot čelá, ∧ ‖ ∧ s pósvista pýl'!
> Móln'i ot vzórov ‖ begút vperedí,
> Dúby grjadóju ‖ ležát pozadí...

Or in the poem *Snigir'* (1800):

> Čtó ty zavódiš' ‖ ∧ pésnju voénnu,
> Fléjte podóbno, ‖ ∧ mílyj Snigír'?
> S kém my pojdëm ∧ ‖ vojnój na giénu?
> Któ tepér' vóžd' naš? ‖ ∧ Któ bogatýr'?...
> ...Nét tepér' múža ‖ ∧ v svéte stol' slávna:
> Pólno pét' pésnju ‖ voénnu, Snigír'!

If one considers as normal the usual dactylic tetrameter with feminine caesura in the second foot (Vixr' polunočnyj ‖ letit bogatyr'... etc.), there are two possible metrical variations: a catalectic masculine ending (S cepi sorvav ʌ ‖ ves' vozdux pokryla...) or anacrusis variation in the second hemistich with omission of the initial unstressed syllable (Čërnaja tuča ‖ ʌ mračnye kryla); it is also possible to have a combination of both forms of truncation with "omission" of two syllables (T'ma ot čela ʌ ‖ s posvista pyl'...). The variations in the Warsaw Ode are more diversified; most of the verses of *Snigir'*, on the other hand, come close to the metrical type noted in Karamzin's poetry.

In recent times Bal'mont has made wide use of the catalectic caesura. A four-stress line in a binary or ternary meter is broken down in such cases into two hemistichs, each with two stresses, which frequently show rhythmic and syntactic parallelism. Cf., for example, the iambic tetrameter with hypercatalectic caesura:

> Xočú byt' dérzkim, ‖ xočú byt' smélym,
> Iz sóčnyx grózdej ‖ venkí sviváť.
> Xočú upít'sja ‖ roskóšnym télom.
> Xočú odéždy ‖ s tebjá sorváť...

We see the same thing in another sample — constant feminine hypercatalectic endings both in the caesura and at the end of the line:

> Ja vól'nyj véter, ‖ ja véčno véju,
> Volnúju vólny, ‖ laskáju ívy,
> V vetvjáx vzdyxáju, ‖ vzdoxnúv, neméju,
> Leléju trávy, ‖ leléju nivy...

And the same in yet another sample: amphibrachic with constant dactylic endings (hypercatalexis at the caesura and at the line end):

> Nejásnaja ráduga. ‖ Zvezdá otdalёnnaja.
> Dolína i óblako. ‖ I grúst' neizbéžnaja.
> Legénda o sčástii, ‖ bor'bój vozmuščёnnaja,
> Lazúr' neponjátnaja, ‖ nemája, bezbréžnaja...

Metrical parallelism of the hemistichs with catalectic caesura and catalectic feminine ending (dactylic hexameter):

> Véčno bezmólvnoe Nébo, ‖ smútno prekrásnoe Móre, —
> Óba okútany svétom ‖ mёrtvenno-blédnoj Luný.
> Véter v prostránstve smutílsja, ‖ smólk v neutéšnom prostóre —
> Nébo i véter i Móre ‖ grúst'ju odnóju bol'ný...

The regular alternation of lines with catalectic caesura and lines without caesura was shown in the example from Bal'mont ("Ja mečtoju lovil...").

In the following excerpt the odd lines are anapestic tetrameter with catalectic feminine caesura (and feminine ending) while the even lines are anapestic trimeter (with masculine ending):

> Vosxodjáščee Sólnce, ‖ umirájuščij Mésjac,
> Káždyj dén' ja ljubljú vas i ždú.
> No sil'née, čem Mésjac, ‖ i nežnée, čem Sólnce,
> Ja ljubljú zolotúju zvezdú...

This division of the tetrameter line into two groups, each with two stresses, and the use of a strong (catalectic) caesura together with the corresponding movement of the rhythm and intonation was adapted from Bal'mont and popularized by Igor Severjanin. Cf., for example:

> Èto býlo u mórja, ‖ gde lazúrnaja péna,
> Gde vstrečáetsja rédko ‖ gorodskój èkipáž...
> Koroléva igrála ‖ v bášne zámka — Šopéna,
> I, vnimája Šopénu, ‖ poljubíl eë páž...

Examples of the catalectic caesura from Western languages testify to the importance of this phenomenon in the process of canonizing or discarding the principle of syllabism. In the Middle Ages, French syllabic versification admitted a hypercatalectic feminine ending at the caesura of a decasyllabic line (the so-called "epic caesura" in the words of F. Dietz). Cf. for instance:

> Quant vient en mai ‖ que l'on dit as lons jors
> Que Franc de France ‖ repairent de roi cort,
> Reynauz repaire ‖ devant el premier front...

From the Renaissance on, this licence is regarded as inadmissible. But Spanish poetry, for example, according to the investigations of Prof. D. K. Petrov, preserved it even during the classical period.[16] In iambic pentameter the English poets also make wide use of this licence as one of the relics of the freer, purely tonic system; in the medieval period we find the epic caesura even in the work of Chaucer, a poet much concerned with the accuracy of syllable counting (cf. "And in his har*pyng*, ‖ whan that he hadde sunge"), and it occurs also in Shakespeare and his contemporaries, in Milton, and in the nineteenth century. Shakespeare (*Macbeth*): "But how of Caw*dor*? ‖ The thane of Cawdor lives... What thou

---

[16] In this regard, cf. the study by Prof. D. K. Petrov — unfortunately, not yet printed at this time — dedicated to a metrical analysis of the tragedy by Lope de Vega *The Duchess of Amalfi* (1618), from which the courtesy of the author has enabled me to borrow the following example: Hija, n(o) es mucho ‖ que a tu padr(e) assombres... (line 1884). On the epic caesura in old French verse, cf. Tobler, p. 94; Stengel, p. 50; in English verse, J. Schipper, I, p. 26, 54.

art pro*mised*: ‖ yet do I fear thy nature..." etc.). On the other hand, the rebirth of the ballad and the ballad line, together with anacrusis at the beginning of the line, emancipates the caesura by the introduction of catalexis.

The caesura is most conspicuous when the hemistichs are united by caesural rhyme. Caesural rhyme can be either regular or sporadic. Sporadic rhyme does not form an integral part of the metrical structure of the poem. Cf. the English ballads and, correspondingly, Žukovskij's translation *Zamok Smal'gol'm*:

> Do rassvéta podnjávšis', konjá osedlál
> Znamenítyj Smal'gól'mskij barón.
> I bez ótdyxa gnál mež utĕsov i skál
> On konjá, toropjás' v Broterstón...

Regular internal rhyme is, on the contrary, an important element in the metrical pattern. Cf. V. Solov'ĕv's:

> V bylýe gódy ljubví nevzgódy
> Soedinjáli nás,
> No plámja strásti ne v nášej vlásti,
> I moj ogón' ugás.

Regular internal rhyme, creating the sense of closure at the end of each hemistich as if it were an independent rhythmical unit, naturally raises the question as to the conventionality of the line boundary. We could, for instance, arrange Solov'ĕv's poem in hemistichs:

> V bylýe gódy
> Ljubví nevzgódy
> Soedinjáli nás...etc.

In fact, the line and the hemistich, the period and the line are all relative concepts. We prefer to regard the line as that rhythmical unit which preserves the most stable unity within the limits of the stanza; in this sense we regard the hemistich as a part of the line and the period as a combination of lines. In all European languages the syllabic group tends to be of a fairly consistent average length, which holds good not only in the more usual poetic and lyric meters but also in prose, to the extent that artistic prose can be broken down into uniform, more or less "rhythmical" groups: the average length is (7)-8-9-(10) syllables, corresponding in our syllabo-tonic system to the iambic (or trochaic) tetrameter, the anapestic (or amphibrachic) trimeter, and in purely tonic systems to the three-stress line. It is possible that the number of syllables is determined by purely physiological conditions, by, for example, the normal quantity of breath exhaled. The meters which exceed these normal line boundaries possess less stability and exhibit a tendency to fall into hemistichs with an obligatory metrical cut — i.e., caesura. In the Russian ten-syllable line (iambic pentameter) or in the twelve-syllable line with four stresses (the amphibrachic tetrameter, for example) such a caesura, as we have seen, is optional, although in the majority of cases there is at least a mobile syntactic cut. In the iambic (or trochaic) hexameter it is already obligatory: but there is a difference in principle between the caesura and the line boundary — a difference in the treatment of the preceding stress. Lines which exceed the customary maximum of twelve syllables are perceived by us rather as metrical periods — i.e., as complex higher units. On the other hand, shorter lines (e.g., of six or especially of four syllables) tend to be linked to a larger group, if this is not hindered by a special catalectic ending or by rhyme, etc. Contrary to the author's express desire, as shown by the typography, we involuntarily group Bal'mont's short lines into larger rhythmical groups, thus converting end rhymes into internal rhymes. For example:

> Útrom ráno, ‖ iz tumána,
> Sólnce výgljanet dlja nás
> I osvétit, ‖ i zamétit
> Vséx, kto ljúbit ètot čás...

In all of these cases, of course, the relative distinctness of the caesura is of primary importance. A strong caesura — together with rhythmic-syntactic parallelism of the hemistichs, and catalexis, and caesural rhyme — contributes to the separation and independence of the hemistichs. We therefore tend to regard a long line with such a caesura, other things being equal, as two independent lines. For example, the following twelve-syllable trochaic lines from Brjusov, in spite of their being united graphically, break down into three independent lines:

> Bliz medlítel'nogo Níla,
>   tám, gde ózero Merída,
>   v cárstve plámennogo Rá,
> Tý davnó menjá ljubíla,
>   kak Ozírisa Izída,
>   drúg, caríca i sestrá!
> I kloníla piramída
>   tén' na náši večerá...

The deciding factor in many cases is the artistic will of the author, who uses graphic devices to indicate that rhythmical grouping of lines which he had in mind at the moment of creation and which should be reproduced in the reading. When there are no such external signs — as, for example, in many medieval manuscripts — the question remains open and frequently gives rise to numerous disputes which themselves reveal the arbitrariness of such grouping.[17] Thus, in tonic verse, with very few exceptions (e.g. the Russian iambic hexameter), there is no qualitative difference, no difference in principle, between the caesura and the line boundary; there is only a quantitative distinction, with the possibility always left open for the occurrence of transitional types.

25. RHYTHMIC MODIFIERS.
RELATIVE STRENGTH OF THE STRESSES

Having determined the metrical scheme of a poem, we can then consider the rhythm of the separate lines. The individual rhythmical variations are to be explained by variations on the metrical scheme which are conditioned by the sum total of the rhythmic modifiers affecting verse. Most prominent among these modifiers are those which account for the deviations in the number and distribution of the stresses which were discussed above in connection with the Russian syllabo-tonic meters. They consist, as we know, of the *omission* of metrical stresses, the *hypermetrical stressing* of metrically weak syllables and *displacement* of stresses: as a general term we can use the word "*replacement*" ("hypostasis", according to Brjusov), if it be thoroughly understood that this is simply a convenient label. In addition to replacement, however, there are a number of other no less important factors which affect the rhythm of the line. These include: 1) the relative strength of the stresses, 2) the distribution of the word boundaries, 3) rhythmic-syntactic patterns. It is necessary to devote a brief discussion to these.

The question of the relative strength of the stresses has already been touched on in connection with the general principles of Russian prosody. The basic defect of the theory of verse which applies the concept of the "foot" to the *rhythm* of syllabo-tonic verse is, as we have seen, the artificial reduction of all accentual relationships to the formula: stressed vs. unstressed (on the analogy of the classical long vs. short), which ignores the fact that in reality the stresses affecting the rhythm of an actual line of verse are determined by the relationship of one to another which implies a great many different degrees. The application of phonetic methods to the study of rhythm in western European verse made it imperative to

---

[17]   On the line boundary, cf. *Rifma*, pp. 49-50; on caesural rhyme, *ibid.* p. 51 ff.

distinguish a comparatively large number of gradations in the concept of stress. Thus Franz Saran (*Deutsche Verslehre*, p. 49 ff.) distinguished nine different degrees of stress: out of these, three serve to differentiate the usual "stressed syllable" (vollschwer, mittelschewr, halbschwer — shown by the figures + 3, + 2, + 1), three are used for the "unstressed" syllable (halbleicht, volleicht, überleicht: −1, −2, −3), two designate special cases of logical or emphatic foregrounding of stressed syllables (überschwer 2 and überschwer 1: + 5 and + 4), and finally, the weak initial syllables of a phrase or sentence are marked as a medium (or zero) degree of stress (indifferent — designated as 0). The basic degree of stress is represented by the full accent (vollschwer), which corresponds to the strength of a stressed syllable outside the context of a sentence (in lexicalischer Isolierung). The two lower degrees of stress (mittelschwer, halbschwer) belong to autonomous words which are subordinated to a more significant utterance within the sentence. The three non-stressed degrees are determined by the varying degree of semantic and accentual independence of unstressed syllables (the heavier ones are proclitics and enclitics, and those "heavy" suffixes which retain some degree of stress; the weaker ones — unstressed syllables which have undergone various degrees of reduction). For example:

$$0 \quad 3 -3 -1 \quad 2 \quad -3 -2 \quad 3 \quad \quad 4 \quad -2 \quad 2 -3 \quad 1$$
Von alledem konnte in Rom nicht die Rede sein.

Maurice Grammont in his study of the rhythm of French verse (*Petit traité de versification française*, p. 98 ff.) uses five different degrees of stress (shown by the numerals: 5-1), between which he thinks it possible to set up various intermediate grades ($1\frac{1}{2}$, $2\frac{1}{2}$, etc.). Cf.

$$2 \quad \quad 1 \ 3 \quad \quad 1 \ \ 1 \quad \ 2 \quad \quad 2\tfrac{1}{2} \quad 4 \quad \quad 1 \ 2 \quad 1 \quad \quad 4$$
Deux liards | couvriraient || fort bien | toutes mes terres,
$$1\tfrac{1}{2} \quad 1 \ \ 1 \quad \ 2 \quad \ 1\tfrac{1}{2} \quad 5 \quad \quad 1 \ \ 1 \ 1 \quad 2\tfrac{1}{2} \quad \ \ 2 \quad 4$$
Mais tout le grand ciel bleu || n'emplirait pas | mon coeur...

Anticipating other investigators (1875) A. Ellis (*Remarks*, p. 442 ff.) experimented with the phonetic analysis of English verse and arrived at nine different degrees of stress and the same number of degrees of length and intonational level. He regarded three basic degrees of stress as absolutely essential for any metrical analysis: the *strong* (8), the *mean* (5), and the *weak* (2); he himself distinguished nuances within each degree (e.g. superstrong — 9, strong — 8, substrong — 7, supermean — 6, etc.) Cf.:

<pre>
2   2   6   8   8   2   2   6   6   8
</pre>
In the black sky glimmers the pale cold moon
<pre>
5   5   2   5   2   2   8   7 2 2 6
</pre>
Sad ghost of night, and the stars twinkle around...

Of course, it is far from true that all the gradations of accentuation isolated by so nuancé a phonetic analysis actually play a role in our perception of verse rhythm. In our study of Russian prosody, however, we were
faced with the necessity of setting up at least two categories of stressed
syllables — strong and weak ("semi-stressed"), and this distinction sometimes has a substantial effect on the rhythmical movement of the verse. Cf.

<pre>
    2   1   2   2   2
</pre>
Žurča eščë bežit || za mel'nicu ručej...
<pre>
    2   1   2   2   2
</pre>
No prud uže zastyl || sosed moj pospešaet...
<pre>
    2   1   2   2   2
</pre>
Ljublju eë snega: || v prisutstvii luny...

Cf. also Fet's systematic weakening of the odd accents in the trochaic
tetrameter:

<pre>
        1   2   1   2
</pre>
Èti gory, èti doly,
<pre>
        1   2   1   2
</pre>
Èti moški, èti pčëly
<pre>
        1   2   2
</pre>
Ètot zyk i svist...

We should at the same time distinguish at least two categories of unstressed syllables: the completely weak unstressed syllable as well as that
partial de-stressing of monosyllabic ambiguous words which permits them
to retain the qualitative identity of the vowel and a certain minimum
strength corresponding to their semantic independence. In this connection we noted heavier and lighter forms within the de-stressed words.
It would seem that an abundance of such monosyllabic words in metrically weak positions, even though they are de-stressed, contributes to a
certain weighting of the line:

...no obmanút' on ne xotél
Dovérvčivost' duší nevínnoj.
Tepér' my v sád pereletím
gde vstrétilas' Tat'jána s ním...

Among the unstressed syllables which are somewhat stronger than those of the weakest level, one must also reckon those unstressed syllables and enclitics in the binary meters (designated by Šengeli as "intense" syllables) occurring in words with an "anapestic" beginning and "dactylic" ending. Cf. "Kogda ne v šutku *za*nemog... I lučše vydu*mat'* ne mog... Takoj prekrasnoj *i* bezgrešnoj..." etc.

In Russian, however, the differentiation of various degrees of stress and non-stress does not play any substantial role in view of the fact that it has *no semantic function* within the word, i.e., it has no connection with differences of meaning and operates only in the larger syntactic whole along with other devices for foregrounding the units of the utterance (word order, intonation). The situation is different in the Germanic languages, especially in German. Here, a compound word has two stresses of unequal force which serve to define the semantic relationship obtaining between the parts of the word. (cf. Váterlànd, Nébelkleìd, Táugenìchts, wáhlverwàndt — and also the semantic difference between úbersètzen "convey across a river" and ùbersétzen "translate"). In the same way, those "heavy" suffixes and verbal prefixes which retain their semantic independence are marked by a clear secondary stress (cf. Váterschàft, Tráurigkeìt, Fínsternìs, áufgegàngen, unertrénnbàr, and so on). Thus, the linguistic material shows phonetically a possibility of rhythmic differentiation that is alien to Russian. German iambic verse, which seems to us monotonous because of the metrically regular alternation of stresses without any "deviation", becomes rhythmically expressive in German pronunciation as a result of the varying strength of the stresses. In Gretchen's monologue, for instance, which is in the monotonous metrical form of the two-stress line, there obtains a complex play of accents due to the shifts of the stronger of the two, back and forth from the beginning to the end of the line, corresponding, as it were, to the movement of the rhythmical tension. Cf.:

Nach ihm nur schau ich	(4—2)
Zum Fenster hinaus	(2—3)
Nach ihm nur geh ich	(4—2)
Aus dem Haus.	(1—3)
Sein hoher Gang,	(2—3)
Seine edle Gestalt	(2—3)
Seines Mundes lächeln	(3—3)
Seiner Augen Gewalt	(3—3)
Und seiner Rede	(2—3)
Zauberfluss	(4—2)
Sein Händedruck	(3—2)
Und, ach! sein Kuss	(3—4)

However, the extent to which the relative strength of the stresses is differentiated is greatly affected by the rhythmical style of the poem, which is closely bound up with the sense and the artistic style in general. In a meditative elegy or in a lyrical, melodious poem the dynamic differences of stress are frequently leveled out; the stresses are held to one level and do not show sudden fluctuations beyond a certain maximum force. E. Sievers[18] has already pointed this out, citing as an example the lyrical, meditative excerpt from the first monologue of Goethe's *Faust* ("O sähst du, voller Mondesschein..."). Cf. Fet's *Melodija*:

> Mésjac zerkál'nyj plyvët po lazúrnoj pustýne,
> Trávy stepnýe unízany vlágoj večérnej...

Any logical foregrounding of individual words (e.g. *travy* stepnye unizany *vlagoj* večernej... or: travy *stepnye* unizany vlagoj *večernej*) would here be unjustified, and the verse itself suggests no such special prominence for any of the words. The situation is different in conversational (or rhetoric) verse with its strongly highlighted emphatic accents and logical intonations.[19] For example:

Minúty-dvé oní-molčáli	(2-3, 1-3)
No-k-néj-Onégin-podošël	(1-2-3)
I-mólvil: "Vý-ko-mné-pisáli	(3, 1-1-3)
Ne-otpirájtes': já-pročël	(3, 1-3)
Duší-dovérčivoj priznán'ja	(2-3, 3)
Ljubví-nevínnoj izliján'ja.	(2-3, 3)
Mne-vaša-ískrennost' milá...	([$\frac{1}{2}$]-1-1-3) etc.

If the relative stress alternations are regularized in accordance with a metrical law in such a way that one stress is the stronger or main stress and another is the weaker or secondary stress, then we may speak of the "dipodic" character of a given meter.[20] A dipodic alternation is often found in music in the so-called "composite rhythms", e.g. $\frac{1}{4}$ time with

---

[18] Cf. Ellis, "Remarks" in the *Trans. of the Philol. Soc.*, 1875-76, pp. 442-46. Ellis discussed this question still earlier in his *Essentials of Phonetics* (1848), p. 75 ff. and in *Early English Pronunciation*, I (1869), pp. 333-335 and 927-953. There is also in use another notation in which the strongest stress is designated as 1, the next weaker as 2, the next as 3, and so on. Cf. Ed. Sievers, *Grundzüge der Phonetik*, § 653, p. 242.

[19] These two types are mentioned by Ed. Sievers in *Rhythmisch-melodische Studien*, p. 68, where he uses the first monolog of Faust as the example. Cf. "O siehst du, voller Mondesschein..." (lyrical tone of the monolog, leveling of the dynamic and melodic intervals) and "Weh! Steck ich in dem Kerker noch!"... (tone of declamatory pathos, extreme dynamic and melodic fluctuations). Cf. also V. Žirmunskij, "Melodika stixa'. Po povodu knigi B. Èjxenbauma", *Mysl'*, No. 3, p. 118.

[20] On the problem of dipody cf. Wundt, III, p. 29 ff., and especially A. Heusler *Zur Geschichte der altdeutschen Verskunst* (Breslau, 1891), pp. 1-12.

the stronger down-beat on the first quarter and the weaker down-beat on the third quarter, or $\frac{6}{8}$ time with the stronger down-beat on the first eighth and the weaker down-beat on the fourth eighth. It still plays a significant role in that folk poetry which has not lost its link with musical performance: F. A. Korš finds dipodic alternation in Russian folk poetry, for instance in the *bylina*.[21] From music the dipidoc alternation penetrated into classical metrics, where iambs, for instance, always have a dipodic character ($\cup \doteq \cup - ...$); hence the terms: iambic "dimeter" or "trimeter" for the four-foot or six-foot iambic line; i.e. a two-measure iambic or three-measure iambic (where two feet equal one measure or dipody). More complicated is the question as to the dipodic character of modern tonic meters which have lost all ties with music. Some Russian theoreticians (e.g. A. Belyj, Vjačeslav Ivanov) see Russian iambic and trochaic tetrameters as dipodies, because they very frequently omit the third stress and the next most frequent omission (especially in the trochee) is the first stress, as a result of which the second and fourth feet become the most stable positions for the strong stress. [22] These considerations are used to justify the view which sees the first + second, and third + fourth feet in iambic and trochaic meters as complex "di-iambic" or "di-trochaic" feet which become paeons on losing a stress, or choriambs when a stress is shifted from the second to the first syllable, and so on. As for terminology, as was mentioned earlier, this introduction of four-syllable feet leads only to a complication of the nomenclature.[23] From a theoretical point of view one must object to this doctrine on the grounds that the alternation of strong and weak accents in the dipodic structure is a peculiarity of the poetic meter, while the omission of stresses in iambic and trochaic, even though it may occur principally in the odd feet, serves to characterize only the rhythm of individual lines ("... I na porfirnye stupeni || Ekaterininskix dvorcov..."), so that the term "dipody", when applied to the phenomena of rhythm, acquires a quite unusual sense. In tonic verse, however, there can be genuine dipodies — under special conditions, to be sure. Thus, the ordinary four-stress line divided by a strong caesura (with "catalexis", for example) into two hemistichs is grouped into dipodies,

[21] F. Korš considers the *bylina* line in terms of classical quantitative versification as an "anapestic dimeter with weakening of all the long syllables except the last" (*O russkom narodnom stixosloženii*, pp. 3-5).
[22] On the iambic tetrameter as "iambic dimeter" cf. Belyj, *Simvolizm*, pp. 349, 354, 400, and *passim*. And earlier still: F. Korš, note to page 5.
[23] From the point of view of terminology, Tomaševskij argues against the dipody in Russian iambics ("*Russkoe stixosloženie*" pp. 32-33).

since the stress preceding the caesura will be stronger than the initial stress. Cf., for example:

Xoču byt' dérzkim, ‖ xoču byt' smélym   (1, 2 ‖ 1, 2)
Iz sóčnyx grózdej ‖ venkí svivát'   (1, 2 ‖ 1, 2)

In such examples, however, the concept of "dipody" is completely covered by the more usual term "hemistich".[24]

26. WORD BOUNDARIES

The foot is an abstract unit of metrical repetition, a part of the pattern, not of the actual verse as it is spoken. The actual verse consists of *words*, not of *feet*, as V. Čudovskij correctly insisted (cf. above, § 11). For the rhythm of the line, however, it is not a matter of indifference how the word divisions are distributed within it (the so-called "word boundaries"). Klopstock contrasted "word feet" (Wortfüsse) and "metrical" feet (Versfüsse): in the word, as a semantic unit held together by a stress (as opposed to the abstract, schematic foot), he sought a theoretical foundation for his experiments with purely tonic and free verse.[25] Following him, Radiščev, in his articles on the hexameter, also proposes to study verse "by word feet according to the precept of Klopstock" (*Apologija Tilemaxidy*). From that time on, the question of the foot and the word and their mutual relationship has remained one of the crucial problems of versification. Most recently in Russia V. Čudovskij, B. Tomaševskij and G. Šengeli have paid special attention to it.

From the point of view of phonetics, the word is not always the unit according to which the linguistic material is divided. The borders of stress groups or stress units need not coincide with the word boundaries.

---

[24]   B. M. Èjxenbaum (*Melodika stixa*, pp. 95-96) speaks in these terms of the division into dipodies.

[25]   Klopstock (*Vom deutschen Hexameter*, 1779): "As a result of the use of artificial feet required by the rules there arise *word feet*, which are the real parts of the line and are the only ones perceived by the hearers, who are totally indifferent to artificial feet." Among modern writers Skeat examines word feet in his preface to *Chaucer* (where he calls them "speech waves") (Cf. *Introduction*, p. 84 ff.). J. Minor (p. 154 ff.) considers the question of the non-coincidence of "metrical" and "word" feet (*Wortfüsse* and *Versfüsse*). Fr. Saran speaks of the foot as an element in the abstract metrical scheme: "The foot is by no means to be regarded as an actual element in a given rhythm. The foot is a part of the meter, that is to say, of the metrical pattern. It exists only for the person who scans the line or considers it from the point of view of the pattern." It is therefore incorrect to say that the actual line "consists of feet": the components of the actual line are the "rhythmic groups" (*rhythmische Gruppen, Glieder*), which are not coterminous with the boundaries of the "feet".

Thus in the Germanic languages there is apparently a tendency to begin the accentual group from the stress, i.e., from the point when the stream of exhalation is increased in force. Cf. the examples cited by Sievers: "Wo-sind-die-Ge|fangenen?" or "Er-hat-das | Buch..."[26] This question has not been sufficiently investigated with regard to Russian. In any case the word in Russian is, to a certain degree, an independent phonetic unit insofar as the pre-stress syllables undergo reduction according to a different rule from that which applies to the post-stress syllables. However that may be, the speaker of a given language conceives words as semantic units rather clearly separated one from the other; in this sense the distribution of the word boundaries becomes a factor in the rhythmic structure in spite of the absence of temporal breaks (pauses) between words.

The word boundaries do not usually coincide with the boundaries of the feet. The early theoreticians of Russian verse regarded this non-coincidence as one of the conditions of rhythmical euphony. Samsonov, for example, writes: "Verse is much smoother and therefore more pleasant when the feet do not end at the same places as the words." (p. 229). When this rule is disregarded, the verse becomes rhythmically monotonous and disintegrates, as it were, into separate feet ("broken meter"). Cf. Bal'mont's *Čeln tomlen'ja* where this device is used as a result of the author's desire to emphasize the alliteration of the initial consonants:

Véčer. | Vzmór'e. | Vzdóxi | vétra ||
Veličávyj | vózglas | vóln. ||
Búrja | blízko. | V béreg | b'ëtsja ||
Čúždyj | čáram | čërnyj | čeln || ...

One cannot, of course, exclude the use of this one-to-one correspondence as a rhythmic device endowed with peculiar expressive qualities. Cf. Nikitin's:

Kipít | vodá, | revët | ruč'ëm, ||
Na mél'nice | i stúk | i gróm, ||
Kolësa-to | v vodé | šumját, ||
A brýzgi | vvérx | ognëm | letját ||
Ot pény-to | bugór | stoít, ||
Čto móst | živój, | ves' pól | drožít || ...etc.

In languages with a constant stress on the last syllable, like French, or on the penultimate syllable, like Polish (and to a certain extent like Italian, which has a predominance of feminine endings) a regular distribution of

---

[26]   Ed. Sievers, *Grundzüge der Phonetik*, p. 235; cf. note 49 above. On the problem of the word boundaries within the line, cf. R. Jakobson, *O češskom stixe*, pp. 28-29.

word boundaries means at the same time that the line will be divided into regularly recurring feet which threatens to make the internal structure of the line completely monotonous. Cf., for instance, the experiments made by the Belgian poet Van Hasselt:[27]

> Allons, | mes oiseaux | si légers, | si fidèles,
> Au bord | de vos nids | déployez | vos deux ailes;
> Oiseaux | du printemps | par la brise | emportés,
> Chantez!

It was probably an unconscious desire to avoid the rhythmical mono-tony of such verse that led to the establishment in the Romance languages (and in Polish) of the freer "syllabic" system of versification, which does not require the stresses to be distributed within the line according to a uniform metrical pattern. When the word boundaries do not coincide with the borders of the feet, diverse rhythmical effects appear, thanks to the interaction of stress and word boundary. Thus the iambic line may ac-quire a trochaic cadence if the word divisions occur after unstressed syllables: e.g. "Moj djadja | samyx | čestnyx | pravil..." Or a dactylic cadence can appear in an anapestic line, as in Nekrasov's: "I nasmešlivyj | vnutrennij golos... Zaxvatilo vas | trudnoe | vremja..." and so on. Usually the arrangement of the word boundaries changes from line to line, which makes it possible to have a very great many rhythmical com-binations thanks to the customary omission (in the binary meters) of stresses at various places in the line. Thus in the following excerpt from *Evgenij Onegin* each line has its own particular configuration of stresses and word boundaries. If, however, these lines were considered only from the point of view of stress, they might appear to be rhythmically monotonous, since seven of the eight lines show the simplest of all variations of the iambic tetrameter: the stress on all even syllables or on the second, fourth and eighth. Cf.:

> U nóči | mnógo | zvëzd | preléstnyx,
> Krasávic | mnógo, | na Moskvé;
> No járče | vséx | podrúg | nebésnyx
> Luná | v vozdúšnoj | sinevé.
> No ta, | kotóruju | ne sméju
> Trevóžit' | líroju | moéju,
> Kak veličávaja | luná
> Sred' žën | i dév | blestít | odná...

There are about forty combinations which the word boundaries and stresses of the iambic tetrameter can in practice form (cf. G. Šengeli, p.

[27] Cf. L. Kastner, p. 340 ff.; Edm. Stengel, p. 8.

139 ff.). The individual style of a poet which appears in his selection from these possibilities can be established by statistical calculation. B. V. Tomaševskij, in his work on the rhythm of Puškin's iambic tetrameter and pentameter, has studied this question exhaustively and demonstrated statistical methods for the study of a poet's individual manner as shown in his way of combining stress and word boundaries. For purposes of notation the most convenient system is that suggested by V. Čudovskij and B. Tomaševskij. Under this system a figure is used to indicate the number of syllables in each word while an exponent to that figure shows which of the syllables bears the stress. Thus, in the excerpt quoted above:

$$\text{line 1: } 3^2 + 2^1 + 1^1 + 3^2$$
$$\text{line 2: } 3^2 + 2^1 + 3^3$$
$$\text{line 3: } 3^2 + 1^1 + 2^2 + 3^2$$
$$\text{line 4: } 2^2 + 3^2 + 3^3$$

and so on.[28]

27. RHYTHMIC-SYNTACTIC FIGURES. ENJAMBMENT

By the term "rhythmic-syntactic figures" we shall understand the various interrelationships of the rhythmic and syntactic elements of verse, thus extending the meaning which was given to the term by O. M. Brik in his discussion of rhythmic-syntactic parallelism.[29] There arises here, among others, the question of the "run-on line" (Fr. enjambement), a question which was introduced into traditional metrics because of its great practical importance but which was treated as a rather isolated and accidental phenomenon. For us enjambment is certainly not the only, but merely the most revealing example of the bearing of syntactic factors upon rhythm.

The compositional arrangement of the verbal material of a poem, as was shown at the beginning (cf. § 1), concerns not only the distribution of words and stresses in the line but extends also to the harmonic ordering of syntactic groups. In lyrics which retain the original connec-

---

[28] The first Russian theoretician to devote attention to the distribution of the word boundaries was A. Belyj, who gave them the unhappy designation "pauses" (*Simvolizm*, p. 276). The problem was made the subject of a special study by V. Čudovskij (especially in *Neskol'ko myslej*, p. 84 ff.); he is also the coiner of the cumbersome term "phonophoria". Statistical material relating to this question, aside from that of B. V. Tomaševskij, is to be found in G. Šengeli's *Traktat*.

[29] On the term "rhythmic-syntactic figures", cf. *Kompozicija liričeskix stixotvorenij*, p. 3.

tion with singing there is still preserved that arrangement of rhythmical and syntactic elements by which the longer syntactic group (e.g. the sentence) corresponds to the longer rhythmical period, while the shorter syntactic group (e.g. the syntactically independent part of the sentence — the phrase) corresponds to the shorter rhythmical unit. Cf. in the Russian folksong:

> Ne sxodít' li mne mladén'ke | do zelëna sáda ||
> V gósti nádobno pozvát' by dorogógo drúga ||
> Posulílsja ko mne mílyj | sízym golubóčkom ||
> Priletál síz golubóček | sél na teremóček... || etc.

Or in the French song:

> Quant on veut cueillir les roses |
> Il faut attendre le printemps |
> Quant on veut aimer les filles |
> Il faut qu'elles aient seize ans ||

Modern lyric poetry has to a considerable degree retained the harmonic grouping of the song lyric: line, period and stanza usually constitute independent syntactic groups maintaining the appropriate degrees of mutual subordination. Cf. Bal'mont's poem, cited at the beginning of this book (§ 1) or Puškin's:

> Dlja beregóv otčízny dál'noj |
> Ty pokidála kráj čužój; ||
> V čás nezabvénnyj, v čás pečál'noj |
> Ja dólgo plákal pred tobój || .

Where the line is broken by the caesura into two hemistichs the metrical grouping into half-lines normally coincides with the syntactic grouping. Cf., for example, Puškin's:

> Redéet oblakóv | letúčaja grjadá...
> Zvezdá pečál'naja | večérnjaja zvezdá.
> Tvoj lík oserebríl | uvjádšie ravníny,
> I drémljuščij zalív, | i čërnyx skál veršíny...

In some cases the rythmical grouping of the line is matched by the syntactic parallelism of the hemistichs, i.e., an identical sequence of similar syntactic elements (e.g. subject + predicate || subject + predicate). Such *rhythmic-syntactic parallelism* is often accompanied by anaphora, i.e., by the repetition of the same word at the beginning of corresponding rhythmic-syntactic groups. Examples of this are especially numerous in dipodic constructions, that is, when there is a strong (catalectic) caesura. Cf. Bal'mont's:

> Xočú byt' dérzkim, xočú byt' smélym...
> Ja búdu sčástliv, ja búdu mólod...
> Laskáju trávy, leléju nívy...
> Vosxodjáščee sólnce, umirájuščij mésjac... and others.

Such two-part parallelism can also be seen in non-caesural meters — e.g., in the iambic or trochaic tetrameter. Cf. Puškin's:

> V čás nezabvénnyj, v čás pečál'nyj...
> Tvojá krasá, tvoí stradán'ja...
> Dar naprásnyj, dár slučájnyj...
> Mčátsja túči, v'jútsja túči...

Along with direct parallelism there is also a reverse parallelism — the so-called *chiasmus*. For example:

> B kosmátoj šápke, v búrke čërnoj...
> Sérdce pústo, prázden úm...

In the iambic pentameter, in line with the most common type of stress distribution (on the second, sixth and tenth syllables) one frequently encounters a three-part parallelism. Cf. Blok's "O doblestjax, | o podvigax, | o slave..." In *Boris Godunov*: "Izmenčiva, | mjatežna, | sueverna... I putaet, | i v'ëtsja, | i polzët... Ty milost'ju, | raden'em | i ščedrotoj..." Cf. also the type with stresses on syllables four, six and ten: "Čto ni korol', | ni papa, | ni vel'moža... Za ix grexi, | za slavu, | za dobro..." and numerous others.[30]

The rhythmical significance of syntactic parallelism is to be found chiefly in the equality of the stress relationships — i.e., in the identical sequence and strength of the stresses, to which one must add identical intonation (melody) and in certain cases identical number of words and identical distribution of the word boundaries. In a short non-caesural line, this phenomenon can create the appearance of a metrical cut: an optional "syntactic caesura". Furthermore, the parallelism of the rhythmical movement is accompanied by a parallelism in the arrangement of the semantic elements, that is to say, the rhythmical structuring includes not only phonetic but also semantic elements. In this sense V. A. Čudovskij's observation is quite accurate: the two isometric lines "Al'fons saditsja na konja" and "Bogat i slaven Kočubej", which are identical with regard to the distribution of the stresses and word boundaries $(2^2+3^2+3^3)$, show essential differences in rhythm owing to the different ordering of the syntactic elements (the relative positions of the

---

[30] On rhythmic-syntactic parallelism as a device of composition cf. *Kompozicija liričeskix stixotvorenij*, p. 3.

subject and predicate). This question, however, has not yet been sufficiently studied in Russian metrics.[31]

When the metrical and syntactic divisions do not coincide, what results is the so-called "run-on line" (enjambment). In modern lyric poetry, cf. Anna Axmatova's:

> Čém xúže ètot vék predšéstvujuščix? | *Rázve*
> Tém, čto v čadú vesélij i trevóg
> On k sámoj čërnoj prikosnúlsja jázve
> I iscelít' eë ne móg.

Or in another of her poems:

> Nastojáščuju néžnost' ne spútaeš'
> *Ni s čém,* | i oná tixá...

The most characteristic feature of enjambment is that it contains within the line a *syntactic pause* which is stronger than that at the beginning or end of the same line. Depending on the distribution of this pause, one can distinguish two kinds of enjambment: one internal syntactic pause terminates a phrase carried over from the preceding line (the second example above; the French term is *rejet*), and the other begins a phrase carried over into the following line (example one — French: *contre-rejet*). Often, however, both types are to be seen in one enjambment. Cf. in *Evgenij Onegin*:

> ...Rebját dvoróvaja sem'já
> *Sbežálas' šúmno.* | *Ne bez dráki*
> Mal'číški razognáli psóv...

The absence of syntactic and metrical coincidence is possible also in the caesura. In such cases it is customary to speak of *caesural* enjambment. For example in Puškin's iambic pentameter:

> ...Igráet na licé ⦙ eščë bagróvyj cvét;
> Oná živá eščë ⦙ segódnja, | *závtra* — nét...
> ...Xolódnaja tolpá ziráet na poèta,
> Kak na zaézžego ⦙ *figljára:* | esli ón
> Glubóko výrazit serdéčnyj tjážkij stón...

The question has often been raised as to what kind of syntactic elements are so closely bound that separating them creates enjambment. In answer, various authors have pointed out the connection of the subject with the predicate, of the predicate verb with the direct object, of the modifier with the modified, and so on.[32] In this form, however, the

---

[31] Cf. V. Čudovskij, "Neskol'ko utverždenij", *Apollon*, 1917, No. 4-5, p. 67.
[32] Cf. Tred'jakovskij, *Novyj sposob*, rule III, pp. 26-27. Cf. also Tobler, pp. 114-115.

question is improper: one can adduce sufficient examples in which close
syntactic ties are disrupted without causing enjambment. The subject is
separated from the predicate in Puškin's:

> Pred ním pustýnnye ravníny
> Ležát zelënoj pelenój...

And here the predicate verb from the direct object:

> ...Blagogovéja, vsé *čitáli*
> *Priméty* gnéva i pečáli...

Or the modified from the modifier:

> ...Voobražájas' *geroínej*
> Svoix vozljúblennyx *tvorcóv*...

In all of these cases enjambment occurs only when there is within the line
a significant syntactic pause giving rise to a closer linkage of the syntactically bound parts of the sentence. Cf.

> ...Pred ním — pustýnja; | i *ravníny*
> *Ležát* zelënoj polosój...
> ...Pred ním pustýnnye ravníny
> Ležát, | i *tëmnoj polosój*
> Raskínulsja... and so on.

Thus, the presence of enjambment is determined not so much by the
absolute significance of one syntactic pause or another as it is by the
relationship between the syntactic break occurring in the middle of the
line and that occurring at the line's end. In connection with this an
important role is played by word order: e.g., inversion, which contributes
to the isolation of syntactic elements, and creates more distinct boundaries between the linked parts of the syntactic group. Cf. Puškin's:

> No v sérdce xána *čúvstv inýx*
> Taitsja *plámen'* bezotrádnyj...

The significance of inversion in enjambment was already clear to the
Russian theorists of the eighteenth century. Tred'jakovskij, for instance,
who would not permit caesura to separate syntactically bound parts of
of the sentence, admitted such division when the word order was inverted.
He considered "unsatisfactory" any metrical cut which divided the subject from the predicate:

> [P]   [S]
> Stixotvorčestvom *našli* || *mnogi* slavu v ljudjax...

But the same line seems to him "fairly good" with inverted order:

[P] [S]
Stixotvorčestvom *naši* ‖ v ljudjax slavu *mnogi.*

He also regarded a caesura between the predicate verb and the direct object as "unsatisfactory":

[Vb] [Obj.]
Nyne ja už ne *ljublju* ‖ *stixotvorstva* stara...

But with inversion the line was acceptable:

Stara ja už ne ljublju ‖ nyne *stixotvorstva.*

The same thing applied to an interruption between the adjective modifier and the modified noun. Cf. the "unsatisfactory" enjambment:

Presečeniem *xudoj* ‖ *stix* byt' možet xudšij

With inversion:

"Presečeniem *xudoj* ‖ byt' *stix* možet xudšij..."

French theoreticians, in their turn, made the same observations. A. Tobler (*Vom französischen Versbau*, pp. 120-121) cites some examples. Thus, Racine's line with inverted order "*De leurs champs* dans leurs mains ‖ portant *les nouveaux fruits*" would have been inadmissible had it been "Portant *les nouveaux fruits* ‖ *de leurs champs* dans leurs mains". Cf. other examples of inversion and isolation from Racine: "Toujours de *ma fureur* ‖ interrompre *le cours*" and "Je fuis *de leur respect* | l'inutile *longueur*" and many others.

The problem of how run-on lines are to be *read aloud* has been the subject of considerable dispute. When the syntactic and metrical groupings clash, a decision can be made in favor of one or the other: while some theoreticians recommend that verse be recited *according to the sense*, others demand a reading which preserves the *metrical pattern*. The problem is especially acute with respect to dramatic blank verse, which generally makes extensive use of enjambment. Cf. the lines of *Mocart i Sal'eri*:

> ...Otvérg ja ráno prázdnye zabávy;
> Naúki, čúždye múzyki, býli
> Postýly mne; ‖ uprjámo i nadménno
> Ot nix otrëksja ja i predálsja
> Odnój múzyke. ‖ Trúden pérvyj šág

I skúčen pérvyj pút'. ‖ Preodolél
Ja ránnie nevzgody; ‖ remesló
Postávil ja podnóžiem iskússtvu. ‖
Ja sdélalsja reméslennik: ‖ perstám
Pridál pospéšnuju, suxúju béglost',
I vérnost' úxu. ‖ Zvúki umertvív,
Múzyku ja raz"jál, kak trúp. ‖ Provéril
Ja algébroj garmóniju. ‖ Togdá
Uže derznúl, v naúke iskušénnyj,
Predát'sja nége tvórčeskoj mečtý. ‖

The realistic style of theatrical speech which was traditional at the end of the nineteenth century divided verse lines "according to the sense" and strove to give them a "natural" — i.e. prose, conversational — intonation. The extreme example of this manner is to be seen in the performance by the Moscow Art Theater of Puškin's small tragedies. If one discards the prosaic, conversational intonation, which is clearly inappropriate to poetic speech, there remains the possibility of interpreting run-on lines of blank verse as a special sort of "free iambic" with a varying number of syllables per line. E.g.: "Nauki, čuždye muzyki, byli postyly mne. Uprjamo i nadmenno ot nix otrëksja ja i predalsja odnoj muzyke. Truden pervyj šag, i skučen pervyj put'. Preodolel ja rannie nevzgody. Remeslo postavil ja podnožiem iskusstvu. Ja sdelalsja remeslennik. Perstam pridal pospešnuju, suxuju beglost'..." and so on.

In the majority of cases, modern theoreticians of German and English verse interpret the blank verse of Schiller, Shakespeare and Milton in this way; they regard the ten-syllable line as merely a graphic convention.[33]

To this is opposed the musical (or more exactly, metrical) style of reading which has been widely followed in recent times and which originated with the poets themselves. The verse line, according to the champions of this view, is a real unit, the limits of which are determined not only by the regular number of syllables and metrical accents, but also by special phenomena appearing at the end of the line (hypercatalectic clausula with feminine ending in iambic verse). Any lack of agreement between the syntactic and metrical divisions is an artistically planned dissonance, which is resolved, after several such disagreements, when the syntactic pause finally coincides with the end of the line. E.g.

Vsé govorját: nét právdy na zemlé.
No právdy nét i výše: ‖ Dlja menjá
Tak èto jásno, kak *prostája gámma.* ‖‖

[33] Thus Minor, p. 205-6; H. Paul, p. 136; P. Verrier, I, p. 181.

In reading, therefore, the boundary of the line should be marked by an appropriate *pause*, i.e., in some cases by *silence* or only by *slowing down* at the last stress or by a special *intonational* clausula. According to Maurice Grammont, who made a special study of this problem (*Le vers français*, p. 35 ff.), syntactic incompleteness occurring with enjambment causes a *rising* intonation of the voice instead of the usual terminal *falling* intonation. This raised inflexion serves at the same time as a means of placing extra emphasis on a word participating in the enjambment. Grammont cites a great many examples in which the run-on line is used for expressive purposes by the French romantics. Hugo, for example;

> Tout à coup la nuit vint et la lune apparut
> *sanglante...*

Or:

> ...Comme un cèdre au milieu des palmiers
> *règne*, et comme Pathmos ⋮ *brille* entre les Sporades...

Analogous examples for Russian verse are cited by B. V. Tomaševskij, who compares them with "the graphic device of italics" (p. 80). In *Mocart i Sal'eri*, for example:

> A nýne sám skažú — ja nýne
> *zavístnik*. Ja zavíduju : *glubóko*,
> Mučítel'no zavíduju. — O, nébo...

In rhymed verse also:

> ...I vsé prinját' svoí starális' méry
> Čtob srázu byt' zaméčennymi. Vdrúg
> V sebjá vtjanúli životý kur'éry...

In many cases enjambment contributes to the syntactic isolation of a word which, in prose, would normally be joined to the word following it to form a more or less stable phraseological unit. Thus, in the example taken from Axmatova: "Čem xuže ètot god [*Sic*: vek] predšestvujuščix? *Razve-tem*, čto v čadu veselij i trevog..." Set apart by enjambment, the word *razve* acquires an unusual significance. The same thing is to be seen in Puškin's *Domik v Kolomne*:

> ...V nej vkús byl obrazóvannyj. *Oná*
> Čitála sočinén'ja Èmína.

In prose we should be obliged to read: "V nej vkus byl obrazovannyj. *ona-čitala* sočinen'ja Èmína..." Here the metrical break corresponds to the syntactic interruption symbolized by several dots or by a dash.

The same sort of thing is easily possible in blank verse. Cf. *Mocart i Sal'eri*:

> Ja sčástliv býl : ja naslaždálsja mírno
> Svoím trudóm, uspéxom, slávoj; *tákže*
> Trudámi i uspéxami druzéj...

In all such cases, failing to observe the boundaries of the line and the intonational pause at the end means to frustrate not only the metrical intention of the poet but also the artistic sense of his verse.[34]

One must mention, moreover, that the cases of enjambment which are justified on grounds of semantic expressiveness constitute — in spite of M. Grammont's theory — only a minority of all such cases, especially in the work of poets who habitually employ this device. The artistic significance of enjambment resides in the very fact of the non-coincidence of metrical and syntactic groupings; this is perceived as an individual deviation from a uniform, "normal" kind of syntactic structure. When seen against the background of the traditional coincidence of metrical and syntactic groups, such deviations appear always as acts of poetic freedom, as evidence of a striving toward more individual, compositionally unbound forms — i.e., as a romantic reaction against the metrical canon. At the same time they can serve as an expression of artistic naturalism, freeing itself from metrically clear-cut compositional forms

---

[34] In the most recent poetry the most extreme example of a device for disrupting rhythmical and syntactic composition has been the widespread use of enjambment with non-autonomous (auxiliary) parts of speech. Cf. Verlaine's:

> ... Deçà, delà
> Pareil à la |
> Feuille morte...

And among the Russian poets, Mandel'štam's

> ... I sovsém ne vernëtsja — *ili*
> On vernëtsja sovsém drugój...

Similar examples are to be found earlier also, especially in blank verse. Thus, from Shakespeare: The king, your father, was reputed for | A prince most prudent... And from German poetry (Minor, p. 205): ...Schwärzer, *als* | Die Nacht... | or ...um | Dich zu veredeln... or ...zu schätzen *und* | Zu schirmen...

One might also include in the category of enjambment those cases in which a more important syntactic pause coincides with a less important metrical division, e.g., when there is a stronger syntactic pause at the caesura than at either the beginning or end of the given line. Cf. Puškin's

> ...Ved' èto, nakonéc, i žítelju berlógi,
> Medvédju nadoést. | Nel'zjá že célyj věk
> Katát'sja nam v sanjáx s Armídami mladými...

In classical poetics enjambment which ended with the caesura was regarded as less reprehensible. Cf. Ostolopov, *Slovar'*, II, p. 364.

and the pronounced stanzaic structure of the song lyric; this is especially so in dramatic blank verse and in narrative genres. In general, the run-on line is associated with "colloquial" verse and develops at times when poetry is emancipating itself from music. Conversational poetry acquires a great deal of structural freedom and strives to approximate actual speech and free "spoken" inflexions; this at the same time destroys the precise structural boundaries characteristic of the earliest song-like verse. Thus, insofar as romanticism tends toward a song-like, musical sort of lyric, it will avoid enjambment and will rather encourage the various forms of rhythmic-syntactic parallelism between adjacent hemistichs and lines (cf. for example, Fet and Bal'mont).

In the historical development of enjambment the two most interesting moments are, first, the rigid subordination of syntax to meter during the Classical epoch and, second, the struggle for a freer verse structuring during the period of Romanticism. During the Renaissance in France (cf. Ronsard and the Pléiade poets) the rhymed Alexandrine couplet made the freest possible use of enjambment. Malherbe and the other poets of the Classical period decreed correct syntactic divisions, and Boileau formulated the desired orthodoxy in his famous rule:

> Que toujours dans vos vers le sens coupant les mots
> Suspende l'hémistiche, en marque le repos.

Alexandrine verse, paired into even couplets and divided by the caesura into two hemistichs, acquired during the Classical era that monotonous harmony against which the Romantics polemicized so violently. Very often this syntactic structuring was accompanied by the device of making the hemistichs neatly parallel to or contrasting with each other. Cf. Racine's *Bérénice*:

> Combien tout ce qu'on dit ‖ est loin de ce qu'on pense;
> Que la bouche et le cœur ‖ sont peu d'intelligence!
> Avec combien de joie ‖ on y trahit sa foi!
> Quel séjour étranger ‖ et pour vous et pour moi!...

Or from the same source:

> Quoi! Dans ce même jour ‖ et dans ces mêmes lieux
> Refuser un empire, — et pleurer à mes yeux!

More noticeably in the eighteenth century poets, e.g. Voltaire (*Oedipe roi*):

> Finissez vos regrets, ‖ et retenez vos larmes:
> Vous plaignez mon exil, ‖ il a pour moi des charmes;

> Ma fuite à vos malheurs ‖ assure un prompt secours;
> En perdant votre roi ‖ vous conservez vos jours...

The reaction sets in at the end of the eighteenth century. André Chenier already makes wide use of enjambment at the caesura and at the end of the line. The Romantics — Victor Hugo and his school — assert enjambment as the fundamental principle of the new versification; as was shown earlier (§ 24), the Romantic elimination of the caesura was essentially nothing more than this use of caesural enjambment. Cf. V. Hugo (M. Grammont, p. 44 ff.):

> ...Il fit scier son oncle ‖ *Achmet* entre deux planches
> *de cèdre*, afin de faire ‖ *honneur* à ce vieillard...

> ...Parce qu'on est jaloux ‖ *des autres*, et honteux
> *de soi*...

> ...Tu t'es fait de valet ‖ *brigand* et de bandit
> *courtisan*...

Similar phenomena are to be seen in England with the development of the so-called "heroic couplets" in iambic pentameter. During the Middle Ages in Chaucer and during the Renaissance in Shakespeare and his contemporaries, enjambment is used with complete freedom. During the period of Classicism Pope and his school insist that the boundaries of the couplet, line and hemistich be strictly observed: the device of casting adjacent hemistichs and lines in parallel or antithetical constructions reaches the point of an importunate affectation, far exceeding analogous phenomena in the history of French verse. Cf. Pope's *Eloisa to Abelard*:

> ...I ought to grieve, ‖ but cannot what I ought;
> I mourn the lover, ‖ not lament the fault;
> I view my crime, ‖ but kindle at the view,
> Repent old pleasures, ‖ and solicit new;
> Now turn'd to heav'n, ‖ I weep my past offence,
> Now think of thee, ‖ and curse my innocence...

During the Romantic period the poets reverted to the practice of the Middle Ages and the sixteenth and seventeenth centuries. Thus Shelley and Keats, restoring its earlier freedom to the iambic pentameter, create a verse whose rhythmical character sharply differs from that of the eighteenth century "heroic couplet": enjambment occurs between single lines and even between one couplet and another. Cf. Shelley's *Julian and Maddalo*:

He ceased, and overcome leant back awhile,
Then rising with a melancholy smile
Went to a sofa, || and lay down, and slept
A heavy sleep || and in his dreams he wept
And muttered some familiar name, and we
Wept without shame in his society...

In Russian poetry we note several revealing changes in the practice of Puškin. His "southern poems" have very few cases of enjambment when compared to later poems, e.g., *Mednyj vsadnik*. The same can be said about the first chapters of *Evgenij Onegin* in comparison with later stanzas. Cf. Chap. VII of *Onegin*:

> ...No nýne...pámjatnik unýlyj
> Zabýt. || K nemú privýčnyj sléd
> Zaglóx. || Venká na vétvi nét...

Or:

> Byl véčer. Nébo mérklo. || Vódy
> Struílis' tíxo. || Žúk žužžál.
> Už rasxodílis' xorovódy,
> Už za rekój, dymjás', pylál
> Ogón' rybáčij. || V póle čístom...

In *Mednyj vsadnik*:

> ...Ili činóvnik posetít,
> Guljája v lódke v voskresén'e,
> Pustýnnyj óstrov. || Ne vzrosló
> Tam ni bylínki. || Navodnén'e
> Tudá, igrája, zanesló
> Domíško vétxij. || Nad vodóju
> Ostálsja on, kak čërnyj kúst...

Puškin's *Domik v Kolomne* is an example of this later manner in the iambic pentameter, as opposed, for example, to *Gavriiliada*. Cf.:

> Četyrëxstópnyj jámb mne nadoél:
> Im píšet vsjákij. || Mál'čikam v zabávu
> Porá b ego ostávit'. || Ja xotél
> Davným davnó prinját'sja za oktávu.
> A v sámom déle: || ja by sovladél
> S trójnym sozvúčiem. || Puščús' na slávu...

Enjambment penetrates into the iambic hexameter along with the influence of André Chenier. Cf. verses written in 1824:

> ...Davnó tvoéj iglój uzóry i cvetý
> Ne oživljálisja. || Bezmólvno ljúbiš' ty
> Grustít'. || O, ja znatók v devíčeskoj pečáli!
> Davno glazá moí v dušé tvoej čitáli.

As for blank verse, the tradition of enjambment in dramatic blank verse goes back, as we have said, to the plays of Shakespeare. In the epic and didactic poem it goes back to Milton and to his eighteenth century disciple Thomson (cf. *The Seasons* 1725-1730). Both Shakespeare and Milton make extensive use of this device. In Germany, the plays of Schiller are in this regard more freely constructed than the more lyric poetic dramas of Goethe. In Russian, Puškin's small tragedies show an abundance of run-on lines while *Boris Godunov* still makes very sparing use of them. An example from *Mocart i Sal'eri* was cited above (cf. pp. 163-164).

V. PURE TONIC VERSIFICATION

28. THE THEORY OF TONIC VERSIFICATION

Pure tonic verse is based on a count of the stressed syllables; the number of unstressed syllables between the stressed syllables is a variable quantity. The general pattern of such verse is x ⊥ x ⊥ x ⊥ x, where x = 0, 1, 2, 3... We thus distinguish two-stress, three-stress, four-stress lines, and so on. The organizing principle of such verse is the recurrence of a strong syllable following a more or less extended group of weak ones; the rhythmical attention is directed toward catching the strong syllables which recur after groups of varying length. That is why purely tonic verse is always easiest to write in those languages which have a clear-cut dynamic accent, i.e., a sharp contrast of stressed and unstressed syllables, as in the Germanic languages. When the attention is focussed on the stressed syllables, groups of unstressed syllables — even though they contain varying numbers of syllables — may be perceived as equivalent to each other.

Of course, the number of unstressed syllables between stresses is of essential importance in shaping the rhythm of individual lines or of the poem as a whole: since, however, such syllables form no part of the compositional structure, they belong to the area of rhythm, not meter. Moreover, although the number of unstressed syllables between stresses is a variable quantity, it normally varies within certain limits. These limits follow naturally from the necessity of perceiving the rhythmical portions linked together by the stresses as equivalent to each other. The more it is possible to have sharp fluctuations in the number of unstressed syllables between stresses — and, in general, the greater the number of unstressed syllables — the more difficult it is to hold the unstressed groups together by means of the stress, and as a consequence the verse gives the impression of being somehow less orderly with regard to its rhythm and approaches the natural freedom of accentuation which characterizes colloquial language or literary prose. However, a strongly marked stress (as we see, for example, in Majakovskij) is capable of uniting around itself a more extensive group of unstressed syllables. In the so-called *dol'niki* the usual value of x is 1 or 2. Cf. Blok's:

> Vxožú ja v tëmnye xrámy,
> Soveršáju bednyj obrjád.
> Tam ždú ja Prekrásnoj Dámy
> V mercán'i krásnyx lampád.
> V tení u vysókoj kolónny
> Drožú ot skrípa dveréj,
> A v licó mne gljadít, ozarënnyj
> Tol'ko óbraz — liš' són o néj...

Cf. also Axmatova's:

> Nastojáščuju néžnost' ne spútaeš'
> Ni s čém, i oná tixá.
> Ty naprásno beréžno kútaeš'
> Mne pléči i grúd' v mexá...

The same relationship exists also in German Romantic *dol'niki* and, in general, in lyric stanzas, especially those with a song-like quality. The use of three syllable intervals between stresses creates an impression of weakened rhythm, an approximation of colloquial prosaic rhythms. Cf. Blok's *Iz gazet*:

> Prošlí časý. Prixodíl čelovék
> S olovjánnoj bljáxoj na tëploj [*Sic.* Žirmunskij: *temnoj*] šápke.
> *Stučal i dožidalsja u dv*eri *čelov*ek.
> Niktó ne otkrýl. Igráli v prjátki.

And from the same source:

> ...Segódnja ostávila dóma platók
> Deti *prjatali eg*o po uglam...
> ...Skazála: kúšajte. *Vstala na kol*eni
> I, *klanjajas', kak m*ama, krestíla detéj...

The same poem furnishes examples of four-syllable intervals:

> ...*Zaprygali na sten*e, pri svete fonarej...
> ...Sosčital i zapla*kal i postuč*al u dverej...
> ...Deti prisly*šalis', otv*orili dveri...

Characteristic examples are to be seen also in the "sprung lines" (*preryvistyestroki*) of Bal'mont. Cf. *Boloto*:

> ...Na versty i *versty šelestj*a*ščaja* osoka,
> Nezabudki, kuvšinki, kuvš*inki, kamyš*i.

Bolóto raskínulos' vla*stno i širóko*,
Šépčutsja *stébli v izumrúdnoj* tiši...

It is extremely rare to find two metrical stresses side by side in Russian
dol'niki (x = 0). However, in the same poem by Blok, there is the line:

...Zvenjáščaja dvér' xlópnula vnizú...

But in recent times interesting experiments have been made in this direction. Cf. for instance *Ballada o dezertire* by the young poet Pozner,
where the precise meter (the ballad *septenary*) and the syntactic pauses
between adjacent stresses permit the realization of this rare rhythmical
construction:

> ...On bežit — čas, on bežit — dva, ‖ on bežit — tretij čas.
> I solnce pogaslo, i mesjac vzošël, ‖ i mesjac opjat' pogas.
> I vintovkoj kažetsja každyj sučok, ‖ i soldatom každyj kust.
> No les — *tix*, nebosvod — čist, ‖ A gorizont — pust...

In the poem *Naš Marš* Majakovskij systematically uses the device of
placing the stresses near each other as the basis for the "drum rhythm"
of the refrain:

> Béjte v plóščadi buntóv tópot.
> Výše górdyx golóv grjadá!
> My razlívom vtorógo potópa
> Peremóem miróv gorodá
> *Dnej byk peg.*
> Medlenna let arba
> *Naš bog — beg*
> Serdce — naš baraban...

In Germanic poetry, especially in the old German epic, the close proximity
of two stresses as well as polysyllabic interstress intervals were habitual
devices. And in the work of Majakovskij and the poets of his school the
predominant metrical stress frequently unites a lengthy polysyllabic
group — sometimes, an entire syntactic segment held together by the
phrase stress (cf. below, § 31). In the usual *dol'niki*, the order of interstress intervals contained within a certain number of syllables is not
arranged by any rules. One encounters, however, rhythmical forms, in
which the alternation is defined by a definite rule: $x_1 = 1$, $x_2 = 1$, $x_3 = 2$, $x_4 = 2$. Cf. Fet's lines:

> Izmúčen žízn'ju, kovárstvom nadéždy,
> Kogdá im v bítve dušój ustupáju,
> I dněm i nóč'ju smežáju ja véždy
> I kak to stránno porój prozreváju...

On the analogy of the Greek and Latin "mixed" ("polymetric") meters, we call this variety of purely tonic verse "logaoedic". It is found most frequently in imitations of classical lyric meters, but it is occasionally encountered in original tonic verse, though it is not used with complete consistency (cf. Fet's "V tiši i mrake..." and "Izmučen žizn'-ju..."; in neither of these examples is the alternation pattern carried through with complete consistency). If a regular sequence of interstress groups, varying in number of syllables, is maintained throughout an entire poem or a considerable part of it, then the arrangement of the unstressed syllables becomes an intrinsic part of the metrical scheme. (E.g. in the example cited above: $- \acute{-} - \acute{-} - - \acute{-} - - \acute{-} -$). Since in such a meter, there is a regular, recurrent sequence of stressed and unstressed syllables, it is sometimes broken down into syllabo-tonic "feet". Thus the example given above might be viewed as a combination of two iambs and two anapests with a hypercatalectic feminine ending. However, in view of the polymetric structure of logaoedic verse such a grouping would always be arbitrary. For example, one might regard the lines of this same stanza as consisting of one iamb and three amphibrachs with a catalectic ending. Both divisions are equally justified, since they are concerned with an abstract metrical scheme and change nothing in the actual rhythm of the verse. This contradiction, however, reveals how arbitrary is the very principle of dividing a verse into feet when there is no absolute equality among the interstress intervals.

Although pure tonic verse is organized on the principle of stress-counting it in fact admits, as does syllabo-tonic verse, rhythmical *variations* such as the *omission* of a metrical stress or the *hypermetrical stressing* of metrically weak syllables. The practice of omitting stresses causes tonic verse to resemble the binary meters, and it is to be accounted for chiefly by the influence of analogous rhythmical variations in the usual syllabotonic meters.[1] Cf. Tjutčev's lines (for the iambic type):

> O kak na sklone našix let
> Nežnej my ljubim *i* suevernej...
> ...O ty, poslednjaj*a* ljubov',
> *ty* i blaženstvo *i* beznadežnost'...

Or Fet (the dactylic type with weakened initial stress):

> ...*i* nepodvižno, na ognennyx rozax,
> Živoj altar' mirozdan' ja kuritsja...

[1]   Those who adhere to the theory of pauses see a pause in such cases in the place of an accented syllable, e.g.: Peterburgskaja vesna... (the first pause replaces a stressed syllable). Such a construction is entirely fictitious and violates the basic principle of purely tonic verse, the principle of syllable counting.

Cf. also Gumilëv (the anapestic type with a "substituted" tribrach):

> ...Belosnežnye koni rinut
> V oslepitel'nu*ju* vysotu...

The same thing in Axmatova, with a slight weakining of the second stress:

> ...Polulaskovo polulenivo
> Pocelu*em* ruki kosnu*l*sja...

In another of Axmatova's poems — with an approximation of the "iambic" cadence:

> ...I gljadit mne v glaza suxie
> Peterburgska*ja* vesna...

Cf., however, Mandelštam, where there is no specific syllabo-tonic cadence:

> ...I slučajnyj ritm — tol'ko slučaj,
> *Neožidannyj Akvilon*...

And in Gumilëv:

> ...Slovno *moloty gromovye*
> Ili vody gnevnyx morej...

On the other hand, purely tonic verse, following the pattern of the ternary meters, admits supplementary stresses on metrically weak syllables. Cf. Fet's:

> ...Eščë temnee *mrak* žizni vsednevnoj...
> ...I plamja tvoë uznaju *solnce* mira...

And Axmatova's:

> ...I zagadočnyx drevnyx likov
> Na menja pogljadeli oči.
> *Desjat'* let zamiranij i krikov,
> *Vse* moi bessonnye noči...

Gumilëv:

> ...Zolotoe serdce Rossii
> *Merno* b'ëtsja v grudi moej

Puškin in *Skazka o rybake i rybke*:

> ...Starik *lovil* nevodom r*y*bu,
> Staruxa prjala svoju prjažu...

Omitted stresses and hypermetrical stresses are possible in pure tonic verse to the extent that they leave intact the inertia of the predominant metrical stresses. When there are a great many additional stresses not called for by the meter, a line may seem to be in danger of rhythmic disintegration; it displays something like the free alternation of stress characteristic of colloquial speech or rhythmical prose. However — as we see from the example of Puškin's poem above or from his *Pesni zapadnyx slavjan*, and most recently from the work of Majakovskij and his school — our rhythmical feeling is very flexible and habitually subsumes under one metrical law rhythmical variations of extremely diverse types.

The first attempts to deal theoretically with Russian *dol'niki* derived, as one would naturally expect, from the usual syllabo-tonic schemes. Belyj's theory of rhythmic "deviations" prompted investigators to regard the peculiarities of purely tonic verse as deviations from traditional metrics. Belyj himself considered the *dol'niki* of the Symbolists to be verse lines with "pauses".[2] This point of view receives its best defense in the works of the Moscow poet Sergej Bobrov (*Novoe o stixosloženii Puškina*, 1915; *Zapiski stixotvorca*, 1916). He regards *dol'niki* as variations of the anapest with "pauses". When in the interstress intervals (or before the first stress) there appears one syllable instead of the two required by the anapestic pattern, the place of the omitted second syllable is occupied by a "pause". Cf. Blok's:

> Ja stojal mež dvumja fonarjami
> ∧ I slušal ∧ ix golosa.
> Kak šeptalis', zakryvšis' plaščami,—
> Celovala ix noč' ∧ v glaza...

As in Belyj's method, the pauses are plotted as points on a grid and are connected with lines to form figures representing the deviations from the meter. In those instances when three or four unstressed syllables — instead of two — occur between stresses, these deviations are marked as "quartoles" or "quintoles". The rhythmical wealth of the lines containing pauses depends, just as it does for Belyj in the iambic meter, on the abundance and variety of the deviations from the metrical pattern.

The inadequacy of Bobrov's theory is to be seen first of all in the fact that tonic versification, unlike the classical metrical patterns built on the principle of quantity, takes no account of "empty" time (*chrónos kenós*, in classical terminology; time not occupied by sound): in tonic versification, time, as was pointed out above (cf. § 3), is not a *substantive* part of the metrical structure but only the abstract schematic *form* of the sequence

---

[2] *Simvolizm*, p. 557; the examples are from Z. Gippius, V. Brjusov, and A. Blok. A curious remark: "Only five or six years ago Russian criticism regarded the use of pauses as an intolerable novelty, as the simple inability to write verse."

or the *count* of the metrically significant units, the *syllables*. Of course it is always possible to make an artificial pause between stresses at a word boundary when it is called for by Bobrov's scheme; in many cases, however, there is in fact no pause between adjacent words since the semantic division into words is far from always identical with the phonetic division into rhythmic-syntactic groups. It is in any case impossible to prove that this "pause" is more significant in those cases when a syllable is "dropped" between stresses (as, for example, in the line: "I slušal ʌ ix golosa") than it is in other situations (e.g. at the syntactic break: "Kak šeptalis', zakryvšis' plaščami"). In our verse the pause is in reality not a metrical phenomenon at all; it is exclusively a feature of recitation. Bobrov's basic notion is apparently that metrical units, like musical measures, should possess a certain *isochronism* (i.e., identical temporal length), and this is disrupted by variations in the syllable count; and therefore, in those instances when one syllable instead of two stands between stresses, the incomplete temporal unit is filled out with a pause. From the metrical point of view, however, the one essential feature which appears to be fundamental in pure tonic verse, is that a two-syllable group is recognized as being equal to a three-syllable group (more rarely, to a four-syllable group). The question of what device is used to realize this equality in recitation, the question of whether and to what degree this promotes the isochronism of the rhythmical sections — these problems can be resolved only by experimental means, but they do not alter the metrical composition of the phenomena discussed here. Such equalization is apparently achieved in the majority of cases not by a pause at all, but rather by speeding up or drawing out the pronunciation of groups of syllables to compensate for differences in the number of syllables in different groups; a stressed syllable, in particular, lends itself most easily to lengthening.[3] It is evident that Bobrov arrived at his theory of pauses not by studying the actual sound of Russian *dol'niki* but simply by applying the customary syllabo-tonic scheme, which he found it necessary to adapt, with the help of Belyj's rhythmic "deviations", to the new system of Russian metrics.[4]

[3] On the substitution of the stressed syllable for length, cf. p. Verrier, I, p. 79 ff., 164 ff.; B. Tomaševskij, *Russkoe stixosloženie*, p. 38; J. Minor, pp. 14, 29, 59-60, considers that the temporal equalizing of the interstress groups is peculiar to verse having a varying number of unstressed syllables between stresses, in contrast to ordinary iambs and trochees; in this he sees the difference between the quantitative (*quantitierend*) and syllabic (*silbenzählend*) systems.
[4] G. Šengeli uses the term *lejma* instead of "pause" to indicate the "falling out" of one or more syllables (p. 81).

Treating the anapest as the basic metrical scheme of Russian *dol'niki* is also completely arbitrary. The example from Blok ("Vxožu ja v tëmnye xramy...") shows that one-syllable and two-syllable intervals can frequently be completely equivalent; in the anacrusis in this example, for instance, the one-syllable opening occurs five times, the two-syllable opening — three times; between stresses there are six one-syllable intervals and ten two-syllable. Fet's poems ("V tiši i mrake..." and "Izmučen žizn'ju...") reveal an approximately equal number of one and two-syllable intervals. These poems can with equal justification be regarded as anapestic with "pauses" or as examples of a binary meter (e.g. iambic) permitting the "substitution" of three-syllable feet ("triplets"). Open to criticism for the same reason is Tomaševskij's terminology (*Russkoe stixosloženie*, p. 38) which speaks of a "contraction" (rather than "pauses") in the ternary meters. In the examples from Blok and Fet cited above one would be equally justified in speaking of the "contraction" of an anapestic foot (two-syllable interstress group) or of the "expansion" of an iambic foot (one-syllable interval). The theory of "pauses" is totally unacceptable for the poetry of Majakovskij or for Old German alliterative verse, which differ from the song-like *dol'niki* not in principle but only in degree.[5] Here, extended groups of syllables are united around the predominant metrical stress and these groups, regardless of their obvious inequality in number of syllables, are also perceived as equivalent rhythmic units. It is completely impracticable to reduce such verses to "anapests" or, indeed, to any syllabo-tonic scheme.

Nor does Bobrov's theory offer any considerable convenience as a system of notation. Based on the principle of "deviation", it repeats all the major defects inherent in Belyj's parent system: individual deviations (pauses, quartoles, etc.) are isolated from the total picture of the rhythm. It is much more convenient to note down rhythmic variations by using figures to indicate the number of unstressed syllables between stresses. For instance, in Blok's poem ("Vxožu ja..."): 1, 1, 2; 2, 1, 2; 1, 2, 1; 1, 1, 2. The arrangement of the word divisions can, when necessary, be indicated by special marks; e.g. in the second stanza: 1, 2^0, 2^1; 1, 1^0, 2^1 ... and so on.

All this, of course, does not eliminate the fact that one notices in some cases a certain kinship between the dominating rhythm of a poem

5 For a contrary opinion, cf. R. Jakobson, *O češskom stixe*, p. 102, where he undertakes to prove the difference in principle between the verse of A. Blok and Majakovskij. According to Jakobson, the *dol'niki* of Blok are "syllabic in orientation" and deviations from the syllabic principle "remain in a minority" (?).

written in pure tonic verse and the traditional syllabo-tonic schemes. In Tjutčev's poem *Poslednjaja ljubov'* the iambic cadence predominates ("O kak na sklone našix let...") and it is this circumstance which leads to the omission of the metrical stresses, a characteristic feature of Russian binary meters. In the same way many poems of Blok and Axmatova resemble the ternary meters (amphibrachs and anapests). Theoretically, this resemblance is rendered almost predictable by the fact that the Russian ternary meters, like the *dol'niki*, are not inclined to omit stresses and can consequently be counted by stress groups. Historically, the Russian Romantic *dol'niki* originated from the ternary meters, and the earliest examples of *dol'niki* depart from the orthodox syllabo-tonic patterns only in isolated "deviations" ("contractions", "pauses"); cf., for example, Lermontov's poem quoted below: "Pocelujami prežde sčital..." (p. 200) and others. There thus occur transitional forms between the syllabo-tonic and the purely tonic systems.

English iambics furnish an interesting example of such transitional forms. Shakespeare and his contemporaries, Milton, and the majority of the nineteenth century poets were quite ready to admit in their iambic pentameters disyllabic as well as monosyllabic intervals between the stresses. Cf. Shakespeare's: "Succeeding his father Bolingbroke did reign... At any time have recourse unto the princes... I was then present, saw them salute on horseback... Put in their hands their bruising irons of wrath..." Shelley: "To curtain her sleeping world. You gentle hills... Hoping to still these obstinate questionings..." Tennyson: "He laughed and yielded readily to their wish..." and many others. More rarely one encounters in one and the same line two or even three such deviations. Shakespeare: "Of your great predecessor, King Edward the Third... Given to captivity me and my utmost hopes..." and so on. Still rarer is the use of three unstressed syllables between accents. Cf. Shelley: "The broad and burning moon lingeringly rose..." Tennyson: "And there were none but few goodlier than he..." etc.

Historically, the use in English iambics of two unstressed syllables between stresses results from a confluence of many causes. In many cases we have a phonetically weak vowel which is in the process of appearing or disappearing (e.g. shuddering, lingering and so on; cf. Tennyson's, "Faltering and fluttering in her throat, she cried..."). Other examples, not less numerous, are to be explained by the elision of a final vowel before the initial vowel of a following word — or, more exactly, not by elision (i.e., the disappearance of the final vowel), but by a certain flowing together of the two vowels which permits their being considered metrically as one syllable (so-called "synaloephe"); the same feature is well known in Italian poetry. According to the findings of Robert Bridges, Milton made extensive use of such elision under the influence of classical and Italian models.[6] To these phonetic conditions promoting the use of disyllabic intervals one must add the influence of the freer metrical forms. We have examples of hypermetrical caesura (the so-called "epic caesura" of the French decasyllabic line) which, in view of the fact that the syntactic break in English iambic pentameter is very mobile, can occur at any foot where there is a strong syntactic pause. Disyllabic anacrusis is admitted under the same circumstances (cf. above §§ 23-24). One must also mention here the influence exerted by the traditional national tonic verse. The Romantic poets of the mid-nineteenth century undoubtedly imitated the archaic manner of Shakespeare or Milton, finding in these deformations of the "orthodox" iambic meter an esthetic charm to which the earlier writers had accustomed the English ear. Hence it is clear that individual instances of disyllabic intervals are related to the predominant iambic pattern as "deviations". If the number of such deviations is extremely large, then we may be said to have crossed

---

[6]   On "elision" cf. especially R. Bridges, pp. 9-37; for a criticism of Bridges' theory, cf. G. Saintsbury, *A History of English Prosody*, II, 258-272. In English verse the term "elision" covers a variety of phenomena. 1) Historical changes in the number of syllables: a) a vowel which is in the process of disappearing or has already done so, as in the words champion, obedience, conscience, vision, weltering, suffering, popular, credulous, luminous, threatening; b) a new vowel in the process of forming or already formed, as in tire, fire [-ɑiə(r)] or power, flower [-ɑuə(r)]. Where such weak vowels are concerned the poet can use the archaic form or the modern form, or both together. 2) The occurence of two vowels side by side, in which case the first vowel does not constitute a metrical syllable — as in, classical, French, and Italian poetry. Cf. Milton's: He effected... in glory above his peers... to our native heaven... for God is also in sleep... and rapture so oft beheld... be it so, for I submit... The almighty... The Aonian Mount... and so on. Syllabic r, l, m, n at the end of a word are on the same level as vowels; in colloquial speech this phenomenon probably arose out of the merged pronunciation of adjacent words: in prevocalic position the sonants, in accordance with a general phonetic rule, lose their syllabic function. Cf. the temple [tɛmpl] — the temple-of God [təmpləv-]. Modern literary pronunciation, however, retains an independent post-stress syllable in all positions. In verse, nevertheless, elision is allowed. Examples from Milton: ... a pillar of fire... savour of death... purple and gold... abominable, inutterable, and worse... Iron or solid rock... garden of God... etc. But in English verse, as opposed to French and Italian, the elision is not obligatory but merely *optional* (cf. R. Bridges, p. 34). Cf. Milton: The image of a brute... (the first two syllables maintain their independence), but: The image of God in man... (elision). In pronunciation, on the other hand, as in Italian, the elided vowel is not completely lost but merely coalesces with its neighbor (*Verschleifung, synaloephe*), while the degree of such coalescence shows considerable individual differences. It is clear from this that the spread of such a metrical tradition threatens to topple the very principle of syllable counting.

the border-line and to be dealing with a system based on a count of stresses, i.e., a purely tonic system.

And so it is possible to have transitional cases which play a significant role in the historical process. Their existence, however, does not lead us inevitably to the conclusion that both systems must be reduced, as Bobrov and certain other investigators would suggest, to a single metrical principle: one must seek the peculiar qualities of each system not in transitional cases but in the most typical manifestations of each system.

29. GERMAN TONIC VERSE

In the poetry of the Germanic nations purely tonic verse is a legacy of the national art: versification based on the principle of counting the dynamic peaks is most natural in languages having a strong dynamic accent. The counting of the syllables between stresses — and along with that the principle of dividing verse into feet — appears in Germanic poetry under a foreign influence: during the Middle Ages, under the influence of religious hymns sung in Latin and the syllabic versification of Provençal and French poets, and during the Renaissance, under the influence of metrical theories applying to Germanic tonic verse the classical principle of the foot, a principle which went back in origin to quantitative metrics but then received a fresh interpretation in the poetic practice of the modern European nations.

In the history of German poetry, two developments are of greatest interest for the general theory of tonic versification: 1. the transition from the native purely tonic principle to the new syllabo-tonic system in the chivalric lyric of the Minnesingers and the courtly epic (end of the twelfth century) — under the influence of foreign Romance models; and 2. the rebirth of the native principle of stress-counting and the emancipation from the "foot" during the *Sturm und Drang* and Romantic periods.

The earliest examples of Germanic poetry are in the so-called "alliterative verse"; e.g. the Anglo-Saxon *Beowulf* (ca. 700), the Old Saxon poem *Hêliand* (end of the eighth century), the Old High German *Song of Hildebrand* (end of the eighth century), the Old Icelandic *Edda* (nineth to twelfth centuries) and others. Old Germanic alliterative verse is purely tonic, with four predominant stresses in each line — two in each hemistich. Of the four stressed syllables, three, or at least two, are linked by the alliteration of the initial consonant of the stressed syllable (usually — by virtue of the phonetic principles governing stress in Germanic languages

— the initial consonant of the word). Alliteration was obligatory on the first stressed syllable of the second hemistich, and the other alliterations (one or two) occurred in the first hemistich. Vowels, even of different quality, could also be used in alliteration if they introduced a stressed syllable. Besides the dominant metrical stresses in the line there could be other, secondary stresses, which are to be regarded as supplementary; the number of syllables between stresses, before the first stress at the beginning of a line and after the final stress at the end of a line, was a variable quantity. Nevertheless, we can establish certain basic types of rhythmical variations in the distribution of the secondary stresses and the unstressed syllables; they are formulated by Sievers in his five types of alliterative verse ("Fünftypensystem").[7] It would be incorrect to regard these types as metrical schemes which the poets consciously used as the basis of their verse; these are rather empirical rules, abstracted from the actual rhythmical configurations of the verse — conventional classifications which facilitate the modern observer's statistical analysis of the preferred rhythmical varieties in four-stress poetry. It must be added that the predominant (metrical) stresses stand out clearly in each line, since they always fall on words which, according to the rules of the language, have the greatest phonetic strength: there is no conflict between metrical accent and normal word stress, a phenomenon which is in general characteristic of purely tonic verse.

As examples we can cite the following excerpts. From the *Song of Hildebrand*:

> Hiltibrant enti *h*adubrant | untar *h*eriun twem
> Sunufatarungo | iro saro rihtun
> Gartun se iro *g*udhamun | *g*urtun sih iro swert ana
> Helidos ubar *h*ringa | do si to dero *h*iltiu ritun...

Beowulf:

> ...Ge*w*at tha ofer *w*aegholm | *w*inde gefysed
> Flota *f*amiheals | *f*ugle gelicost
> Oth thaet ymb antid | othres dogores
> Wundenstefna | ge*w*aden haefde
> Thaet tha *l*ithende | *l*and gesawon
> Brimclifu *b*lican | *b*eorgas steape... etc.

Pure tonic versification continued to predominate in early Germanic

---

[7] Ed. Sievers, *Altgermanische Verslehre*, p. 189. A. Heusler (*Über germanischen Versbau*, p. 75) significantly remarks that the "five types" constitute only the possible rhythmical variations of the fundamental metrical pattern (*als Regelungen der Vers füllung*), not independent meters.

poetry even at the time when the influence of Latin models had caused alliteration to be replaced by end rhyme. Thus, the poetic Gospel of the monk Otfrid (ninth century), the first instance of rhymed verse in the German area, in spite of its connection with the Latin hymnal tradition, preserves the native principle of stress counting (four-stress line). At the time when Middle High German peotry was flourishing (from the end of the twelfth century) this native principle begins to interact with the principle of syllabism, imported from the Romance West. Here there is to be seen a fundamental difference of poetic tendencies and styles. Thus the more archaic tendency of the chivalric lyric, which was maintained along the Danube, preserves the purely tonic principle, remaining at the same time free from the thematic and stylistic influences of the Romance (Provençal) lyric; the same is true of those examples of the heroic epic dealing with ancient national themes (*Nibelungenlied*, *Gudrun*, etc.). Cf. from the songs of Kürenberg:

> Swenne ich stan aleine || in minem hemede,
> Und ich an dich gedenke, || ritter edele,
> So erbluojet sich min varwe || als der rose an dorne tuot,
> Und gewinnet mir daz herze || vil manigen trurigen muot...

From the *Nibelungenlied*:

> Do wuohs in Niderlanden || eins richen küneges kint,
> Des vater hiez Sigemunt, || sin muoter Sigelint,
> In einer burge riche || witen wol bekant,
> Niden bi dem Rine: || diu was ze Santen genant...

As we see from these examples, the number of stresses in the line was constant: in the *Nibelungenlied* stanza a seven-stress line is divided into two hemistichs (4+3) and the last line of each stanza has eight stresses (4+4). The number of unstressed syllables between the stresses varies from 0 to 2. It is not unusual to find two immediately adjacent stresses ($x = 0$). In the prestress portion of the line variations are also permitted ($x_1 = 0, 1, 2$). The last syllable of each hemistich and each line always carries a stress (as was already true in the verse of Otfrid); if either hemistich ends on a disyllabic or trisyllabic word, with the stress, as is customary in German words, on the first syllable (hémedè, édelè, aléinè, gedénkè), the last syllable receives an additional metrical stress (the so-called "klingende Endung" — two-stress ending).[8]

On the other hand, under the influence of Romance poetry — the lyrics of the Provençal troubadours, the French courtly epic — German

---

[8] On the two-stress ending, cf. *Rifma*, pp. 240, 266.

verse is at the same time undergoing change in the direction of the syllabic principle. In the work of the Minnesingers, who imitate the fashion of the Provençal poets (Heinrich von Veldecke, Friedrich von Husen, Heinrich von Morungen, et al.), and in the representatives of the courtly epic, which arose under the influence coming from the north of France (as early as Heinrich von Veldecke in his *Eneit*, and especially in the work of Hartmann von Aue, Gotfried von Strassburg, et al.) the new themes of the French Arthurian romances and the new styles were accompanied by the new metrical forms. The transition from purely tonic to syllabo-tonic verse can be reduced to the following changes: 1) The number of syllables between stresses becomes a stable, invariant feature: this makes possible the differentiation between binary and ternary meters (in the former, $x = 1$, the "iambic" type; in the latter, $x = 2$, the "dactylic" type); 2) the number of syllables before the first stress (anacrusis) becomes a stable quantity: e.g., in the binary meters lines beginning with an unstressed syllable (one-syllable anacrusis) are either not mixed with lines starting with a stress (without anacrusis) or they alternate with each other according to a definite stanzaic pattern (for the binary meters, the first case is the "iambic" type, where $x = 1$, and the second is the "tro-chaic" type where $x = 0$); 3) together with lines ending on a stress (masculine ending), there appear lines having a final unstressed syllable (feminine ending), and these also alternate in accordance with a definite stanzaic pattern. The second of these transformations occurred later than the others: variations by means of anacrusis continue to be practised for rather a long time by poets who permit themselves no deviation from the syllabic principle within the body of the line. Cf. Friedrich von Husen's binary meter ("iambic") with a variation of the anacrusis:

> ◡ Ich wand ir e vil verre sin
> Da ich nu vil nahe ware
> ◡ Alrerste hat daz herze min
> Von der fremde groze sware...

One encounters, of course, deviations even in the feature which is basic for the syllabo-tonic system — the constant number of unstressed syllables between the stresses within the line. In epic poetry we find two-syllable intervals alongside one-syllable intervals. Among the lyric poets, those most free in their metrical practice are the ones who hark back to native models, especially the folksong (e.g. Walther von der Vogelweide). The absence of an academic metrical theory based, as in modern times, on classical metrics, and the connection of the Minnesingers' poetry with music naturally promoted the relative freedom of medieval German versification. Nevertheless, wherever Romance poetry is recognized as the model for poetry of the grand style, the syllabo-tonic principle prevails. And as early as the thirteenth century its supremacy is accompanied by those phenomena which customarily attend the supremacy of this system: conflicts with the natural characteristics of the linguistic medium; contradictions between the ideal pattern of alternating stressed and unstressed syllables, prescribed by the metrical scheme, and the actual rhythmic configuration of individual lines. Modern investigators have noted the frequency in medieval German poetry of stress "shifts", "hypermetrical stressing" of unstressed syllables, "suppression" of the natural phonetic stresses by the dominating metrical accents, and other "deviations" (cf. such terms as, for example, Accentversetzung, metrische Drückung, schwebende Betonung, etc.). These divergences become especially significant in the verse of the fifteenth century Meistersingers and the sixteenth century satirical poets (Hans Sachs, Fischart et al.). In their verse the only constants are the total number of syllables and the obligatory stress at the end of the rhythmical unit: thus, thanks to the constantly growing number of deviations from the syllabo-tonic pattern, their syllabo-tonic verse becomes "syllabic" in exactly the same sense that this term has in French verse. Cf. Hans Sachs:

> Ich, Apolo, steig ab vom Himel,
> Zu schawen das Menschlich gewimel,
> Wie es gleich einem Amais hauffen
> Ahn ru[e] thut durch einander lauffen,
> Durch unzal begir und affect.
> Es in sehr grosem irthumb steckt...

The metrical reform of Opitz at the beginning of the seventeenth century, which was similar in its basic features to the reform of Russian versification by Tred'jakovskij and Lomonosov, established the syllabo-tonic system based on the foot for modern German poetry. Opitz, like the Russian theoreticians who came after him, started from classical quantitative metrics, adapting its terms to the tonic versification of the Germans. "Each verse", writes Opitz in his Poetics (*Buch von der Deutschen Poëterey*, 1624, chap. VII), "can be either iambic or trochaic; not that we are able, as were the Greeks and Romans, to reckon with the specific length of the syllables (Grösse der Silben), but from the accents or the tone we recognize which syllable to count as high (hoch) and which low (niedrig)". And further "Although, so far as I know, no one up to the present time, including myself, has strictly observed these rules, it nevertheless seems to me just as necessary for us as it was necessary for the Romans to construct their verse with regard for the length or *quantity*". As compared with his medieval predecessors, Opitz is a great deal stricter about implementing in practise the alternations called for by the metrical scheme. The displacement of the stress from an even to an odd syllable occurs in his verse only at the opening of a rhythmical sequence. Not less important is the distinction which he made at the very beginning between lines starting on a stressed and those starting on an unstressed syllable: owing to the influence of classical metrics, and in contradistinction to the practice of many medieval German poets, he immediately assigns "iambs" and "trochees" to basically different metrical types. The ternary meters — in German terminology, "dactyls" —, which, as we mentioned earlier, do not generally play an essential part in German poetry, make their appearance in the work of Opitz's successors.[9] It is interesting to note that it is in these "dactyls" that there first appears the characteristic feature of old Germanic poetry, the alternation of monosyllabic and disyllabic interstress groups, as well as anacrusis — at first, to be sure, only in specific places in the lines and stanzas, as in the "logaoedic" verse of the classical system (the so-called "mängtrittige Dactylen"). E.g., Birken:

> Komm, du süsseste Stunde,
> Wünsch ich mit heissem Sehnen;
> Da ich werde aufhören zu sterben,
> Da mir der Tod das Leben gebieret...

A second clash between the principle of dividing verse into feet and the native Germanic principle of stress-counting takes place in the middle and latter part of the eighteenth century: a struggle against the system of Opitz ends with the consolidation, alongside the dominant syllabotonic system based on the foot, of a freer system based on the native tradition. This emancipation of verse proceeds along several different paths: we note the influence of folk poetry, the imitation of the forms of archaic German verse (so-called "Knittelvers"), and the adaptation of classical meters (hexameter, "logaoedic"). Regardless of the different origins of these new tendencies, they are equally directed against the tedious "monotony" of orthodox iambs and they all result in the appearance of freer verse forms, in which the interstress groups contain a varying number of syllables.

From a historical point of view, the most fruitful of these new tendencies was the rebirth of the folksong. During the age when the Romance

[9]   On "dactyls" cf. H. Paul, p. 95 ff, and note 71.

principle of syllable-counting was developing in literature of the elevated style, the folksong, allied with music, maintained the native tradition of counting stresses. Cf. the folk ballads in the Herder collection (*Volkslieder*, 1778-1779), copied down in Alsace (1771) by the youthful Goethe, e.g.:

> ...Was zog er aus der Taschen?
> Ein Messer, war scharf und spitz.
> Er stach's seiner Lieben durch's Herze;
> Das rote Blut gegen ihn spritzt...

The normal stanza of the German folksong consists of two metrical periods; each period is divided into two lines with four and three stresses respectively (the ballad septenary); only the endings of the periods rhyme. The number of unstressed syllables between stresses is normally 1 or 2, more rarely 3; and in some cases two stresses stand immediately next to each other. By an old tradition, the line always ends with a stress; disyllabic words (Táschèn, Hérzè) receive a supplementary metrical stress on the final syllable in accordance with the general melodic construction.

The renaissance of folk poetry during the period of *Sturm und Drang* and Romanticism meant not only the liberation of the German lyric from the stylistic stereotypes and traditional themes of French eighteenth century poetry, but also the renovation of metrical forms. In his articles on the folk song and his translations of English and Danish folk ballads, Herder calls attention to the metrical freedom of the folksong and attempts to reproduce it in German. His *Folksongs* (*Volkslieder*, 1778-1779) often show a purely tonic meter, especially in the translated ballads of the first manuscript edition (1772-1773), which was probably well known to the young Goethe, although in the later printed edition Herder cautiously returned in a great many instances to the concept of the foot canonized by traditional metrical theory.[10] Thus, for example, the original version of the ballad *Der eifersüchtige König* (*Junker Waters*):

> ...Oft hab ich geritten durch Sterlingschloss
> Bei Wetter und Regenguss,
> Doch nimmer ritt ich durch Sterlingschloss
> Mit Ketten an Hand und Fuss.
> Oft hab ich geritten durch Sterlingschloss
> Bei Wind un Wetter allein,
> Doch nimmer ritt ich durch Sterlingschloss
> Um nimmer zu kehren ein...

---

[10]   Cf. Lohre, *Von Percy zum Wunderhorn* (1902) (= *Palaestra*, XXII), p. 13 ff.

Cf. also the ballads translated from Danish; e.g. *Erlkönigs Tochter*:

> Herr Oluf reitet spät und weit,
> Zu bieten auf seine Hochzeitleut;
> Da tanzen die Elfen auf grünen Land,
> Erlkönigstochter reicht ihm die Hand...

The first attempt to use the folk ballad meter in an original work executed in the folk manner is to be seen in Goethe's first version (1773) of the ballad *Der König von Thule*, later included in *Faust*:

> Es war ein König in Thule,
> Einen goldnen Bächer er hätt'
> Empfangen von seiner Buhle
> Wohl auf des Todes Bett...

Goethe subsequently returned often to this meter in those poems written in the spirit of the folksong. An especially great influence on his contemporaries was exercised by his *Schäfers Klagelied*:

> Da droben auf jenem Berge
> Da steh ich tausendmal,
> An meinem Stabe gebogen,
> Und schaue hinab in das Tal...

During the last quarter of the eighteenth century, purely tonic verse was consolidated in German poetry chiefly as a *ballad* meter. It is true that Bürger, in the majority of his ballads (e.g. *Lenore, Der wilde Jäger*) continued to use iambic verse; cf., however, *Des Pfarrers Tochter von Taubenhain* (1781):

> Im Garten des Pfarrers von Taubenhain
> Geht's irre bei Nacht in der Laube.
> Da flistert's und ströhnt's so ängstiglich,
> Da rasselt, da flattert und sträubet es sich,
> Wie gegen den Falken die Taube...

In his ballad *Erlkönig*, Goethe introduces the four-stress line with paired masculine rhymes after the example of the Danish ballad of the knight Olaf, translated by Herder, whence also come the rhythmical theme of galloping and the image of the seductive daughters of the forest king (cf. above). Žukovskij's translation has, in place of the purely tonic line, the usual ballad amphibrach. Cf. Goethe's:

> Wer reitet so spät durch Nacht und Wind?
> Es ist der Vater mit seinem Kind.
> Er hat den Knaben wohl in dem Arm,
> Er fasst ihn sicher, er hält ihn warm...

Even Schiller sometimes introduces into his classical ballads, which are far removed from the folk tradition, the characteristic devices of tonic meters. Cf. *Der Taucher*:

> "Wer wagt es, Rittersmann oder Knapp',
> Zu tauchen in diesen Schlund?
> Einen goldnen Becher werf' ich hinab,
> Verschlungen schon hat ihn der schwarze Mund.
> Wer mir den Becher kann wieder zeigen,
> Er mag ihn behalten, er ist sein eigen!"... etc.

Tonic verse is widely used in the lyric songs of the German Romantics, who, like Goethe, imitated the folksong. *Des Knabens Wunderhorn* (1805-1808), a collection of folksongs published by Arnim and Brentano, opens a new era in the history of the German lyric: Brentano, Eichendorf, Uhland, V. Müller, E. Mörike and others are followers of this folksong tradition. By analogy with the Russian lyric meters of most recent times, we designate this folksong verse by the general term *dol'niki*. Cf. the Romantic *dol'niki* of Eichendorf:

> Es schienen so golden die Sterne,
> Am Fenster ich einsam stand
> Und hörte aus weiter Ferne
> Ein Posthorn im stillen Land.
> Das Herz mir im Leib entbrennte,
> Da hab' ich mir heimlich gedacht, —
> Ach, wer da mitreisen könnte,
> In der prächtigen Sommernacht!...

We Russians are most familiar with the Romantic *dol'niki* through the lyrics of Heine, who continues the tradition of Goethe, the Romantics and German folksong. Cf. *Lorelei* (for A. Blok's translation cf. above § 4):

> Ich weiss nicht, was soll es bedeuten,
> Dass ich so traurig bin.
> Ein Märchen aus alten Zeiten
> Das kommt mir nicht aus dem Sinn...

It should be mentioned that in Romantic verse, liberated from its ties to music, the customary folksong device of the two-stress ending in the odd lines involving a supplementary metrical stress on the last syllable of a disyllabic word is transformed into a simple feminine ending. Thus, instead of the alternation of lines with four and three stresses, characteristic of the ballad "septenary", we find three-stress lines with an alternation of feminine and masculine endings (Sterne — stand — Ferne — Land, etc.).

Alongside the Romantic *dol'niki* of the ballad type, there was another source of the new versification: the old Germanic "broken line" (Knittelvers). This meter goes back historically to the syllabic twelve-syllable verse of Hans Sachs.[11] After Opitz's reform establishing the regular alternation of stressed and unstressed syllables, this archaic verse fell into literary disrepute. Writers of poetry in the elevated style employed it only in parodies of old-fashioned doggerel, and a correct appreciation of the ancient system of versification was thus gradually lost. Such verses were read with the modern predilection for stress, and consequently appeared as not quite correct four-stress lines. That is the form in which this verse was reproduced in the parodies: account was no longer taken of the number of syllables, the number of stresses was normally in the vicinity of four. This same type of verse was used not only for parody but also for satire. The literary revolution of the 1770's lifted Hans Sachs's "broken" verse from the lower rungs of literature and upheld it in opposition to the orthodox iambics of the eighteenth century poets. Goethe was captivated by Hans Sachs; he read him, as did his contemporaries, in accordance with the established tradition and used broken verse in literary parodies and satires written in the spirit of the "carnival farces" (Fastnachtspiele) of Hans Sachs. A satirical character is to be seen also in the unfinished poem *Der ewige Jude*, but along with the vulgar comical elements and the intentionally rude satire there appears the lyrical pathos characteristic of the times. These same heterogeneous elements are combined in the first version of *Faust* (1775). The monologue of Faust with which the action opens approaches the tradition of a market-place puppet show; it is intentionally based on the phraseology of everyday speech and seeks the extreme and naturalistic effects of vulgar clownish humor. Suddenly, however, this rather rudely comic tone is interrupted by intense emotional pathos and lofty lyrical inspiration: in such cases the "broken" line usually yields to the iambic.[12] It is by such means, through the tragicomedy of the new style based on the organic native national tradition, that the "broken line of Hans Sachs" enters into poetry of the elevated style. Its metrical peculiarities are: four stresses, a varying number of unstressed syllables between stresses, irregular anacrusis, paired rhymes, and an arbitrary mixture of masculine

---

[11] For the history of *Knittelvers*, cf. J. Minor, pp. 354-68; Flohr, *Geschichte des Knittelverses vom 17 Jahrhundert bis zur Jugend Goethes* (Berlin, 1893). The name comes from the word *Knittel* (*Knüttel*) — "bludgeon" — and originally was used to mean *versus rhopalicus*. Brjusov's translation, "chivalric verse" [*rycarskij stix*], is therefore incomprehensible (cf. *Osnovy stixovedenija*, p. 122).

[12] Cf. Max Morris, *Goethe-Studien* (1902²), Bd. I: *Die Form des Urfaust*, pp. 1-13.

and feminine endings. An iambic movement is on the whole predominant, but with considerable variations, including possibly as many as three unstressed syllables between stresses in individual lines. Cf. in the first version (*Urfaust*):

> ...Heisse Magister, heisse Doktor gar,
> Und ziehe schon an die zehen Jahr,
> Herauf, herab, und quer, und krumm,
> Meine Schüler an der Nas herum...
> ...Zwar bin ich gescheiter, als alle die Laffen,
> Doktors, Professors, Schreiber und Pfaffen,
> Mich plagen keine Skrupel noch Zweifel,
> Fürchte mich weder vor Höll noch Teufel...

Following Goethe, Schiller employed the "broken" line in *Wallensteins Lager*. Especially rich in rhythmical variations is the sermon of the Capuchin monk, which is also composed in the style of vulgar popular humor:

> ...Und das römische *Reich* — das Gott erbarm!
> Sollte jetzt heissen: römisch *Arm*,
> Der *Rheinstrom* ist worden zu einem *Peinstrom*,
> Die *Klöster* sind ausgenommene *Nester*,
> Die *Bistümer* sind verwandelt in *Wüsttümer*,
> Die *Abteien* und die *Stifter*
> Sind nun *Raubteien* und *Diebesklüfter*...

It is interesting to compare the "broken" verse of *Faust* with the ballad meter of *Erlkönig*. In both cases Goethe employed a four-stress line with paired rhymes. It is true that, in contrast to the amorphous non-stanzaic composition of the "tirade" of Faust, we have in the ballad a regular stanza of eight lines (*Sic.* Žirmunskij means four lines) organized on a rigid pattern, with none of the syntactic enjambments so numerous in Faust, and with masculine rhymes only. However, the fact that a difference of impression is produced by identical meters depends not so much on any such differences in formal structure as it does on the difference in the general content and style of the poetry: the four-stress line acquires a totally different emotional coloration and a different meaning. Instead of the rude, broken speech intentionally based on colloquial language, there appears in *Erlkönig* an emotionally heightened pathetic tone, the solemnity and severity of the classical ballad in the grand style. Similar contrasts can be seen by comparing *Faust* or *Erlkönig* with the Romantic *dol'niki* of the folksong style: here also, one and the same meter in different stylistic environments acquires a different artistic expressiveness (a different *ethos*, in the terminology of classical and German

theoreticians) which depends only to a slight degree on the purely metrical differences of the verse itself. In the case of Russian *dol'niki*, Blok
and Axmatova furnish us with examples of the same contrast. (cf. below,
§ 31).[13]

Finally, among the most important sources of purely tonic verse in
modern German poetry we must consider the impact and peculiar application of certain classical meters (the hexameter and the logaoedic
line). The metrical revolution of Klopstock, who first made wide use of
the classical models, as well as the metrical reforms of Herder and Goethe,
were inspired by the attempt to disrupt the monotonous patterns of
syllabo-tonic verse based on the concept of the foot. Of all the tendencies
mentioned here, the adoption of the classical meters was the earliest
manifestation of the new tastes: it was the first serious blow to the syllabic
principle which had become consolidated after the reforms of Opitz, and
in this sense it prepared the way for the rebirth of the freer metrical forms
of the folksong. On the classical meters, cf. below, § 33.[14]

30. ENGLISH TONIC VERSE

The history of English versification shows the same basic stages in the
struggle of the syllabo-tonic principle, drawn from foreign models, with
the more unrestrained native tonic verse; there is, however, an essential
difference in that the national traditions of English poetry were stronger
than those of German, so that the syllabic principle achieved complete
predominance only in rare instances. Thus, at the beginning of the Middle English period, alongside the metrical Gospel of the monk Orm
(*Orrmulumm*, ca. 1200), which, under the influence of the Middle [*sic*! Ed.]
Latin poets, observed the monotonous alternation of long and short
syllables, there is also the epic of *King Horn* (mid-thirteenth century),
written in purely tonic verse with paired rhymes which is linked to the
native tradition. Along with Chaucer and his school (second half of the
fourteenth century) who were brought up in the spirit of French poetry and
the strict observance of syllable-counting, the fourteenth and fifteenth centuries in the north of England and in Scotland saw the unexpected rebirth
of the ancient principle of alliteration and purely tonic verse — sometimes

---

[13]   Cf. J. Minor, p. 332: "If the content demands pathetic declamation, then we have
verse which is hardly to be distinguished from music; if the content offers an obstacle
to measured delivery (*taktierender Vortrag*), then the verse frequently approximates
prose." Cf. also V. Žirmunskij "Melodika stixa", *Mysl'*, No. 3, pp. 123-24.
[14]   On the role played by Klopstock, cf. H. Paul, p. 98 ff.; Fr. Saran, p. 324 ff.

accompanied by end rhyme and complex stanzaic constructions (*Sir Gawain and the Green Knight*, Langland's religious poem *Piers Plowman*, and others). During the Renaissance the syllabo-tonic principle, aided by the example of classical verse theories and earlier promoted by Chaucer, was finally established, at least for poetry of the elevated style: it was used by Spenser, Shakespeare and Milton.[15] But the struggle of the unruly linguistic material against the monotonous metrical scheme is more noticeable in these poets than in the German continuators of Opitz: English iambics admit not only displacement of the stresses (cf. § 15 above), but frequently also disyllabic interstress groups alongside the customary monosyllabic intervals, and in certain cases lines beginning with a stress ($x^1 = 0$) (cf. §§ 23, 28 above). A strict and uniform regularity in the alternation of stressed and unstressed syllables, with no displacement of stresses within the line, without any disyllabic interstress groups, may be observed for a short time during the heyday of English Classicism (first half of the eighteenth century) in the heroic couplets of Pope and his school. Immediately after Pope, however, from the middle of the eighteenth century, there began a literary reaction deriving from the style and rhythm of Milton (Thomson, Gray). And the following period of Romanticism led in England, too, to the rebirth of the national form of purely tonic verse.

As in Germany, the source of the new metrical forms was folk poetry. The folk ballads collected by Percy (*Relics of ancient english poëtry*, 1760) use, for the most part, the same seven-stress ballad line (septenary) which was preserved in the German folksong (4+3 stresses). Cf. the beginning of the famous ballad, *The Hunting of the Cheviot*, from a 16th century manuscript:

> The Percy out of Northumberlond
> And a vow to God made he,
> That he should hunt on the mountains
> Of Cheviot within days three,
> In the maugre of doughty Douglas
> And all that with him be...

Or cf. the ballad *Child Waters*:

> Child Waters in his stable stood
> And stroaketh his milk-white steed.
> To him came a fair young lady,
> As ere did weare woman's weed...

---

[15] On English theoreticians of the Renaissance, cf. J. Schipper, vol. I, §§ 3-7; Saintsbury, *History of English Prosody*, vol. I, p. 167 ff.

The first imitations of the English ballads used the customary iambs and amphibrachs (or anapests), only gradually introducing the anacrusis symptomatic of a less restrained metrical pattern (cf. § 23 above). Southey, however, in his ballad *The Old Woman from Berkeley* (1798), translated by Žukovskij in conventional ternary meter, used the purely tonic line of folk poetry:

> And in He came with eyes of flame,
> The Devil to fetch the dead,
> And all the church with his presence glow'd,
> Like a fiery furnace red.
> He laid his hand on the iron chains,
> And like flax they moulder'd asunder,
> And the coffin-lid, which was barr'd so firm,
> He burst with his voice of thunder... etc.

Somewhat later, Sir Walter Scott joined this tendency in his ballads on historical national themes. Cf. his *Eve of St. John* (in Žukovskij's translation — *Zamok Smal'gol'm* — written in ordinary ballad amphibrachs):

> The Baron of Smaylhome rose with day,
> He spurr'd his courser on,
> Without stop or stay, down the rocky way,
> That leads to Brotherstone...
> ...The Baron return'd in three days space,
> And his looks were sad and sour;
> And weary was his courser's pace,
> As he reach'd his rocky tower...

In the same year, 1798, when Southey wrote his poem of the *Old Woman*, the English Romantic Coleridge introduced a looser metrical principle into the literary genre founded by him, the romantic poem (*Christabel*, 1798-1800). Later, in 1816, when he brought out the first edition of his *Christabel*, he consciously contrasted his new tonic system with the traditional syllabo-tonic pattern of versification. "The metre of Christabel", he wrote in his preface, "is not, properly speaking, irregular, though it may seem so from its being founded on a new principle: namely, that of counting in each line the accents, not the syllables. Though the latter may vary from seven to twelve, yet in each line the accents will be found to be only four. Nevertheless, this occasional variation in number of syllables is not introduced wantonly, or for the mere ends of convenience, but always corresponds to some transition in the nature of the imagery or passion." The four-stress line of Christabel — which has from zero to two unstressed syllables in the anacrusis, one to two syllables between stresses as was habitual in English *dol'niki,* and the masculine endings which dominate English poetry — really could have from seven to twelve syllables. For example:

> ...The night is chill, the forest bare;
> Is it the wind that moaneth bleak?
> There is not wind enough in the air
> To move away the ringlet curl
> From the lovely lady's cheek, —
> There is not wind enough to twirl
> The one red leaf, the last of its clan,
> That dances as often as dance it can,
> Hanging so light, and hanging so high,
> On the topmost twig that looks up at the sky...

In Sir Walter Scott's romantic poems, written under the influence of Coleridge, whose poem he read in manuscript, the purely tonic four-stress line (often, as in the ballads, combined with a three-stress line) predominates, but reverts for long stretches to the ordinary iambic tetra-meter. Byron's "eastern poems" are also, with few exceptions, written in iambic meter, although in *The Siege of Corinth* he returned to the less restrained manner of Coleridge:

> ...His head was drooping on his breast,
> Fevered, throbbing and oppressed...
> There he sate all heavily,
> As he heard the night-wind sigh.
> Was it the wind through some hollow stone,
> Sent that soft and tender moan?
> He lifted his head, and he looked on the sea,
> But it was unrippled, as glass may be...

During the whole of the nineteenth century the ballad and the romantic poem maintain the native tonic verse line alongside the syllabo-tonic. The interaction of these two metrical systems probably accounts for the existence of the iambic and ternary meters in the work of the majority of the nineteenth century poets, who rejected decisively the strict tech-nique of Pope and his contemporaries and turned to the looser metrical practices of Milton and the Elizabethans.

31. RUSSIAN *DOL'NIKI.* THE SYMBOLISTS. MAJAKOVSKIJ

Pure tonic verse penetrated in various ways into Russian poetry: the romantic *dol'niki* of western European writers, imitation of classical meters, and the influence of folk poetry in varying degrees furthered the emancipation from the traditional system based on the foot. The struggle against the iambics of Lomonosov had already begun with the school of Karamzin and continued through the first decades of the nineteenth century. The hexameter and native Russian verse were opposed to the iambic hexameter as the heroic meter. Certain references to iambics are very characteristic of an age which had wearied of the monotonous syllabo-tonic versification. Thus, the Metropolitan Evgenij Bolxovitinov wrote in 1808 to Count D. N. Xvostov: "...That which we now call tonic poetry, i.e., iambs and trochees, is for our language certainly not tonic poetry, but, as L'vov says in *Dobrynja*, those are 'tight foreign frames.' Our language with its polysyllabic words can't be contained in iambs and trochees and therefore in scansion we sometimes have on one word two accents and sometimes three. Lomonosov sensed this disgraceful situation, for which he himself stands guilty before our poetry, for *he* thought up the idea of squeezing our language into the German pattern, not having taken into account the fact that German has few polysyllabic words. For that reason he himself, in his best odes, avoided four-syllable and even three-syllable words which did not have an accent on the middle syllable." (*Bibliografičeskie zapiski*, 1859, No. 8, pp. 248-9).[16] Vostokov (*Opyt o russkom stixosloženii*, 1812-17) accuses Lomonosov of having "hampered the free movement of his epic with the most monotonous of all lines, the rhymed Alexandrine" (27) following the example of "Frenchmen and Germans" (24). He regrets the fact that "Lomonosov

[16] Cf. also the letter of Metropolitan Evgenij Bolxovitinov to Deržavin (*Moskvitjanin*, 1842, 1, pp. 171-75; cf. note 53). He finds that to write iambs and trochees in Russian is "much more difficult than to write dactyls and anapests, which are more fitted to our language, as was understood by our simple early poets" (p. 174). It is interesting to note the similar judgments of later theoreticians concerning native Russian tonic verse and the historical role of the reform of Tred'jakovskij and Lomonosov. Cf. A. Potebnja, *Ob"jasnenija malorusskix i srodnyx narodnyx pesen*, II, (1887), p. 17 ff.: "Tred'-jakovskij's theory is maintained up to the present time even though from the very beginning it has conscientiously revealed itself to be a bad, self-contradictory theory, since it cannot stand without two kinds of "license", i.e., arbitrary inventions: one is that an unstressed syllable may be taken for a stressed one, for instance, a pyrrhic for a trochee and an iamb; and the other is the exact contrary, viz., a stressed syllable can be taken for an unstressed one, which is supposed to permit two stressed syllables to stand side by side. ... The "reform" only hampered Russian literary versification by its demands that each line have an obligatory number of syllables and by its directions concerning the placement of etymological stresses. But this hindrance, which still operates today, is only temporary; it ıs powerless to change the nature of the language, which makes possible a temporal equalization, not only in singing but in *pronunciation* also, of heterosyllabic syntactic feet. Toward the end of his career Puškin made use of this characteristic of the language in, e.g., those works which are linked together both by content and style: *Janyš Korolevič, Rusalka, Skazka o rybake i rybke* (1832-1833)."

did not choose for his *Petriada*, instead of the monotonous Alexandrine, some freer meter such as anapesto-iambic or dactylo-trochaic" (24). "We are bored," confesses V. V. Kapnist, the champion of Russian versification, to S. S. Uvarov, "by rhymes and by the mixing of iambs with pyrrhics, (!), spondees and amphibrachs (?), and of trochees with pyrrhics, anapests and amphimacers (?), by means of which our Alexandrines and other verses are now for the most part composed..." (*Čtenie v Besede*, XVII, 1815, p. 30). And several years later A. Odoevskij returns to the same subject: "The French have yet another peculiarity: their versification is syllabic, and the accents fall with no particular regularity. But in our poetry six ponderous iambs, very occasionally replaced by pyrrhics, drag along one after the other and beat in our ears like hammers. Surely our Russian language, sonorous and manly, will not be eternally imprisoned in this tight, monotonous jacket for the expression of the stormiest bursts of passion. The tightness, which may permit isolated happy utterances, constrains the fullness of feeling and the unbroken chain of thought..." (1825, *O tragedii Venceslav, peredelannoj Žandrom, Sočinenija*, pp. 553-4). Thus the old "Lomonosov metrics" was seen as the source of wearisome monotony and also as creating an irreconcilable conflict between the spirit of the language, the natural phonetic features of the linguistic medium, and a pedantic "German" system — a conflict giving rise to the well-known "deviations" and "replacements".

At the beginning of the nineteenth century the most weakly represented of the new metrical tendencies mentioned above were the Romantic *dol'niki*, which were to be so significant during the age of Symbolism. They appear first of all in translations from German and English, from the work of the western Romantics, who wrote in the tradition of folk poetry. It is characteristic, however, that in the majority of Žukovskij's translations (*Erlkönig*, Southey's *The Old Woman from Berkeley*, Scott's *Eve of St. John* and so on) the purely tonic meter is replaced by the Russian "ballad" amphibrachs or anapests with masculine endings. *Dol'niki* first occur in Žukovskij's translation of *Schäfers Klagelied* (1818):

> Na tú znakómuju góru
> Stó ráz ja v dén' prixožú;
> Stojú, sklonjásja na pósox,
> I v dól s veršíny gljažú.
> Vzdoxnúv, medlítel'nym šágom
> Idú vo sléd ja ovcám,
> I částo, částo v dolínu
> Sxožú, ne čúvstvuja sám...

Lermontov used *dol'niki* in an early translation of a ballad by Byron (from *Don Juan*). With the exception of the anacrusis, his lines show only isolated departures from the ternary meter:

> Beregís'! Beregís'! Nad burgósskim putëm
> Sidít odín čërnyj monáx;
> On bormóčet molítvu vo mráke nočnóm,
> Paníxidu o próšlyx godáx.
> Kogda *Mávr prišël* v naš *rodímyj dóm*,
> Oskvernjájuči cérkvi poróg,
> On bez *dál'nix slóv* výgnal vséx černecóv, —
> Odnogó tol'ko výgnat' ne móg.

We observe *dol'niki* also in a free translation from Heine, with, however, rhythmical deviations from the ballad stanza of the German original. Monosyllabic and disyllabic intervals alternate here according to a definite metrical pattern (two iambs, three anapests, feminine ending) — as in "logaoedic" verse:

> Oní ljubíli drug drúga tak dólgo i néžno,
> S toskój glubókoj i strást'ju bezúmno-mjatéžnoj,
> No, kak vragí, izbegáli priznán'ja i vstréči,
> I býli pústy i xládny ix krátkie réči.
> Oni rasstális' v bezmólvnom i górdom stradán'i,
> I mílyj óbraz vo sné liš' poróju vidáli;
> I smért' prišlá: nastupílo za gróbom svidán'e, —
> No v míre nóvom drug drúga oní ne uználi.

In his translation from Uhland (*O legt mich nicht ins dunkle Grab...*), Tjutčev used a combination of three-stress and two-stress tonic lines. In the first line, of the dactylic type, the initial stress is noticeably weakened. In the fifth line between the second and third stresses there are three unstressed syllables, and it could, in a different context, have been read as an iambic tetrameter. Cf.:

> Ó, ne kladíte menjá
> V zémlju syrúju.
> Skrójte, zarójte menjá
> V travú gustúju.
> Puskáj dyxán'e veterká
> Ševelít travóju, —
> Svirél' poët izdaleká,
> Svétlo i tíxo oblaká
> Plyvút nado mnóju...

In translating Heine, Russian poets were confronted with the problem of *dol'niki* in a specially acute form. Fet and Apollon Grigor'ev repeatedly used *dol'niki* in such translations.[17] For example, Fet's:

> Ty vsjá v žemčugáx i v almázax,
>   Vsjá žízn' dlja tebjá — blagodát',
> I óči tvoí tak preléstny, —
>   Čegó ž tebe, drúg moj, želát'?
> K tvoím očám preléstnym
>   Ja sózdal céluju rát'
> Bessmért'em dýšaščix pésen, —
>   Čegó ž tebe, drúg moj, želát'?
> Očám tvoím preléstnym
>   Danó menjá terzát',
> I tý menja ími sgubíla, —
>   Čegó ž tebe, drúg moj, želát'?

Fet also used *dol'niki* in translating the romantic "melodies" of Thomas Moore (e.g., *Proščaj, Tereza! Pečal'nye tuči...*) and introduced isolated "contractions" into his translations of Goethe's *Erlkönig*. This tradition of importing *dol'niki* in translations was continued by A. Blok in his versions of Heine. Cf. *Opjat' na rodine*:

> Véčer prišël bezmólvnyj
> Nad mórem tumány svilís';
> Taínstvenno rópščut vólny,
> Kto-to bélyj tjánetsja v výs'...

Simultaneously with the translations, and perhaps under their influence, the romantic *dol'niki* also began to penetrate into original Russian lyric poems. One can find, during the age of Puškin, isolated examples in the work of A. Bestužev-Marlinskij, Xomjakov and Podolinskij. B. M. Èjxenbaum (*Lermontov*, p. 39) gives several examples from Lermontov: alongside the disyllabic intervals there sometimes appear trisyllabic groups (at the caesura). E.g., *Melodija*:

> Est' čúdnaja árfa, s *kolybéli* oná
> Do sámoj mogíly igráet,
> Sokrýta glubóko, *ne vidná*, ne slyšná,
> Nigdé, nikogdá ne smolkáet...

Several examples are to be found in Lermontov's poems of the year 1831, probably owing to the influence of the English poets. Deviations from the ternary meter are usually very insignificant and are limited to occasional

---

[17] *Dol'niki* in Fet's translations from Heine: *Vo sne ja miluju videl, Oni ljubili drug druga, Ja plakal vo sne...* and *Dva grenadera.* From Goethe: *Lesnoj car'.* From Moore: *Proščaj, Tereza...* In Grigor'ev's translations from Heine: *Oni menja isterzali, Pregre zilsja snova mne son byloj, Žil byl staryj korol,* and from Goethe: *Lesnoj car'.*

instances of one-syllable interstress intervals ("contractions") and isolated examples of anacrusis:

> Pocelújami prézde sčitál
> Ja sčastlívuju *žizn' svojú*,
>   No tepér' ja ot sčást'ja ustál,
> No tepér' nikogó ne ljubljú.
>   I slezámi kogdá-to sčitál
> Ja mjatéžnuju *žizn' mojú*,
>   No togdá ja ljubíl i želál,
> A tepér' nikogó ne ljubljú.
>   I ja sčët svoix lét poterjál,
> I *krýl'ja* zabvén'ja lovljú:
>   Kak ja sérdce unést' by im dál!
> Kak by véčnost' im brósil mojú!

In the early editions of the poems which Tjutčev wrote during the first half of his life one encounters interesting deviations from the syllabo-tonic system (e.g. in *Sovremennik* of 1836). In his collected *Poems* of 1854 all such deviations were corrected to conform to school metrics — not, perhaps, without the intervention of Turgenev. In the original version of the poem *Son na more* the anacrusis was present:

> I móre i búrja kačáli naš čëln,
> Ja, sónnyj, byl prédan vsej príxoti vóln...
> *Vkrug menjá*, kak kimvály, zvučáli skalý,
> *Oklikálisja* vétry i péli orlý...

But cf. the 1854 version: "Krugóm, kak kimvály... I vétry svistéli..." And in an iambic poem one finds ternary lines which convert the iambic tetrameter into a purely tonic three-stress meter (unless, of course, one chooses to regard this poem as written in octosyllabic lines of the French syllabic type):

> Molčí, skryvájsja i taí
> I čúvstva i mečtý svoí
> Puskáj v duševnoj glubiné
> *Vstajút i zaxódjat oné*
> *Kak jásnye zvëzdy v nočí*:
> Ljubújsja imi i molčí...

The poem *Poslednjaja ljubov'* (1854) should perhaps be regarded as a vestige of the manner adapted from the German models. It is written in a four-stress meter, close to the iambic tetrameter type, with the metrical accent in certain lines (especially in those approaching the iambic pattern) falling on phonetically weak syllables. We thus have omissions of stress similar to those which are customary in Russian binaries:[18]

[18]   B. Tomaševskij attempts to interpret this poem as iambic pentameter with varia-

O, kák na sklóne nášix lét
Nežnéj my ljúbim *i* suevérnej...
Sijáj, sijáj, proščál'nyj svét
Ljubví poslédnej, zarí večérnej!
Polnéba *o*xvatíla tén'
Liš' tám na západe bródit siján'e
Pomédli, pomédli, večérnij dén'
Prodlís', prodlís', *o*čarován'e... etc.

Dol'niki are also to be seen in the work of Fet; e.g.

Svečá nagoréla. Portréty v tení
Sidíš' priléžno i skrómno ty.
Starúške zevnúlos'. Po óknam ogní
Prošlí v te dál'nie kómnaty.
Nikák komará ne progóniš' ty próč', —
Poët i k svétu vsë prósitsja...
Vzgljanút' ty ne sméeš' na lúnnuju nóč',
Kudá dušá perenósitsja... etc.

In the poems "Izmučen žizn'ju, kovarstvom nadeždy..." and "V tiši
i mrake tainstvennoj noči..." the four-stress line assumes the "logaoedic"
form (two iambs, two anapests, feminine ending) for considerable
stretches at a time. For the rest, however, it is free of such regularity.
In isolated lines one finds weakened stresses and also heavy supplementary stresses on metrically weak syllables, as in the ternary meters:

---

tions of the endings at the places of the caesura-like syntactic breaks (*Russkoe stixosloženie*, pp. 60-61). It is interesting to point out in the work of other poets of the
Romantic school the existence of rejected editions which contain lines deviating from
the syllabo-tonic scheme. My student, N. P. Kolpakova, has kindly brought to my
attention the following example from Fet. In the edition of 1850 of *Èolova arfa* line
18 read "Slyšu ja bezzvučnuju drož'..." but in later editions became "Slyšu ja ι bezzvučnuju drož'..." In the 1850 edition of *Tixaja zvëzdnaja noč'* lines 5-6 read: "*Deva,
radost' ljubvi!* Zvëzdy, čto oči tvoi...", which was replaced in subsequent versions by
"Drug moj, v sijan'i nočnom, kak mne pečal' prevozmoč'...?" S. I. Bernštejn has
called my attention to a manuscript variant of A. Tolstoj's *Kolokol'čiki* (A. Kondrat'ev,
Graf A. K. Tolstoj. Materialy dlja istorii žizni i tvorčestva (1912), pp. 91-92); stanzas
IX-X:

Ja prislúšajus' k vám,
Cvétiki stepnýe,
Rússkim ljúdjam peredám
Ja delá bylýe!
Gój ty, véter, ne šumí
V zelënoj rakíte,
Kolokól'čiki moí,
Zveníte, zveníte!

The refrain with displaced stress (Zvenite, zvenite!) is repeated two more times. Thus
Tjutčev, Fet, A. Tolstoj all searched unconsciously for new metrical forms, and at the
same time they all consciously gave way to the dominant tradition.

Izmúčen žízn'ju, kovárstvom nadéždy
Kogdá im v bítve dušój ustupaju,
I dněm i nóč'ju smežáju ja véždy
I kák-to stránno porój prozreváju
...i nepodvížno na ógnennyx rózax
Živój altár' mirozdán'ja kurítsja;
V egó dymú, kak v tvórčeskix grězax,
Vsja síla drožít, i vsja véčnost' snítsja... etc.

In the work of the Russian Symbolists, from the beginning of the 1890's, various types of romantic *dol'niki* become more and more widespread. *Pesnja* by Z. Gippius, written in 1891, makes use of the four-stress tonic line in combination with shorter lines in the same stanza:

...Uvý, v pečáli bezúmnoj ja umiráju,
   Ja umiráju,
Stremljús' k tomú, čegó ja ne znáju,
   Ne znáju.
I èto želán'e ne znáju otkúda,
   Prišló otkúda.
No sérdce xóčet i prósit čúda,
   Čúda! ...

It is interesting that *Pesnja* begins with lines which can be completely accommodated within the iambic metrical pattern, both pentameter and hexameter (combined in the stanza with shorter lines). When, however, we compare them with further stanzas, where the pattern is purely tonic, even these lines must be read as *dol'niki*, each odd line having four stresses (three in the first). The dominant metrical stresses prevail over entire phrase groups (e.g., tol'ko-nebo, takim-pustym, nad-moim-serdcem, etc.). Thus, out of the rhythmical cadences characteristic of syllabo-tonic versification itself there arises the possibility of new metrical forms. Cf.:

Oknó moë vysóko nad zemlëju
   Vysóko nad zemlëju.
Ja vížu tol'ko nébo s večérneju zarëju
   S večérneju zarëju.
I nébo kážetsja pustým i blédnym
   Takim pustým i blédnym.
Ono ne sžálitsja nad sérdcem bédnym,
   Nad moim sérdcem bédnym...

Z. Gippius used the customary four-stress line in her poem *Cvety noči* (1894):

Ó, nočnómu čásu ne vér'te!
On ispólnen zlój krasotý.

V ètot čás ljúdi blízki k smérti,
Tól'ko stránno žívy cvetý...

Beginning with the early 1890's we find *dol'niki* also in the work of
V. Brjusov, especially in the "city poems" of 1896. Brjusov alternates
trisyllabic interstress intervals with the usual disyllabic and monosyllabic
intervals, which imparts to his *dol'niki* the character of a broken meter
reproducing the free rhythms of colloquial speech:

S opúščennym *vzórom*, v *pelerínočke* béloj
Oná mimo nás proskol'znúla nesmélo,
S opúščennym vzórom, v pelerínočke béloj...
...I tól'ko nébo — vsegdá golubóe, —
Sijálo, prekrásnoe, v strógom pokóe,
Odnó liš' nébo, vsegdá golubóe!...

Or:

Edvá ej býlo četýrnadcat' lét
Tak zadúmčivo gásli línii bjústa.
O, kák ej ne šël puncóvyj cvét
Símvol strástnogo čúvstva!...

Or:

Est' čtó to pozórnoe v móšči priródy,
Nemája vraždá k lučám krasotý.
Nad mírom skál pronósjatsja gódy.
No véčen tól'ko mír mečtý...

Lyric *dol'niki* appear somewhat later in the work of Brjusov. In, for
example, the poem *Grjaduščie gunny* (1905):

Gdé vy, grjadúščie gúnny,
Čto túčej navísli nad mírom?
Slýšu vaš tópot čugúnnyj
Po eščë ne otkrýtym Pamíram.
Na nás ordój op'janéloj
Rúxnite s tëmnyx stanóvij —
Oživít' odrjaxlévšee télo
Volnój pylájuščej króvi...

It is at a comparatively late time (*Tol'ko ljubov'*, 1906) that we find the
"sprung lines" of Bal'mont (*Boloto, Staryj Dom*) which also contain
up to three unstressed syllables between stresses. For example:

... Kto v mërtvuju glúb' vraždébnyx zerkál
Kogdá to *brósil bezotvétnyj* vzgljád
Tot zérkalom *skóvan*, i *vysókij* zál
Naselën tenjámi, i *ljústry v nëm gorját*

In the work of Vjačeslav Ivanov *dol'niki* also occur only in isolated instances (*Xvala Solncu, Attika i Galileja*) and deviations from the general type of binary meter are limited to scattered cases of "contraction". Cf., however, the following instance of a four-syllable interstress group (at the caesura):

> O, Sólnce! vožátyj, ángel bóžij
> S rasplávlennym sérdcem v razvérstoj grudí!
> Kudá nas vlečёš' ty, na nás nepoxóžij,
> Putí ne *vídjaščij pred sobój* vperedí...

In spite of the fairly numerous examples of *dol'niki* at the end of the nineteenth and beginning of the twentieth centuries, the use of this meter in the older generation of Russian Symbolists did not go beyond the stage of metrical experiment in isolated poems. A feature of all these experiments is the presence of the dominant syllabo-tonic basis (usually a ternary meter), deviations from which occur now in one, now in another line, and are perceived as "contractions" (or "expansions") of the basic meter — most frequently in the anacrusis or caesura. This was the period in the history of purely tonic verse when the term *pauznik* and the theory of "pauses" attracted attention. In Blok's *Stixi o Prekrasnoj Dame* (1900-1905) Russian tonic verse entered upon a new period of its development. Here for the first time *dol'niki* became an integral part of the Russian poetic language, a verse form on an equal footing with the old syllabo-tonic meters. In this regard, Blok's role in the history of modern tonic versification resembles the role of Lomonosov in establishing the syllabo-tonic principle: both had predecessors, but they were both first in implanting a new system by writing poems in which this system appeared as an organic attribute of their poetic style.

In the *dol'niki* of Blok there are usually one or two unstressed syllables between stresses. One distinguishes three-stress and four-stress lines, with differing endings. The more usual is the three-stress line:

> Potemnéli, poblékli zály.
> Počernéla rešёtka okná.
> U dveréj šeptális' vassály:
> — Koroléva, koroléva bol'ná...

An example of the four-stress line:

> Nevérnaja! Gdé ty? Skvoz' úlicy sónnye
> Protjanúlas' dlínnaja cép' fonaréj,
> I, pára za pároj, idút vljublёnnye,
> Sogrétye svétom ljubví svoéj...

It is rare to find three (and rarer to find four) unstressed syllables between stresses in the usual *dol'niki* of the lyric type (but cf: Koroleva, koroleva bol'na...); such verses are concentrated in a special group of poems written in broken, colloquial rhythms, e.g. *Iz gazet* (cf. § 28 above) and others. Cf.:

> ... Njánjuška sé*la zadú*malas'
> *Lúčiki pobežáli,* — tri lúčika.
> "*Njánjuška, o čém* ty zadúmalas'?
> — Rasskaží pro svjatógo múčenika..."

After Blok, *dol'niki* became the general property of Russian poetry. Numerous examples are to be seen in the work of Kuzmin, Gumilëv and others. In Axmatova's work, in contrast to the singing style of Blok, they acquire the character of intentionally casual, intimate, colloquial speech: the poetry strives, as it were, to approximate the free rhythm of prose. The change in the general character of the meter (of its *ethos* in German terminology) is connected not so much with its rhythmical peculiarities (stressing of metrically weak syllables, syntactic enjambment) as with the choice of words, the conversational phraseology, the curtailment of direct emotional expressiveness — in a word, with the general alteration in the thought and style of the verse. Cf., for example:

> Býlo dúšno ot žgúčego svéta,
> A vzgljády egó — kak lučí.
> Ja tól'ko vzdrógnula — étot
> Móžet menjá priučít'...

Nor does the metrical system of Majakovskij offer anything principally new. Here also we have purely tonic verse, usually with three or four stresses per line, in the customary stanzas of four lines with alternating rhymes. The number of unstressed syllables between stresses, however, can fluctuate sharply; one finds frequent departures from the usual one or two-syllable intervals commonly seen in lyric *dol'niki*. Sometimes the dominant metrical stresses unite about themselves rather extensive groups of syllables, and sometimes they fall on immediately adjacent syllables. For the four-stress line, cf. *Vojna i mir*, 5:

> O, kakíe | vétry, | kakógo | júga
> sveršíli | čúdo | sérdcem | pogrebënnym?
> Rascvetájut | glazá | tvoí, — | dva lúga.
> Ja kuvyrkájus' | v níx — | vesëlyj | rebënok...
> ...Gúb | ne xvátit | ulýbke | stolícej.
> Vsé | iz kvartír | na plóščadi | vón!
> Serébrjanymi | mjačámi | ot stolícy | k stolíce
> raskínem | vesél'e, | sméx, | zvón!
> Ne pojmëš', | èto vózdux, | cvetý-li, | ptícy-l'!

I poët, | i blagouxáet, | i pëstroe | srázu,
no ot ètogo | kostróm | razgorájutsja | líca,
i sladčájšim | vinóm | p'janéet | rázum...

Or the three-stress line of *Oblako v štanax*, 3:

Kák vy sméete | nazyvát'sja | poètom
i, séren'kij, | čiríkat', | kak pérepel?
Segódnja | nádo | kastétom
Kroít'sja | míru | v čérepe...

It is more usual to find four and three-stress lines alternating within a stanza in no particular premeditated order. E.g. in *Oblako v štanax*, 2:

Slúšajte! | Propovéduet, | mečás' | i stenjá,
Segódnjašnego | dnjá | krikogúbyj | Zaratústra!
Mý — s licóm, | kak záspannaja | prostynjá,
s gubámi, | obvíššimi, | kak ljústra,
Mý — | katoržáne | góroda | leprozórija,
Gde zóloto | i grjáz' | iz''jazvíli | prokázu, —
My číšče | veneciánskogo | lazór'ja,
morjámi | i sólncami | omýtogo | srázu.

But alongside the usual four or three-stress line it is also possible, as in the free iambics of the eighteenth century (in Krylov, Bogdanovič and Griboedov), to find shorter lines alternating with longer lines according to no fixed pattern. For example, *Vojna i Mir*, 3;

Prišlí, | rassélis' | v zemnýx | dolínax,
gósti | v strášnom | narjáde.
Mráčno | poígryvajut | na šéjax | dlínnyx
ožerél'ja | jáder...

Or, from the same source:

... I tám, | gde Ál'py, | v zakáte | gréja,
výlaskali | v nébe | lëd | sčekí, —
oblakóv | galleréej
naxoxlílis' | zórkie | lëtčiki...

It has been pointed out, as though it were a peculiarity of Majakovskij's metrical system, that in his verse individual word stresses are subordinated to the predominating stresses of phraseological groups. In the examples cited above such consolidated groups, each constituting a single rhythmical unit, are: "kak-vy-smeete..., no-ot-ètogo..." Such examples, however, can be found in ordinary ternary verse or in *dol'niki*. More extended phraseological groups are integrated in the following stanza from *Oblako v štanax*, 2:

Ja rán'še | dúmal, — | *knígi délajutsja* | ták:
Prišël | poèt, | *legkó razžál* | ustá,
I srázu | zapél | vdoxnovénnyj | prosták, —
požálujsta!

Or, from the same source:

U menjá | v dušé | ni odnogó | *sedógo vólosa,*
I stárčeskoj | néžnosti | nét v nej!
Mír | ogromív | móšč'ju | gólosa
Idú — | krasívyj | dvadcatidvuxlétnij...

Such cases, however, are very rare in Majakovskij's poetry. And, more-over, in free stanzaic composition which unites lines with a differing number of stresses, they can also be interpreted as longer, five-stressed lines. Cf., for example: Ja ran'še | dumal: | — knigi | delajutsja | tak...

And thus the difficulties of Majakovskij's prosodic technique for a reader brought up on older poetic models lie not in peculiarities of the metrical system but in his particular rhythmical devices: word groups of the most varied size are subordinated to the predominant metrical stresses, but are, nevertheless, perceived as equivalent metrical units.

The graphic devices used by Majakovskij should not lead us astray: they do not represent either the line divisions or the division of the lines into metrical parts (stress groups); their fundamental role is to break the line down into *semantic and syntactic groups,* thereby emphasizing the *declamatory pauses* and serving the cause of *semantic expressiveness.* Cf. *Oblako v štanax* (I use a single bar to show metrical divisions and a double bar to indicate line boundaries):

Vy dúmaete, | èto brédit | maljaríja? ||
Èto býlo, |
býlo | v Odésse. ||
"Pridú | v četýre," — | skazála | María. ||
Vósem'. |
Dévjat'. |
Désjat'. ||
Vót i véčer |
v nočnúju | žút' ||
ušël | ot okon, |
xmúryj, |
dekábryj. ||
V drjáxluju | spínu | xoxóčut | i ržút ||
kandeljábry. ||

In any case, Majakovskij's verse is not "free verse" — unless one means free in the sense that his stanzaic composition is free, like the "free iambics" of Krylov's fables. It is the tonic system of Blok's *dol'niki* in its further development and implementation.

32. IMITATIONS OF CLASSICAL METERS:
THE DACTYLO-TROCHAIC HEXAMETER

The first *imitations of classical meters* in modern European poetry were unsuccessful attempts to adopt the quantitative principle of classical metrics: poets strove to compose modern verse after the example of the ancients by alternating long and short syllables without regard for the stress accent.[19] During the second stage of the process of adapting the classical meters, it was realized that an essential difference existed between the phonetic material of classical and modern verse: the former recognized variation in length, the latter — in degree of stress. And so the reproduction of the classical model had to be limited to reproducing the metrical design of the ancient pattern but in terms of the phonetic material native to a given linguistic system. Thus was established the principle which remained dominant up to our own day: the long syllable of the classical meter was replaced in tonic versification by a stressed and the short syllable by an unstressed syllable. In this process feet with two or more long syllables (especially spondees) were destined to create considerable difficulties in view of the fact that the foot (or the rhythmical unit) in tonic versification contains only *one* stress, which dominates a group of unstressed syllables (on the problem of the spondee, cf. below, p. 212 ff.).

For the rest, poems reproducing classical meters according to this principle do not in any way differ from other verse constructed under the native tonic or syllabo-tonic system: it is only from the point of view of their origin that we single out a special group of meters, which we designate as "classical". But this difference in historical origin should not be allowed to obscure the identity in principle which the "classical" meters share with certain "native" forms when one considers the meter itself. In the history of the struggle against the syllabic principle the imitation of those classical meters having unequal numbers of syllables played a role equal in importance with the revival of the folksong and other analogous phenomena.

[19] On experiments in quantitative meters, cf., for the Germans, H. Paul, p. 89; for the English, J. Schipper, I, p. 8; R. Bridges, p. 106. In Russia, Meletij Smotrickij (1619) tried to establish a quantitative system on a purely orthographic basis. Cf. V. Perec, *Istoriko-literaturnye issledovanija* (1900), vol. I, chaps. I-II.

Among the classical meters the most popular and the most longlived in the literatures of modern nations is the *hexameter*. The classical hexameter, as has already been indicated, was a dactylic line of six feet. According to the rules of metrical versification, it admitted the replacement of each dactylic foot (except the fifth) by a spondee, and the sixth foot was obliged to be disyllabic (trochee or spondee). The Russian hexameter is also a six-foot dactylic line with a feminine (catalectic) ending. Dactyls can follow one after the other for a considerable stretch within a poem; cf. Gnedič *Iliada*

> (*Iliad*), VI: ...Rék i priblížasja k sýnu, prostër k nemu rúki Priámid:
> Vspját' otklonílsja mladenéc, i k pérsjam rabýni pitávšej
> S kríkom priník, ustrašásja ljubéznogo ótčego vída:
> Médi gremjáščej bojásja i kónskij zrja grében' užásnyj,
> Grózno nad šlémom vysókim navíššij i zýblemyj vétrom...

Usually, however, the spondee, which lent considerable variety to the ancient meter, was replaced by Russian poets with the trochee. In this way such a "dactylo-trochaic hexameter" line as "Gnęv, o boginja, vospoj Axillesa Peleeva syna..." is equivalent to the line "Gnęv, boginja, vospoj Axillesa Peleeva syna...", where the dactyl of the first foot is replaced with a trochee. Cf. from Žukovskij's *Undina*:

> Rýcar' s glu*bókim* *čúvstvom* ljubví *smotrél* na Undínu.
> Mnóju l', on dúmal, daná ej dušá *il' nét*, no prekrásnej
> Ètoj duší ne byválo na svéte: oná kak nebésnyj
> Ángel. — I slëzy Undíny s nežnéjšim učástiem drúga
> Ón otirál, *celúja* ej óči, ustá i laníty...

In their use of the "dactylo-trochaic" (tonic) hexameter, Russian poets rely on the practice of the Germans. Cf. Klopstock's *Messias*:

> *Sing' un*sterbliche Seele, der *s*ündigen Menschheit Erlösung,
> Die der Messias auf Erden in *seiner M*enschheit vollendet,
> U*nd d*u*rch* die er Ádams Geschlecht zu der Liebe der Gottheit,
> Leidend ge*tötet* und verherrlichet, wieder erhöht hat...

Or Goethe's *Hermann und Dorothea*:

> Hab' ich den Markt und die Strassen doch *n*ie *so* einsam gesehen!
> Ist doch die Stadt wie ge*kehrt*! *Wie au*sgestorben! Nicht fünfzig
> *Däucht* mir, blieben zur*ü*ck *von* allen unsern Bewohnern!...

The development of the dactylo-trochaic hexameter from the middle of the eighteenth century was linked, as was the spread of the *dol'niki*, with the reaction against the domination of syllabo-tonic versification. Klopstock, who adapted this meter to German in his *Messias* (1748 and afterwards), had only a few insignificant predecessors in Germany:[20] as an innovator, he supplied the justification for his metrical reform in theoretical articles.[21] Iambs seemed to him monotonous; German as a linguistic medium would not accomodate itself to the mechanically repeated alternation of stressed and unstressed syllables, and this gave rise to the customary violations of the meter ("deviations") or the suppression of the natural verbal stresses (Silbenzwang). The hexameter introduced the indispensable variety into poetry and permitted a wider exploitation of the verbal material, which was easily fitted into its flexible pattern. It is interesting to compare the hexameter with old Germanic alliterative verse, which Klopstock regarded as having a "polymetrical" structure (altdeutsche Polymetrie), i.e., involving — as in the hexameter — a disruption of the syllabo-tonic pattern.

In Russia, Tred'jakovskij was already experimenting with the hexameter (cf. in particular his *Tilemaxida*). His example, far from calling forth emulation, repelled his contemporaries.[22] The spread of the new meter was linked up with the metrical experiments of the last quarter of the eighteenth century: Radiščev came forward with his *Apologia Tilemaxidy i šestistopov* and in his *Putešestvie* (in the chapter entitled *Tver'*), he proposed the hexameter as a heroic line to replace the six-foot iambic lines of Lomonosov and Xeraskov. "If Lomonosov had translated Job or the psalmist in dactyls and if Sumarokov had written Semira or Dmitrij in trochaic verse, then Xeraskov also would have taken it into his head that one might write in some measure other than iambic, and would have earned more glory for his eight years' labor by describing the

---

[20]   On Klopstock's predecessors in the adaptation of classical verse measures, cf. H. Paul, p. 97 ff. Gottsched (*Kritische Dichtkunst*, XII, §§ 13, 14) gives examples of experiments in the tonic hexameter. Historically important for the eighteenth century were the experiments of Kleist (*Der Frühling*, 1746-49), who used the hexameter with a monosyllabic anacrusis (an *amphibrachic* line of six feet). This archaic form, which was supplanted in Germany by Klopstock's *Messias*, was reflected in Russia in the experiments of Voejkov (translation from the *Georgics* of Virgil in *Vestnik Evropy*, 1815, VI) and somewhat earlier in the work of Merzljakov (where it was mingled with amphibrachic pentameter; cf. *Vestnik Evropy*, VII (1808), for a translation from the *Odyssey*). Cf. Vostokov, *Opyt*, p. 38 ff.

[21]   Klopstock's articles on the hexameter and the classical meters: *Von der Nachahmung des griechischen Silbenmasses* (1756); *Vom deutschen Hexameter* (1769); *Vom gleichen Verse* (1773); *Fragmente über Sprache und Dichtkunst* (1779); *Vom Silbenmasse Merkwürdigkeiten der Literatur* (1770). Also cf. *Briefwechsel zwischen J. G. Voss und Klopstock* (in the book by Voss, *Zeitmessung der deutschen Sprache*, 1831², p. 200 ff.). Cf. Fr. Muncker, *Klopstock*, 1900².

[22]   Lomonosov gave examples of dactylo-trochaic verse in his *Pis'mo*. Among the metrical experiments of Sumarokov, published posthumously by Novikov, there is a fragment of his translation of *Télémaque* in hexameters (Vol. I, p. 313).

capture of Kazan' in a verse form appropriate to the epic." Radiščev was already dreaming of translating Homer into hexameters and criticized the iambic translation of Kostrov: "I am not astonished that the ancient tricornered hat has been set on Virgil's head à la Lomonosov, but I should like to see Homer appear among us not in iambs but in verse similar to his own, in hexameters; and though Kostrov is not a poet, but a translator, he might have started a new epoch in our versification, advancing the progress of poetry itself by a whole generation." Among Karamzin and his friends this question, apparently, had already been long resolved. Thus, Karamzin wrote, in 1788, to I. I. Dmitriev: "If you yourself take it into your head to sing your mighty deeds and those of all our army, then please, sing in dactyls and trochees, in Greek hexameters and not in those six-footed iambs which, in heroic poems, are insufferable. Be our Homer, not our Voltaire." (*Pis'ma N. Karamzina k I. Dmitrievu*, pub. 1866). It is interesting that Karamzin regarded the hexameter as a logaoedic line with regular alternation of binary and ternary feet: "Two dactyls and a trochee, two dactyls and a trochee." His example: "Truby v poxode gremeli, kriki po vozduxu mčalis'."

At the beginning of the nineteenth century the question of the hexameter was again the subject of debate. The first attempt by Gnedič (from the sixth canto of the *Iliad*) was printed in the *Čtenie v Besede ljubitelej russkogo slova*, (XIII, 1813). Along with this experiment appeared the letters of S. Uvarov and N. Gnedič proposing the dactylo-trochaic hexameter as the heroic line to replace the six-foot iambic line, which was characterised as "tedious", "monotonous", and so on. V. Kapnist came forward as the opponent of the hexameter in the same *Beseda* (*Čtenie*, XVII, 1815): he also admitted that iambs "bored" contemporary poets, but found the hexameter unsuited to the Russian language and recommended that the heroic line be drawn from the tradition of folk poetry. D. Samsonov, in *Vestnik Evropy*, took up a conservative position, rejecting both the hexameter and the native Russian verse line: he deemed it feasible to lend the required variety to iambic verse by shifting the caesura and by varying the positions of the "pyrrhics". Vostokov's *Opyt o russkom stixosloženii* (1812-17) went far toward summing up these disputes: written principally for the purpose of defending the tradition of folk poetry, it was the first attempt to lay a serious theoretical foundation for the new metrical experiments by introducing the concept of a special system of versification based exclusively on the counting of stresses. The second edition of this book (1817) contains a special section (pp.

50-60) devoted to the history and theory of the Russian hexameter.[23]

The question of replacing a dactyl with a trochee instead of with the classical spondee occupies a central place in these disputes about the hexameter. Tred'jakovskij, who was the first to make extensive use of the dactylo-trochaic hexameter, also defends this replacement on theoretical grounds.[24] N. Gnedič, in his translation of the *Iliad*, allowed such replacement but thought it necessary to avoid too frequent application of the device "in this first attempt, in order that the meter, still unfamiliar to the ear, not impede the reader." (*Čtenie*, XIII, 71). D. Samsonov, on the other hand, could not reconcile himself to the use of a meter in which the alternation of trochees and dactyls was not regulated by any rule whatsoever: "Our verses please us owing to the fact that they present us with a regular sequence of high and low syllables; but how can one expect such a sequence from verses in which dactyls and trochees may be capriciously placed anywhere?" (*Kratkoe rassuždenie*, *Vestnik Evropy*, 1817, XCIV, 248). Vostokov, on the contrary, saw in this device the chief advantage of the hexameter over monotonous iambic verse and accused N. Gnedič of a too cautious use of the trochee: "In my opinion, such

[23]   The history of the Russian hexameter is given in detail by Vostokov in the second edition of his *Opyt* (1817), p. 51 ff. On the argument about the hexameter in Russian verse, cf.: *Čtenie v Besede ljubitelej russkogo slova*, XIII (1813), S. Uvarov, "Pis'mo k N. I. Gnediču o grečeskom èkzametre". Gnedič's answer is on p. 69 of the same number. — XVII (1815): "Pis'mo V. V. Kapnista k S. S. Uvarovu o èkzametrax". Uvarov's answer to Kapnist is printed on p. 47 of the same number. — Dor. Samsonov, "Kratkoe rassuždenie o russkom stixosloženii", (*Vestnik Evropy*, vol. XCIV (1817), p. 219 ff. — A. Vostokov, *Opyt o russkom stixosloženii* (1817), sec. ed. (the chapter on the hexameter is in a new section: "Kritičeskoe obozrenie stoposložnyx razmerov", pp. 34-65). — N. Gnedič, "Zamečanija na Opyt o russkom stixosloženii g-na Vostokova, i nečto o Prozodii drevnix" (*Vestnik Evropy*, XCIX (1818), p. 98 and 187 ff.). — D. Samsonov, "Nečto o dolgix i korotkix slogax, o russkix gekzametrax i jambaz", (*Vestnik Evropy*, C (1818), p. 260 ff.; an answer to Gnedič's article.) — N. Ostolopov, *Slovar' drevnej i novoj poèzii* (1821), I, 306-335, the article entitled "Exameter" (includes an "excerpt from the investigation of A. F. Voejkov: 'Ob Ekzametrax' pp. 321-333). Among modern writers who have written about the imitation of classical meters, cf. Prof. F. F. Zelinskij, *Russkij èlegičeskij distix* (Ovid's *Heroides*, translated by Zelinskij (1913); Commentary, pp. 210-204); B. I. Jarxo, preface to the *Satyricon* of Petronius Arbiter, pub. by *Vsem. Liter.* (1924), p. 32 ff.

[24]   Cf. *Tilemaxida*, — *Pred"iz"jasnenie ob iroičeskoj piime* (= *Works*, vol. II): "The epic absolutely demands a dactylo-spondaic, or in terms of our tonic verse, a dactylo-trochaic movement..." (p. 9 ff.). "When compelled by necessity, we replace the disyllabic trochee and iamb by the pyrrhic, which in a great many cases is indispensable for filling out a line. And for that reason I have substituted the pyrrhic for the trochee here also, when it was required. And since my heroic verse does not proceed via the trochee alone, but more often prefers the dactyl, a trisyllabic foot, I have, with the same justification and in answer to the same need, sometimes replaced the dactyl by the tribach, which is also a trisyllabic foot" (p. LXX). On the use of classical meters cf. also the preface to *Argenida*, p. LXXI ff.

verses [i.e., unbroken dactyls. V.Ž.] are still more wearisome and monotonous than our Alexandrines, to which pyrrhics lend a certain degree of
variety. The principal advantage of dactylo-trochaic and amphibrachic
hexameters over iambic verse lies in their unrestricted alternation of feet,
which device permits the line to contain more or fewer syllables without
exceeding the limits of the six-foot meter." (*Opyt*, 2d edition, 40). Modern
purists like Prof. F. Zelinskij forbid the use of the trochee, since they
find that it does not correspond to the classical spondee. Taking as
fundamental the rule that "stress corresponds to the long syllable, non-
stress to the short," Prof. F. Zelinskij attempts to reproduce the classical
spondee by a foot with two stresses: this is accomplished by rendering the
second long syllable through a monosyllabic word having its own independent stress. "And even in these cases," writes Prof. F. Zelinskij,
"I have, with a view to sonority, allowed it only following the caesura:
...Protezileju privet šlët za more Laodamija... ...Gde tvoja gordost'
teper'? Gde podvigov rjad mnogotrudnyx? ...Stala tebja stol' vyše,
skol' ty, pokoritel' vselennoj..." (cf. *Russkij èlegičeskij stix — Ovidij,
Geroini*, translated by F. Zelinskij, p. 201).

The point of view of the purists is repudiated the moment we forget
the origin of the dactylo-trochaic hexameter and approach it as a Russian
meter, adapted to and peculiarly metamorphosed in the Russian poetic
tradition. In this sense, the dactylo-trochaic hexameter has as much right
to existence as do the lyric *dol'niki* of Blok: it is a six-stress, purely tonic
line with a feminine ending and without anacrusis, in which monosyllabic
interstress intervals alternate with disyllabic intervals ($x = 1, 2$). Furthermore, as in the *dol'niki*, a disyllabic unit (so-called "trochee") is counted
as the equivalent of a trisyllabic unit ("dactyl"), a feature realized in
declamation by various devices of temporal equalization (slowing down
or speeding up the rate of speaking, pausing, and so forth). On the other
hand, the presence of a hyper-metrical stress in weak position in the
Russian accentual "spondee" is felt, just as in the other types of *dol'niki*,
as a sharp deformation of the metrical pattern, a feature which comes
nowhere near to rendering the effect of a classical "spondee": it forms
a sort of roadblock in the path of the normal flow of the line and the
line becomes labored. This was sensed by Russian theoreticians at the
beginning of the nineteenth century. V. Kapnist found spondees "unsuited to our language and difficult to pronounce" (from a letter to S. S.
Uvarov about hexameters, *Čtenie v Besede*, 1815, XVII, 24; cf. also 26).
It was the opinion of A. Vostokov — and D. Samsonov agreed with him
in this instance — that Russian was altogether "without spondees",

since whenever two stresses occurred side by side one of them "is over-shadowed and yields its place to the other" (e.g. gde on?) or, if each word retains its independent accent (especially in polysyllabic words), then there appears between the stresses "an interval or gap in the voice (pause)" (Vostokov, pp. 21-22; cf. D. Samsonov, *op. cit.*, p. 247). Vosto-kov admits that a "spondee" may replace a trochee "as a sop to conven-tion". Cf. the examples which he cites from Voejkov: "Rezkij *tresk trub* brannyx poslyšal, kipit i trepeščet... or "Vidiš' li? *Znak dan!* vyrvavšis' von iz ogrady..." "But such artificial spondees," he continues, "must be employed with great discretion, to convey, as in these examples, some special sound effect or image; in other cases there is no point in using them *in violation* of normal *Russian stress practises*. It would be better to rely on *pure trochees and dactyls*, on which for the most part depends the fluency of our hexameter." (p. 57).

Disputes similar to these can also be found in Germany, whence Russian poets borrowed the dactylo-trochaic hexameter. Klopstock, as has already been pointed out, freely substituted trochees for spondees and justified his practice in theoretical articles. Representatives of the strict antiquarian school such as August Schlegel, Platen, Foss, the translator of Homer, and others, polemicized against the use of trochees in the hexa-meter.[25] From their point of view such lines as the following, for example, were inadmissible: Goethe: "Edelsteine zierten das Werk und goldene Ranken..." or Schiller: "Körper und *Stimme leiht die Schrift dem* stummen Gedanken". The second syllables of such words as Ed*el*-, stein*e*, etc., were too "light" to fill the place corresponding in classical metrics to the second long syllable of the spondee! German purists attempted to form spondees by using two stresses. Here also, mono-syllabic words were employed to that end. Cf. A. Schlegel's "*Steh! Steh!* riefen sie aus: du bist's der unsern geweihten... Klag nicht, Löwe der Menschen! Der *Welt Heil* wollt ihr verderben..." Or Platen's "Konnten sie nicht ans Ufer den *Sarg ziehen*, weil er so *schwer schien...*" Aside from this device, it is possible to have two adjacent stresses in German in a compound word: one syllable bears the primary stress, the other the secondary, e.g., léblòs, Fálschhèit. It is interesting that the rigorists

---

[25] Those German writers who tended toward a purely classical versification were: I. Foss, K. Moritz, Humboldt, Schlegel, and Platen. Cf. especially K. Ph. Moritz, *Versuch einer deutschen Prosodie* (1786), p. 201 ff.; J. G. Voss, *Zeitmessung der deutschen Sprache* (1831²) (p. 183 ff., *Über den deutschen Hexameter*, p. 200 ff., *Briefwechsel zwischen J. G. Voss und Klopstock*; A. W. Schlegel, *Betrachtungen über Metrik. An Fr. Schlegel* (Werke, Bd. VII), especially p. 187 ff. For a bibliography, cf. J. Minor, pp. 526-527.

believed the secondary stress too weak to reproduce the second long syllable of the spondee: in seeking for combinations which would recreate the "equilibrium" of the two long syllables in the classical spondee ("gleichgewogene Spondeen"), they preferred to use words of this type in such a way that the first, heavy stress would fall on the place of the second long syllable of the spondee, and the second, lighter accent would begin the following dactyl. (Cf. the pattern $|--|-\cup\cup|$ as in the combinations: | denn leb | los... or: | auch Schön | heit...). From this point of view, therefore, instead of such a line as "Düstere *Sturmnacht* zog, und *graunvoll* wogte das *Meer auf*". Foss would prefer the following variation giving "equilibrium" to the spondees: "Düsterer *zog Sturmnacht, graun-voll rings* wogte das *Meer auf*". Wilhelm Humboldt also found the line "*Wenn Krank*heit mich befällt" better suited to the character of the hexameter than the line "Wenn mir die *Krankheit* naht". Cf. also "Brausender *steigt Meer*flut im Orkan..." or "Schweift im *Gefild ein*sam..." or "...es er*folgt Schwachheit* absterbenden Alters". We should also mention the fact that Goethe, who at the beginning was guided purely by ear and made free use of the ordinary dactylo-trochaic hexameter, later bowed for a time to the dictates of the purists and allowed them to correct his hexameters in line with their strict principles.[26]

This practice of making the second stress of the spondee exceed the strength of both its neighboring stresses is undoubtedly an extremely violent distortion of the dactylo-trochaic line, a distortion which, though it is perhaps not without its own peculiar charm, is nevertheless least of all suited to reproduce the equilibrium of the classical spondee. The free alternation of trochees and dactyls in the poetry which Goethe and Schiller wrote when they were not under the influence of the rigorist doctrine shows the practical feasibility of using the dactylo-trochaic hexameter: it is perceived with the same immediacy as are the ballad meters with alternating monosyllabic and disyllabic interstress groups. But as A. Heusler, the historian of the German hexameter, rightly observes, in his critique of the system advocated by Foss and A. Schlegel, it does not correspond to classical versification, either. In the classical system the first long syllable of the spondee is strong (arsis), the second weak (thesis), in accordance with the general character of the dactylic meter, where the first syllable is always strong (arsis). The task of the translator is not mechanically to replace every long syllable with a stress and every short one with an unstressed syllable, but to conserve what was the very essence

---

[26] Cf. A. Heusler, *Deutscher und antiker Vers* (1917) (*Qu. F.*, 123); On Goethe and his "teachers" cf. in particular p. 116 ff.

of the classical system — the alternation of strong and weak temporal units (arsis and thesis). The so-called "trochaic" foot in the hexameter fulfils this requirement with much greater success than the so-called "spondee" consisting of two equal stresses. The spondee in which the thesis carries a stronger stress than the arsis is even less suitable.

Among the rhythmical variations of the Russian hexameter we should mention the omission of one of the metrical stresses (usually the first, as in the dactyl) and the weighting of metrically weak syllables by a supplementary stress (as in the ternary meters). Tred'jakovskij, the first theoretician of the dactylo-trochaic hexameter, permitted extensive replacement of a dactylic foot by a "tribrach" (three unstressed syllables: – – –) or of a trochee by a "pyrrhic". Gnedič defended the substitution of a pyrrhic for a trochee in the first foot: he even favored such an "anapestic" opening. Cf. examples from Gnedič himself: "*no* Adrasta živym ulovil Menelaj ratobornyj..." or "*i* Priam, i narod znamenitogo v branjax Priama..." (*Otvet S. S. Uvarovu*, 21). "Russian verses, like Greek, which commence with a compound trochee that does not destroy the form of the hexameter, can be converted into anapestic lines" (*Zamečanija na Opyt o russkom stixosloženii, Vestnik Evropy*, 1818, XCIX, pp. 211-212). Vostokov objected to this: wishing to avoid an anapestic beginning, he demanded that, in Gnedič's examples, "an arbitrary length or stress be placed on the first syllable" (*I* Priam..." etc.). But he himself allowed a line to commence with three unstressed syllables (substitution of a tribrach for the first dactyl): "*No ne toliko* menja sokrušaet sud'ba Iliona..." (Gnedič) (cf. *Opyt*, p. 57). In recent times this substitution has been defended by Prof. F. F. Zelinskij, who is otherwise a champion of the rigorous preservation of the classical hexameter forms; examples: "Prevozmogaet unyn'e žestokaja bol'. Vstrepenuvšis'..." or "V ocepenen'i nemom ruki na lone ležat..." (*Russkij èlegičeskij distix*, p. 202). But Brjusov, concurring in this matter with Vostokov, objected to the anapestic opening: "The replacement of the first trochaic foot by a pyrrhic converts the meter into anapestic; that is why the hexameter avoids such a rhythm." (*Osnovy stixovedenija*, p. 109). As a matter of fact, Gnedič, Žukovskij, Minskij, and others, tended to lighten the first stress in their hexameters rather frequently, and with the same general justification as in syllabo-tonic dactyls and trochees. The practice is also widespread among the German poets who remained relatively independent of the purist demands. Cf. Goethe's: "*Wider*legen kann ich dich nicht; ich sage mir alles... *Wieder*holet politisch und zwecklos jegliche Meinung..."; and often at the caesura after the third stress: "Geh ich gerad in die Stadt | und *über*gebe den Kriegern..." It should be noted that in all such cases where the initial syllable is separated from the nearest strong stress by one or two unstressed syllables, we find in the Russian poets (and even more in the German poets) a lightening, rather than an omission, of the first stress, since the following unstressed syllables are weaker than the first. Therefore in a sequence of dactylo-trochaic hexameters the anapestic beginning ("*i* Priam i narod...") is felt as a rhythmical variation of the dactyl and not as anapestic pentameter; Vostokov probably sensed this when he spoke of "length admitted by convention". One cannot, however, deny that such lightening can also be regarded as a violation of the strict rhythmical style. It is much rarer, of course, to find a metrical stress omitted in the middle of a line; the champions of the strict forms are even more severe in their attitude toward such deviations. Cf. the examples cited in the article by Prof. F. Zelinskij: "Strašno mne *p*ereskočit', ja ispolnena *n*edoumen'ja..." etc.

The weighting of metrically weak syllables by supplementary stresses provoked objections as early as the beginning of the nineteenth century. Vostokov was decidedly opposed to such "impure dactyls". "*Impure dactyls* is the term I reserve for those in which a stressed syllable is placed where a short syllable would be expected. For instance: Šlem probilo naskvoz' i čelo, i v *glub*' kosti proniklo... (Gnedič) or: Tam, nakonec, dve morskie pobedy i v dvux *častjax* sveta..." (Voejkov). "Such dactyls," wrote Vostokov, "can least of all be tolerated in the hexameter." And he continued: "To put the matter briefly, the hexameter, more than any other meter, demands a correct distribution of stresses among the words." (*Opyt*, 58). In recent times, this opinion has also been defended by Prof. F. Zelinskij: "The thesis of the dactyl cannot support stressed sylla bles." E.g.: "Protesilaju privet *šlët* iz rodnogo Laodamija..." (201). As a matter of fact, however, many Russian poets have written hexameters with such additional stresses — sometimes fairly light, sometimes heavy enough to constitute a noticeable interruption of the rhythm, and most often, of course, on monosyllabic words.[27]

---

[27] The rhythmical structure of the Russian hexameter shows important individual differences in the work of various poets. Žukovskij, who at first willingly made use of trochaic feet, subsequently avoided this device. Cf. *Cejks i Gal'ciona*, (1819): in lines 1-50 there are 24 cases, of which 4 are lines with two trochaic feet; *Odisseja*, (1842-49), Book I, lines 1-100 show only 7 cases (in 6 of them the trochee is in the first foot, in the other it is at the caesura); in Book XXII, lines 1-100 do not contain a single example. In Gnedič's *Iliada* the first 50 lines of Book I show 21 cases (five of them lines with two trochees). In Minskij, on the other hand, the first 100 lines of the first book have only two cases (one in the first foot, one at the caesura). Žukovskij permits a lightening of the stress only in compound words: volnoob"jatom, bogopodobnyx, etc.; and occasionally

33. LOGAOEDIC METERS

Imitations of the classical lyrical meters (so-called "logaoedic"), like those of the dactylo-trochaic hexameter, introduced the alternation of inter-stress intervals with a variable number of syllables — with, however, one essential difference: this alternation in any given line or stanza was subject to an invariable compositional rule. Modern poets (German, English, Russian) reproduce the general pattern of such polymetric meters by replacing the quantitative relationships of long and short with a corresponding sequence of stressed and unstressed syllables. Here also, the question of the spondee is uppermost: the purists (especially German) have tried to reproduce the classical spondee by two "counterpoised" stresses, but this is fraught with the same contradictions as were mentioned in connection with the hexameter. A more natural solution, from the viewpoint of tonic versification, is the replacement of the spondee by the trochee or iamb, but in the polymetric schemes this leads to substantial deviations from the metrical pattern of the classical model since it renders impossible the distinction between long-long and long-short combinations, a distinction which plays a role of no little importance in logaoedic structure. Thus in tonic versification the fate of the classical polymetrical schemes is determined not only by the characteristics of the original meter, but also by the nature of the language in which the meter is reproduced.

The source of the German and Russian imitations was, for the most part, the lyric measures of Horace. Let us take as an example the Asclepiad line: **Exegi** monument[um] | **a**ere perennius. In the Latin pattern this is two choriambs divided by a caesura; the first is preceded by a spondee and the second followed by a pyrrhic or an iamb (the last foot is ambiguous):

$$- - - \cup \cup - \mid - \cup \cup - \cup \cup$$

In the Russian version the first spondee is replaced by a trochee. Cf. Vostokov's:

---

at the beginning of the line on monosyllabic conjunctions. Fet is much less strict in this matter. Cf. his translation of *Hermann und Dorothea*, Book I: Gorod — šarom pokati, budto vymoročnyj: i polsotni... Esli ponadobits*ja*. Tol'ko nynče s takoju oxotoj... K obnovlennomu domu, sosed čerez ploščad'. Bogatyj... S zelenovatymi rjumkami — istym bokalom rejnvejna... Cf. Minskij, Book I, 99: Darom bez vykupa ı ne pošlëm gekatombu svjatuju... There is virtually no stressing of metrically un-accented syllables in Žukovskij's *Odisseja*, but this practice is very frequent in Minskij's *Iliada*; cf. Book I, 29: Deve svobody ne dam; *ran'še* pust' eë starost' nastignet; 94: No za žreca svoego, *kogo* car' oskorbil Agamemnon...

Krépče médi sebé | sózdal ja pámjatnik.
Vzjál nad cárskimi vérx | on piramídami.
Dóžd' ne smóet egó, | víxrem ne slómitsja.
Cél'nyj výderžit ón | gódy besčíslenny,
Ne počúet sledóv | býstrogo vrémeni...

The Russian translation is written in purely tonic verse with five stresses, a dactylic ending, and, between two stresses, a strong caesura which is perceived as catalectic. As in all logaoedic verse, the number of unstressed syllables between stresses varies, but the sequence of the interstress intervals follows a regular pattern ($x_1 = 0$, $x_2 = 1$, $x_3 = 2$, $x_4 = 0 \|$ ...etc.) The resemblance to *dol'niki* is even more noticeable in other logaoedic meters. Cf. for example, the Sapphic meter (**Iam satis terris** | nivis **atque dirae**; the pattern: $- \cup - - - | \cup \cup - \cup - -$). In the Russian reproduction the stresses are distributed on every odd syllable, with two unstressed syllables following the caesura: we might characterize this line as a trochaic pentameter with a strong caesura following the third stress and with disyllabic anacrusis at the caesura. Vostokov included the Sapphic among the dactylo-trochaic meters (*Opyt*, 61). Cf., for example, his *Videnie v majskuju noč'*:

> Májska tíxa nóč' razlivála súmrak.
> Gólos ptíc umólk, veterók proxládnyj
> Véjal, zlátom zvëzd ispeščrjálos' nébo
> Róšči dremáli...

Finally, in the tonic version of the Alcaic strophe, we have a four-stress line with a variable number of syllables in the interstress groups which alternate in a regular sequence. E.g. Vostokov (from Horace 11, 19):

> ...Èvóe! Smútnym dúx moj veséliem
> Ob"ját. Volnújus'; Vákxom ispólnena
> Mojá trepéščet grúd'... Poščády,
> Líber! Poščády, grozjáščij tírsom!...

If the modern experts in classical metrics (Vjačeslav Ivanov, Prof. F. Zelinskij, and others) have taught us to reproduce the ancient strophes in rigorous fashion, the attempts of the eighteenth century poets in this direction are hardly less interesting with their "deviations" and "errors", since it is just by this process of *departing from the pattern* that foreign meters have been adapted and acclimatized to Russian tonic versification. Deviations from the correct caesura, for instance, are common; in the Sapphic strophe in such cases the disyllabic group following the third stress loses the character of a caesural anacrusis and the entire line becomes much more similar to the ordinary *dol'niki*. Cf. Radiščev's *Sapfičeskie strofy*:

> Nóč' bylá proxládnaja, svétlo v nébe
> Zvëzdy bléščut, tíxo istóčnik l'ëtsja,
> Vétry néžno véjut, šumját listámi
> Tópoli bély...

Or Sumarokov's translations of Sappho (Ode 11):

> ...Na zlatój ko mné kolésnice ézdja,
> Tý vprjažënnyx gnála k polëtu ptíček,
> V býstrom bége skórost'ju sékla vózdux
> Šéstvuja s néba...

It was very usual for the poets of the eighteenth century to omit metrical stresses in their versions of the classical meters: Sumarokov,[28] apparently, was opposed to this, even though his theoretical strictness was not in accord with his own poetic practice. "Omissions" were especially frequent in the Sapphic line, which in its general composition resembles the binary meters. If these deviations deserve to be censured from the standpoint of strict classical metrics, they are at least understandable when one considers the phonetic characteristics of the Russian language and the poetic tradition developed within it. This, consequently, is one of the normal ways of assimilating a foreign metrical scheme, and the result is the establishment of new, more stable national forms. Cf. Sumarokov's Ode X, written in the Sapphic meter (with rhymes!):

> ...Zrák tvoj v mýsli vlástvuja *obitáet,*
> *Neprestánno* sérdce tobóju táet,
> Vés' napólnen úm moj tobój edínoj,
> Múki príčinoj!
> Búd' pričínoj vmesto togó utéxi,
> *Vozdyxán'i* ty prevratí mne v sméxi,
> Ljúty *prevratí* mne pečáli v rádost',
> Góresti v sládost'!

The route from classical logaoedic meters to purely tonic verse lies across those mixed meters which were created by the poets of the eighteenth and early nineteenth centuries on the model of the lyric strophes of Horace, but with an admixture of feet which had no predecessors in the classical tradition. In Germany, Klopstock, who was the first to

---

[28] Cf. the preface to *Argenida*, p. LXXI: "He did not desire to have a pyrrhic substituted at will for a trochee or iamb even in those verses which we are able to fashion after Greek and Roman models. But I do not see the advantage of such strictness here when such a substitution is not prohibited in purely trochaic or iambic verse."

popularize the classical lyric meters and to defend them theoretically on the grounds of their superiority over the monotonous iambics, created his own polymetrical strophes. It was his habit to preface his poem by a scheme intended to orient the reader in the new meter. E.g. *Die frühen Gräber*:

> Willkommen, o silberner Mond,
> Schöner, stiller Gefährt' der Nacht!
> Du entfliehst? Eile nicht, bleib, Gedankenfreund
> Sehet, er bleibt, das Gewölk wallte nur hin!...

Or *Selma und Selmar*:

> Weine du nicht, o die ich innig liebe,
> Dass ein trauriger Tag von dir mich scheidet!
> Wenn nun wieder Hesperus dir dort lächelt,
> Komm' ich, glücklicher, wieder!...

In all such polymetrical strophes, monosyllabic and disyllabic interstress intervals are combined; in rare instances, stresses fall on adjacent syllables. As compared to *dol'niki*, there is the fundamental difference that the alternation of interstress intervals from one strophe to the next is governed by an invariable rule. In actuality, however, the regularity of the alternation is often brought about by means of an artificial scansion which to a greater or less degree distorts the natural pronunciation of the words (especially of the monosyllabic words). Cf. in the example cited: "...o *die* ich innig liebe..." And from the poem *Die beiden Musen*: "...dort *an* die Laufbahn..., stolz *in* die Schranken..., stolz *auf* die kühne..." and so on. In this we see the struggle of the linguistic medium against a monotonous metrical scheme and the tendency towards complete metrical freedom in distributing the stressed among the unstressed syllables. And, as a matter of fact, Klopstock went all the way from the classical meters, through his own independently created logaoedic schemes, to other, less restricted stanzaic forms where the number of stressless syllables varied from strophe to strophe, and thence to the so-called "free meters", i.e. to purely tonic verse completely liberated from the principle of syllable counting (cf. his odes *Die Genesung*, 1754, *Dem Allgegenwärtigen*, 1758, and others).

As for Russian lyric poetry, this development from the original logaoedic pattern to purely tonic verse is illustrated by Fet's poem beginning "Izmučen žizn'ju..." As has already been indicated, it begins with the regular repetition of a definite combination of binary and ternary feet and with an unvarying caesura, as follows: $- \acute{-} - \acute{-} - \mid - \acute{-} - - \acute{-} -$. The opposition of the linguistic medium is to be seen, in the first place,

mainly at the first stress, which in some lines is noticeably weakened.
In the second stanza the caesura of the last line is displaced from its
regular position. Finally, in the third stanza, in the last two lines, the
stresses are shifted, the number of syllables is altered, and thenceforward
the poem, though it preserves its four-stress line, liberates itself from the
uniform logaoedic pattern. Cf.

> Izmúčen žízn'ju, kovárstvom nadéždy,
> Kogdá im v bítve dušój ustupáju,
> I dněm i nóč'ju smežáju ja véždy
> I kák to stránno poрój prozreváju.
> Eščě temnée mrák žízni vsednévnoj,
> Kak pósle járkoj osénnej zarnícy,
> I tól'ko v nébe, kak zóv zadušévnyj
> Sverkájut zvězd | zolotýe resnícy
> I ták prozráčna ognéj beskonéčnost',
> I ták dostúpna vsja bézdna èfíra,
> *Čto prjámo smotrjú ja iz vrémeni v véčnost'*
> *I plámja tvoě uznajú, sólnce míra!*
> *I nepodvížno, na ógnennyx rózax,*
> *Živój altár' mirozdán'ja kurítsja...* etc.

Original logaoedic schemes (of the dactylo-trochaic or anapesto-iambic
type) are rather widespread among the Russian poets of the eighteenth
century and may be regarded as the first step away from the bondage of
traditional iambs and trochees toward pure tonism. Especially varied are
the examples which one encounters in the *Pesni* (pt. VIII) of Sumarokov.
Cf. *Pesnja* XVIII (in the Sapphic style, with a disyllabic unstressed interval after the first stress):

> Skól'ko ja plákal, búduči v razlúke!
> Skól'ko isčézlo dnéj v nesnósnoj múke!
> Tý vobražálas' vsjákij dén', vsenóšno,
> I povseméstno dúxu býlo tóšno,
> Ne imév otrády.
> Sérdce terzáli vsják čas skórbi ljúty.
> Né byl v pokóe ni odnój minúty,
> Pómnja míly vzgljády... etc.

Or Song XLVIII:

> Ty rúšiš' pokój, svobódu otnjávši,
> A póvod samá mne k ljubví podalá,
> Tý mne nadéždu podávši,
> Opját' vzjalá.
> Počtó bylo vléč', kogdá ne sklonját'sja?
> Ili to zabávno, čtob dúx moj terzát'?
> Už ty móžeš' smeját'sja:
> Nel'zjá otstát' !... etc.

Or Song LXX:

> Gdé ni guljáju, ni xožú,
> Grúst' prevelíkuju terpljú,
> Skúčno mne, gdé ja ni sižú,
> Ljágu, spokójno ja ne spljú;
> Nét mne vesél'ja nikogdá,
> Gór'ko mne, gór'ko zavsegdá!...

In all the examples cited here, as well as in logaoedic verse of the traditional classical type, Sumarokov and other eighteenth century poets permitted the usual omissions of stresses and, by the same token, the artificial, metrically prescribed stressing of monosyllabic words which normally carried only a slight stress. These practices tended to obscure the orthodox regularity of the metrical scheme with rhythmical variations, so that the reader tends to break up the line according to the stress groups and to disregard the division into feet. Thus in the most famous poem of this cycle, with which Sumarokov's collection of songs opens, the strict logaoedic trimeter (dactyl-trochee-trochee) is in reality eclipsed by a freer rhythmical design — a *dol'nik* with two main stresses, the first of which falls sometimes on the first, sometimes on the fourth syllable.

> Blagopolúčny dní,
> Nášimi vremenámi;
> Vésely mý odní
> Xot' net i žénščin s námi:
> Čéstnosti zdés' ustávy,
> Zlóbe, vraždé konéc,
> Íščem edínoj slávy
> Ot čistotý serdéc...

Thus the peculiar devices resorted to in adapting the classical meters to Russian (and German) lyrics led to forms which purists, with an eye to the strict classical tradition, condemned unequivocally. But at the same time these forms enriched the native metrical patterns with new hybrid formations. The historical role of these formations, as the example of Klopstock in Germany showed, could be extremely important — if only in the process of decanonizing syllabo-tonic versification. But, indeed, the syllabo-tonic feet themselves resulted from just such a reworking of native verse patterns with the help of peculiarly adapted classical schemes.

34. RUSSIAN FOLK POETRY

Another source of pure tonism in modern Russian poetry was the imitation of *folk poetry*. Russian folk verse is sung verse, i.e., its rhythmical character is determined principally by the rhythmical structure of the melody. At the same time, however, the musical accents are arranged in accordance with the verbal (or phrasal) stresses, without violating the verbal material, but allowing for the use of accentual doublets (vorota-vorotá, etc.) which exist in various dialects. The only constant element in the line is the number of metrical stresses; the number of unstressed syllables remains a variable quantity. In this sense we are justified in terming folk poetry musico-tonic [muzykal'no-toničeskij].

The study of native Russian versification, in view of its connection with music, exceeds the limits of our present study. But some general information is needed for our orientation in the question of how folk verse forms have influenced literary forms. As our example of folk poetry we shall take the *bylina*, as much because its structure is more transparent and less dependent on the melody as because of its pre-eminent influence on literary verse.

The verse line of the *bylina* has four dominant metrical stresses, two of which form the first hemistich, and two the second. The number of unstressed syllables between stresses varies (usually from one to three syllables), as does the number of syllables preceding the first stress. For the *bylina* line, as for folk poetry in general, the structure of the ending is essential: the *bylina* line generally has a two-stress ending of the dactylic type, the third stress of the verse being obliged to fall on the antepenult and the last stress on the final syllable. If the line ends on a word with a trisyllabic (dactylic) ending, the last syllable is given, in musical performance, an additional metrical stress, e.g., mátuškà, mólodèc and so on. But the same ending can consist of a two-word group with the stronger stress falling on the first and the weaker on the second, e.g.: Kiev-grad, rakitov-kust, dubovyj-stol, or: po čistu-polju, s široka-dvora, etc. In certain *byliny* there is in addition a four-syllable ending of the same type, e.g. pod óbolokì, rostét' — materét', etc. The dominant stresses of the *bylina* line must often be counted not by words but by phrase groups; it is especially common to find indissoluble phrase groups subordinated to one dominant stress, as for example: dobryj-molodec, stol'nyj-Kiev-grad, xleba-kušati, rovno-tri-časa, etc. Furthermore, the rhythmical character of the *bylina* can be greatly altered depending on the individual art of the narrator and his skill in handling the verbal material, which must be fitted into the flexible but at the same time rather strict framework of the four-stress line. It is nevertheless possible to distinguish the two most prominent types of rhythmic arrangement, which were noted (among other, less important varieties) by Gilferding.

Type 1, anapesto-iambic, with interstress intervals usually of one to two syllables. Cf. Rjabinin, *Vol'ga i Mikula*:

> ...Molodój Vol'gá Svatoslávgovič
> Posyláet on célym desjátočkòm
> On svoéj družínuški xoróbroèj
> A ko ètoj ko sóške klenóven'koj;
> Oni sóšku za obži kružkóm vertját
> Sóški ot zemlí podnját' nel'zjá,
> Ne mogut oni sóški s zemél'ki povýdernutì
> Iz omésikov zemél'ki povytrjáxnutì
> Brósit' sóški za rakítov-kùst...

Type II, trochaic, with interstress intervals usually of one or *three* syllables. In the latter case the middle syllable receives a secondary, weaker stress. Cf. Rjabinin, *Il'ja i Solovej*:

> *u* togó li górod*a* Čeríngov*à*
> N*a*gnanó to síluš*ki* čërnym-čern*ò*,
> *a* i čërnym černó kak č*e*rna vóron*à*;
> T*a*k pexótoj*u* niktó tut n*e* proxáživ*àt*,
> N*a* dobróm kon*i* niktó tut n*e* proézživ*àt*,
> Pt*i*ca čérnyj vóron n*e* prolétyv*àt*
> Séryj zvér' da n*e* prorýskiv*àt*...

Although in some *byliny* both types are preserved virtually in their standard form (especially the trochaic), one frequently comes across mixed forms, since neither within the line between stresses nor at the beginning of the line is the number of unstressed syllables strictly regulated. Cf., for example, the trochaic lines from *Vol'ga*: "on svoej družinuškɪ xorobroej" or "Brosit' soški zA rakitov-kust" or, with a dactylic beginning, "Soški ot zemli podnjat' nel'zja..." As an example of the mixed type, consider a Rjabinin *bylina* about Dunaj (interstress intervals of one, two or three syllables):

> Sadíl ix koról' za edínyj stól.
> A kormíl-to ix éstvuškoj saxárnojù,
> A póil-to ix pít'icem medvjányìm.
> Tíxomu Dunájušku Ivánovičù
> Podnosíl k nemu čáru zelená viná,
> To ne máluju stópu — poltorá vedrá.
> Tíxija Dunájuško Ivánovič,
> A skorešén'ko stavál na rezvý nožkí,
> Čáročku on brál vo belý ručkí,
> Brál to on čáročku odnój ručkój, —
> On za ètoju za čáročkoj posvátalsjà

U togó u koroljá litóvskogò,
Na egó na dóčeri ljubímoèj
Na prekrásnoej Oprákse korolévičnòj...

Of the 14 lines here only 4, 7, 11, 13 and 14 belong to the pure trochaic type (intervals of one or three syllables). Line 1 belongs to the pure anapesto-iambic type (one and two syllable intervals). The remaining eight lines belong to the "mixed" form, with intervals of one, two and three syllables. This excerpt, like the entire *bylina*, has four obligatory stresses and is completely free with regard to the number of unstressed syllables between stresses. This is without doubt the dominant form of the *bylina*.

From the point of view of metrics, a group of *byliny* relating chiefly to the historical events of the sixteenth and seventeenth centuries constitutes a special group. In this group we have a trochaic rather than dactylic ending (and, according to F. Korš, a metrical "weighting" of the final syllable). Cf. *Vzjatie Smolenska*:

Posréde-l' bylo Moskóvskogo cárstvà,
Serédi bylo rossíjska gosudárstva,
Kak u svéta u arxángela Mixájlỳ
U Ivána Velíkogo v sobórè

Or in a *bylina* entitled *Ptici*:

A i otčegó-že zimá da načalásjà,
A i krásno léto sostojálòs'?
Začalásja zimá ot morózà,
A i krásnoe léto ot sólncà,
A i bogátaja ósen' ot létà

In the distribution of unstressed syllables these *byliny* and others follow the free pattern of purely tonic verse.

Russian folk poetry began to arouse interest in the middle of the eighteenth century, but only from the end of that century can its direct influence be felt. At first, an attempt was made to measure out folk poetry into the usual syllabo-tonic feet. Tred'jakovskij, relying on folk poetry as tonic verse for the defense of his own reforms, tried to understand its principles. "In these verses feet are for the most part either trochaic, or trochaic with dactyls, or dactyls alone; also iambs, or iambs with anapests, or anapests alone; and a trochee or iamb can be freely replaced by a dactyl. I beg the reader not to take me to task and to forgive me if I quote here certain excerpts from our low but indigenous poetry: I do this only in order to cite some examples" (*Mnenie o načale poèzii*).

Among the examples cited by Tred'jakovskij, we have the following "trochaic" lines:

> Otsta- | vála | lébed' | béla- | ja
> Kak ot | stáda | lebe- | díno- | va

And "trochees with dactyls":

> U ko- | lódezja, | u stu- | dénova
> Dóbryj | mólodec | sam ko- | njá poíl,
> Krásna | dévica | vódu | čérpala...

It is understandable that the attempt to clarify the metrical principles of folk poetry by relying on the devices of syllabo-tonic versification was bound to meet with great difficulties. Thus, Samsonov, the champion of iambs over the metrical innovations of his day, writes: "In olden times not only lyric verse but also narrative verse was written. Whoever takes it into his head to search out rules for such poetry is wasting his time for nothing. The only thing that was given any attention, and that not always, was the equality of the numbers of stresses and the sameness of the endings... Certain people are grieved (about what are people sometimes not grieved?) that such verse has fallen into disuse" (*Vestnik Evropy*, 1817, XCIV, p. 252). As late as the second half of the nineteenth century Šafranov (*O sklade narodno-russkoj pesennoj reči*, 1879) thought it possible to contrast the "phonic" ("prosodic") system of the classical writers with Russian folk versification, which he called a "stylistic" ("internal") system based on parallelism, repetition, etc. And in our times Brjusov has again characterized folk poetry as "semantic versification" (based on a count of "images", and "in general of the meaningful expressions in the line"). In all such theories we see a refusal to admit the existence of any kind of metrical principle whatsoever in Russian folk poetry. At the beginning of the nineteenth century, however, Vostokov had already described Russian folk verse with complete accuracy as belonging to the purely tonic system, based on the counting of stresses, but with attention being paid only to the main stresses in "whole utterances or periods" (i.e. phrase groups). In Russian verse, writes Vostokov (*Opyt*, 105) "not feet are counted, and not syllables, but prosodic periods [in our terminology, phrase groups — V.Ž.], i.e. stresses, by which one must measure the lines of ancient Russian songs." In another place he writes: "Insofar as this meter is based neither on isosyllabism nor on a sequence of feet, dissimilarity in the number of syllables and free placement of the stresses do not constitute substantial faults or discordances in it. This license, indeed, frequently furthers the unimpeded expression of feelings... The number of stresses is the *sine qua non* on which the harmony of Russian poetry is founded." (p. 134). In the *bylina* line Vostokov sees three principal stresses, the last being placed on the antepenultimate syllable. "Three-stress lines with dactylic endings are used in Russian folk tales and narrative songs." (p. 138). In the meters of lyrics and songs he sees more stability in the number of syllables and in the placement of the stresses. "But since this order does not remain always constant in them, and the number of stresses alone is constant, they should be distinguished according to *stresses* and prosodic periods." (p. 108). Finally, Vostokov attaches great importance to the constant ending of the line in folk poetry and classifies the meters principally by means of these endings. He lays especial emphasis on the *dactylic* ending as being pre-eminently characteristic of folk poetry. Further investigations showed, however, that the so-called "dactylic ending" of the *bylina* had an additional metrical stress on the final syllable, a fact which Vostokov himself and all his contemporaries, who were acquainted with *byliny* only through books and were insufficiently experienced in music, could not have noticed. (In this connection, cf. F. Korš, *O russkom narodnom stixosloženii*, p. 8[29]).

---

[29] On Russian folk poetry, cf. the following works: A. Vostokov, *Opyt o russkom stixosloženii* (1812-17). — D. Dubjanskij, *Opyt o narodnom russkom stixosloženii* (Moscow, 1828). — I. I. Sreznevskij, "Neskol'ko zamečanij ob èpičeskom razmere slavjanskix narodnyx pesen", *Izv. Ak. Nauk. po otd. r. jaz. slov.*, vol. IX (1860-61), p. 345 ff.; cf. also the same writer's *Mysli ob istorii russkogo jazyka* (1850), pp. 105-6). — A. F. Gilferding, *Onežskie byliny* (1873), (citations from the second edition of 1894, *Sborn. otd. r. jaz. slov.*, vol. 59, preface, p. 41 ff.) — R. Vestfal', "O russkoj narodnoj pesne", (*Russkij Vestnik*, vol. 143, p. 111 ff.). — S. Šafranov, *O sklade narodno-russkoj pesennoj reči, rassmatrivaemoj v svjazi s napevami* (Petersburg, 1879). — A. S. Famincyn, "O sočinenii g. Šafranova: O sklade narodno-russkoj pesennoj reči", *Zapiski Ak. nauk*, vol. 39, 1881, appendix 8: *Otčët o 23-em prisuždenii nagrad gr. Uvarovu*, pp. 11-197). — P. Goloxvastov, "Zakony stixa russkogo narodnogo i našego literaturnogo", *Russkij Vestnik*, 156 (1881). — A. Potebnja, *Ob"jasnenija malorusskix i srodnyx narodnyx pesen* (1887), II, p. 5 ff. and 17 ff. — P. Sokal'skij, *Russkaja narodnaja muzyka* (Kharkov, 1888). — M. Xalanskij, *Južno-slavjanskoe skazanie o kraleviče Marke* (1895), vol. III, Chap. XX, p. 9. On the *Bylina* Line. — F. Korš, "O russkom narodnom stixosloženii", *Izv. otd. r. jaz. slov.*, I (1896), book 1; by the same writer, "Vvedenie v nauku o slavjanskom stixosloženii", *Stat'i po slavjanovedeniju*, vol. II (1906), pp. 300-78. — V. Brjusov, "O russkom stixosloženii", (in A. Dobroljubov's book *Sobranie stixov* (1900), Preface, pp. 8-19). — A. Maslov, *Muzykal'no-ètnografičeskie očerki*, II: *Byliny, ix proisxoždenie, ritmičeskij i melodičeskij sklad* (1910). — V. Žirmunskij, *Rifma, eë istorija i teorija* (1923), p. 265 ff. — If we agree with F. Korš that the *bylina* line has a dipodic construction, so that one stress (the first) is dominant in each hemistich, we are able to divide the works devoted to Russian verse into the following categories: 1. Vostokov, A. Maslov, and Goloxvastov, who do not take into account the metrical weighting of the final syllable and see three stresses (with a dactylic ending) in the *bylina* line; Goloxvastov considers it most normal to have a stress on the third syllable (anapestic onset), on the seventh and on the eleventh (dactylic

Like the hexameter, Russian folk verse began to be discussed at the end of the eighteenth and beginning of the nineteenth century in connection with the fight against Lomonosov's versification system. In a letter to S. S. Uvarov, V. Kapnist proposed that the Russian line should be used as the heroic measure to supplant the six-foot line and suggested that it was more suited to Russian than the hexameter. "What prevents us," he wrote to the champion of the hexameter, "from devising, in compliance with your own opinion, meters suited to our language, both for the epic and for other genres of poetry? Why should we not attempt to create a metrical scheme built on the very genius of our language?" (*Čtenie v Besede*, 1815, XVII, p. 33). And further: "We discover in our folk songs a multitude of various, delightful poetic meters suited to the expression of every sort of feeling and image..." (p. 36). To the translator of Homer, Gnedič, he proposed the replacement of the six-foot iambic line and the hexameter by the native Russian verse line and desired to see the poems of Ossian in the same metrical form. Vostokov's book *Opyt o russkom stixosloženii* (1812-1817) follows the same practical goal of finding new ways to free Russian literary versification from the fetters of Lomonosov's system. He recommended "the narrative [*skazočnyj*] Russian line" for "*romance* poems in the manner of Ariosto or Wieland" and wanted to introduce their imitators to that true diversity in the distribution of stresses which was inherent in folk poetry and which had been assimilated neither by Karamzin (*Il'ja Muromec*) nor by Xeraskov (several chapters of *Baxariana*).

---

ending) with a normal complement of 13 syllables. 2. I. Sreznevskij, Potebnja, P. Sokal'skij, and M. Xalanskij speak of two principal stresses, one in each hemistich; Xalanskij defines the usual position of these stresses as the third syllable from the beginning (anapestic onset) and the third from the end (dactylic ending). (cf. p. 785) I. Sreznevskij and especially A. Potebnja regard as particularly significant the syntactic unity of the hemistich and the line ("syntactic foot" in the terminology of Potebnja). P. Sokal'skij emphasizes "the inequality of the number of syllables in the hemistichs, each of which has one dominant stress": "This gives rise to a sort of *balancing* of stress in two groups of words which are close but not altogether equivalent..." (p. 264). 3. Šafranov and V. Brjusov refuse to posit an absolute regularity in the distribution of stresses in folk verse and rather emphasize the stylistic elements (parallelism, the count of "significant words", and "images"). As a matter of fact, however, those "significant expressions" or "integral concepts," of which Brjusov speaks ("okean-more, tugoj-luk", etc.) virtually coincide with accentual groups. 4. Gilferding defines the fundamental rhythmical types of the *bylina* line with the aid of the traditional syllabo-tonic schemes (cf. also Dubenskij, p. 54 ff.); he regards "deviations" as the result of the decline of the song tradition. 5. F. Korš and, in particular, R. Vestfal' try to study the structure of the line in connection with the rhythmical structure of its melody, and they deal with the temporal length of the syllables partly in terms of classical quantitative meters.

35. IMITATIONS OF FOLK POETRY

As a matter of fact, the first imitators of folk poetry did not dare or were not able to reproduce the rhythmical variety of the pure tonic line and used in their stylized verse the trochaic tetrameter with a dactylic ending. Thus Karamzin in *Il'ja Muromec* (1794), Xeraskov in *Baxariana* (1802), the young Puškin in *Bova* (1815) and many others. And earlier than any of the others, Sumarokov in his songs (cf. XIX):

> Ó ty krépkij, krépkij Bénder grad,
> Ó razúmnyj, xrábryj Pánin graf,
> Ždët Evrópa čúda slávnova,
> Ždët Rossíja slávy nóvyja,
> Cár' Turéckij í ne dúmaet,
> Čtóby Bénder býlo vzjáti l'zja...

It was in A. L'vov's *Dobrynja* (printed in 1804) that there appeared for the first time an important modification of the basic trochaic meter through the introduction of a strong caesura with a dactyl preceding it — a meter which was to be adapted to Russian poetry by Kol'cov:

> Ó temná, temna | noč' osénnjaja!
> Strášen v tëmnu noč' | i dremučij lés!
> Výjdu, výjdu ja | v pole čístoe
> I poklón otdav | na vse stórony
> Slóvo výmolvlju | bogatýrskoe...

Thus Vostokov in his *Opyt* (1817) was justified in reproaching lovers of Russian poetry for their having chosen, out of all the Russian meters, only the "song" meter, which is "too short and monotonous for large narrative compositions" (p. 162). Vostokov's own experiments (*Rossijskie reki*, 1813; *Izrečenija Konfucija*, taken from Schiller, 1817) show that he had more than a mere theoretical command of pure tonic verse. Cf. *Rossijskie reki*:

> Bespečál'no tekí Volga-mátuška,
> Čerez vsjú svjatúju Rus' do sinjá-morja;
> Čtob ne píl, ne mutíl tebja ljútyj vrag
> Ne bagríl svoeju króv'ju pogánoju,
> Ni nogój on ne toptál beregóv tvoix,
> I v glazá ne vidál tvoix čístyx struj!

As an example of the adaptation of the *bylina* meter to a large epic written in the folk style, cf. Lermontov's *Pesnja pro kupca Kalašnikova* (1837):

> Liš' odín iz níx, | iz opríčnikov,
> Udalój boéc, | dobryj mólodec,

V zolotóm kovšé | ne močíl usov,
Opustíl on v zémlju oči tëmnye
Opustíl golóvušku na šíróku grud',
A v grudí ego bylá duma krépkaja.
Vot naxmúril cár' brovi čërnye
I navël na negó oči zórkie,
Slovno jástreb vzgljanúl s vysotý nebes
Na mladógo gólubja sizokrýlogo, —
Da ne pódnjal gláz molodój boec...

Here the line has three obligatory stresses and a constant dactylic ending. The fourth stress on the last syllable in oral rendering cannot be heard distinctly, but the two-stress ending usually found in *byliny* is reflected in compound endings such as ne močil usov, s vysoty nebes, molodoj boec na široku grud', etc., which are placed on an equal with regular dactyls (iz opričnikov, molodec, etc.). The use of these compound endings as the equivalent of dactyls is a characteristic of all imitations of folk poetry (cf. Sumarokov's "Bender-grad, Panin-graf", L'vov's "dremučij les", Vostokov's "ljutyj vrag, čistyx struj" and so on. As in the *bylina*, Lermontov's poem combines indivisible phrase groups under one dominant, metrical stress: oči-tëmnye, oči-zorkie, etc. Our clear perception of the metrical break (caesura) in the middle of the line is aided by the circumstance that in a great part of the lines this cut immediately follows the stress, as in "Liš' odín iz níx | iz opríčnikov... (cf. lines 1-3, 6-9, 11). On the whole, however, the caesura remains mobile and consequently the rhythmical variety characteristic of the *bylina* is preserved: e.g., feminine caesura "Opustíl on v zémlju | oči tëmnye" or dactylic caesura "Na mladógo gólubja | sizokrýlogo..." Almost without exception, the line begins with an anapest (a practice widespread in the *byliny* also). The predominating pattern for the unstressed groups of syllables between stresses is rhythmically close to the anapesto-iambic type of line: $- - \acute{} - \acute{} | - - \acute{} - -$. Cf. above:

Liš' odín iz níx | iz opríčnikov
Udalój boéc | dobryj mólodec
V zolotóm kovšé | ne močíl usov...

In lines of this type both hemistichs have the same number of syllables, which becomes especially noticeable when the stress preceding the caesura is weakened and both halves end on a dactyl (as in the poetry of L'vov at an earlier time):

...Moja mílaja | dragocénnaja!
Xočeš' zólota, | xočeš' žémčuga...

Or:

> Opozóril on, | osramíl menja,
> Menja čéstnuju, | neporóčnuju

But in this case also the required rhythmic variety is preserved by using a great many lines in which the metrical pattern is implemented in varying ways.

In the songs of Kol'cov this favored variation of the *bylina* line shown above became the dominant metrical scheme. As a composer of lyrical verse, Kol'cov thus arrived at the same isosyllabism which Vostokov believed dominant in the folk song. For example:

> Krasnym pólymem |
>   zarja vspýxnula; ||
> Po licú zemli |
>   tuman stéletsja. ||
> Razgorélsja den' |
>   ognëm sólnečnym; ||
> Podobrál tuman |
>   vyše témja gor; ||
> Nagustíl ego ||
>   v tuču čërnuju || ...

The *bylina* "anapesto-iambic" line here falls into two independent small lines (hemistichs). Both small lines have the obligatory dactylic ending, which is frequently compound, i.e., contains a monosyllabic or disyllabic word with a secondary stress, e.g.: razgorélsja-dèn', podobrál tumàn, po licú zemlì, etc. There is usually also a secondary stress at the beginning of the line on the first or second syllable. If it is on the first syllable we have a sort of trochaic dimeter with a dactylic ending, e.g. Krásnym pólymem... V túču čërnuju. Owing to the stress on the last syllable one could regard individual lines as trochaic trimeter with a truncated masculine ending, e.g. Vyše temja gor... Of course, the trochaic pattern also fits those lines which do not have a stress on the first two syllables: po licú zemli, razgorélsja den', nagustíl tuman... etc. Against the background of this predominant rhythmical cadence, lines which have a stress on the second syllable are felt as deviant; such cases might be regarded as the transposition of the stress of the first foot, which was customary in trochees of the folk variety, e.g.: Zarjá vspýxnula ... Tumán stéletsja... Ognëm sólnečnym (like Slugá i xozjáin, cf. p. 55). Kol'cov's metrical pattern could have been transcribed thus: $\doteq - \acute{-} - \doteq$, where the dot above the syllable mark indicates a weaker, optional stress. On the whole, however, the trochaic rhythm remains nothing more than the overriding rhythmical cadence, while the only obligatory metrical features are the constant number of syllables and the constant stress on the third syllable.

Of the other meters found in Kol'cov's folk songs, the most usual are easily fitted into the traditional syllabo-tonic patterns. We have on the one hand the trochaic trimeter with feminine ending ("Nú taščísja, sívka..."), with the characteristic displacement of the stress of the first foot (cf. § 9 above, e.g. Slugá i xozjáin...); and on the other hand, anapests with dactylic ending in the odd lines ("Osedlaju konja, konja býstrogo..."). Nikitin follows Kol'cov in this respect.

In Russian poetry the three-stress line with feminine ending, widespread in the *byliny* of the sixteenth and seventeenth centuries, had a special fate. This meter was reproduced by Puškin in his *Skazka o rybake i rybke*:

> *Žil* starík so svoéju starúxoj
> U sámogo sínego mórja;
> *Oni* žíli v vétxoj zemljánke
> *Rovno* trídcat' lét i tri góda.
> Starík *lovil* nevodom rýbu
> Starúxa prjála *svoju* prjážu.
> *Raz* on v móre zakínul névod:
> *Prišël* névod s odnóju tínoj;
> *On* v drugój raz zakínul névod:
> *Prišël* névod s travój morskóju
> *V tretij* ráz zakínul on nevod:
> *Prišël* névod s zolotóju rýbkoj...

The individuality of Puškin's line consists not simply in the very free treatment accorded the unstressed syllables; it is principally to be seen in the broad use of phrase-stress, as much as of word-stress. Cf. for example: lovil-nevodom, prišël-nevod, svoju-prjažu. These cases are like the "weighting" of metrically weak syllables in the ternary meters or *dol'niki* and in reading they can be either made somewhat more distinct or subordinated to the dominant metrical stress. "Weighting" of this kind is most noticeable at the beginning of the line (cf. the supplementary stressing of the first syllable of the anapest): e.g., *Žil*-starik so svoeju staruxoj... *Rovno* tridcat' let i tri goda... *V tretij* raz zakinul on nevod. In general, they lend Puškin's tale that broken, almost prosaic, colloquial rhythm which best complies with the artistic intention of the "tale": the metrical scheme is half hidden, it does not stand out so clearly as in the lyric *dol'niki*, but this excerpt nevertheless shows that the inertia of the stress is sufficient to preserve the perception of rhythm.

As Korš and, later, Sergej Bobrov pointed out, the same line was used in the *Pesni zapadnyx slavjan*, with the difference that there are even more supplementary stresses on metrically weak syllables than in the "tale". Cf.:

> *Korol'* xódit bol'šími šagámi
> Vzád i vperëd po palátam;
> *Ljudi* spját — koroljú liš' ne spítsja,
> Koroljá sultán osaždáet,
> Gólovu otséč' *emu* grozitsja
> I v Stambúl otoslat' *eë* xóčet...

Or:

> Radivój *podnjal* žëltoe známja:
> On idët vojnój na basurmána.
> A dalmáty, zavídja *naše* vójsko,
> *Svoi* dlínnye usy zakrutíli,
> Na bekrén' nadéli *svoi* šápki,
> I skazali: "Voz'míte *nas* s sobóju...

Here also one can observe examples of light stress such as otseč'-emu grozitsja, otoslat'-eë xočet, naše-vojsko, svoi-šapki; this sort of thing is common both in *dol'niki* and in the ternary meters. Alongside these we have heavier stresses: korol'-xodit, ljudi-spjat, podnjal-žëltoe znamja. However, the rhythmic inertia of the excerpt as a whole keeps even these supplementary stresses subordinated to the general pattern.

The opinion has been expressed (by B. V. Tomaševskij in his article *O stixe Pesen zapadnyx slavjan*) that Puškin based his metrical experiments on the trochaic pentameter of Serbian songs, and that trochaic pentameter is indeed the meter of these poems also. But the trochaic pattern could be applied to the excerpts cited here only if one were willing to admit every possible kind of deviation from the pattern, including deviation in the number of syllables. The three-stress system, however, regardless of the additional stresses on metrically weak syllables (fairly common even in *dol'niki*) is maintained throughout the *Pesni zapadnyx slavjan* without any deviation whatsoever. And finally, this theory is also to be refuted as regards the origin of Puškin's meter in the *Pesni*. It is probable that Puškin was not so much reproducing his own direct impression of the Serbian song meter as he was following the example and authority of Vostokov, who between the years 1825-1827 published translations of Serbian songs (from the collection of Karadžić) which employed the same meter (three-stress line with feminine ending) as that seen in the later experiments of Puškin.[30] I am inclined to believe

---

[30]   On Vostokov's translations of Serbian songs, cf. *Sev. cvety*, 1825, p. 331 ff.; 1826, p. 43 ff; 1827, p. 269 ff.; *Sorevnovatel' Prosveščenija* (1825), p. 169 ff. Cf. Vostokov's own statement (*Sev. cvety*, 1825, p. 337): "In the Serbian original the meter is trochaic

that these translations of Vostokov provide the immediate source for the metrical form of the *Skazka o rybake i rybke* and the *Pesni zapadnyx slavjan*. Cf., for example, this excerpt (from *Severnye cvety*, 1827, p. 269):

> Poslúšajte póvesti čúdnoj!
> Dočeréj u máteri dévjat'.
> Desjátoju berémenna xódit.
> Boga mólit, čtob mál'čik rodílsja...

Anna Axmatova's poem *U samogo morja* is metrically related to Puškin's *Skazka o rybake i rybke*. This poem is written in a four-stress line with a feminine ending (in some sections a three-stress line is used). Its essential difference from Puškin's style consists in the use of one or two-syllable interstress intervals, as in the lyrical *dol'niki*. And certain basic rhythmical cadences prevail, so that the verse tends toward a logaoedic structure. For example: two dactyls + two trochees:

> Búxty izrézali tëmnyj béreg.
> Vsé parusá ubežáli v móre...

Or:

> Kak ja leglá u vodý — ne pómnju,
> Kak zadremála togdá — ne znáju...

In this verse the supplementary stresses on metrically weak syllables are absent, but on the other hand we have, alongside the principle of syllable-counting between stresses, that characteristic feature of syllabo-tonic versification — the omission of metrical stresses. Cf.:

> *A* nad lampádoj stojál vysóko
> Úzkij malínovyj *ogonëček...*

Or:

> Sólnce ležálo na dné kolódca,
> Grélis' na kámnjax sk*a*lopendry

---

pentameter, with the break at the second foot... In order to preserve the force of the original, the translator has deemed it unnecessary slavishly to follow this meter, which is not used by us and which for Russian verse is perhaps rather tiresome. He has preferred to use a Russian meter of three stresses with a trochaic ending." Cf. also *Sev. cvety*, (1827), p. 277, in the translation of the *Žalobnaja pesnja blagorodnoj Asan-Aginicy* (cf. *Pesni zapadn. slavjan*, No. 17): "We make use here of the Russian narrative meter, with a dactylic ending..." (i.e., the *bylina* line). Nor does A. Jacimirskij (*Puškin*, ed. S. A. Vengerov, vol. III, p. 375 ff.) speak of the possibility of Vostokov's having had any influence on Puškin as regards meter. F. Korš considers the meter of the *Pesni* and of the *Skazka o rybake i rybke* in his article "Razbor voprosa o podlinnosti okončanija Rusalki", *Izv. otd. r. jaz. slov.*, vol. III (1896), Bk. 1, p. 737 ff.). Cf. also *O russkom narodnom stixosloženii*, p. 32 ff., note 25; S. Bobrov, *Novoe o stixosloženii Puškina*, p. 9 ff. and p. 32. Puškin's first attempt at this meter belongs to the year 1827 ("Kormom, stojlami, nadzorom...").

Among the imitations of folk meters, a special place is reserved for the rhymed tonic verse of *Skazka o Balde*. Gogol' asserted that this tale was "even written without meter, only with rhymes". According to L. I. Polivanov "this tale is an example of that *syllabic* verse (?) used in the satyrical legends written under cheap, popular prints. This kind of verse is *syllabic* (?), but since the number of *syllables* in each line is *arbitrary* (!), it might justly be regarded as *cut-up prose* (!) and differs from that only by rhymes, which are for the most part paired." Academician F. E. Korš says "*Balda* is not poetry, but rhymed prose, like the patter of peep-show comedians..."[31] *Skazka o Balde* is nevertheless written in a purely tonic meter, like other compositions in the folk style, the essential difference being that the number of stresses in the line may vary (as in the free iambics of Krylov or, in modern times, in the poetry of Maja-kovskij). Cf:

> ...Vot, móre krugóm obežávši,
> Vysunuv jazýk, mórdku podnjávši,
> Pribežál besënok zadyxájas',
> Vés' mokréšenok, lápkoj utirájas',
> Mýslja: délo s Baldóju sládit.
> Gljád', — a Baldá brátca gládit,
> Prigovárivaja: "Brátec moj ljubímyj,
> Ustál, bednjážka! Otdoxní, rodímyj!
> Besënok otoropél,
> Xvóstik podžál, sovsém prismirél,
> Na brátca pogljádyvaet bókom
> "Pogodí," govorít, "sxožú za obrókom"...

Thanks to the rhymes coupling adjacent lines and to the precise syntactic divisions (almost without any enjambment), the line boundaries (like those of Majakovskij) are clearly felt. The comparatively limited number of unstressed syllables between stresses (one or two, more rarely three syllables, with very rare cases of two adjacent stresses) prevents the line from falling apart and facilitates our perception of accentual groups as equivalent rhythmic units. Moreover, the rhymed couplets are frequently bound together by rhythmic and syntactic parallelism, e.g.:

> ..."Kobýlu podymí-ka tý,
> Da nesí eë polverstý:
> Snesëš' kobýlu — obrók už tvój;
> Ne snesëš' kobýly — on búdet mój"
> Bédnen'kij bés

---

[31]   Cf. S. Bobrov, *op. cit.*, pp. 30-31, where suitable examples are cited.

Pod kobýlu podléz,
Ponatúžilsja,
Ponaprúžilsja,
Pripodnjáv kobýlu, dva šága šagnúl,
Na trét'em upál, nóžki protjanúl...

Thus the rhythmical equilibrium is maintained in the verse, where both the number of stresses and the number of syllables between stresses can change from line to line (as in Majakovskij in modern times).

CONCLUSION

36. GENERAL CONCLUSIONS

Examples of tonic verse with an uneven number of stresses, as for instance in Majakovskij's poetry or in *Skazka o Balde*, confront us with the theoretical importance of the question about the *minimal* conditions distinguishing verse from prose. Pure tonic verse is based on the counting of stresses over a variable number of syllables, but in Puškin's *Skazka* and in Majakovskij the number of syllables varies together with the number of stresses: by what criteria is this verse to be distinguished from an ordinary excerpt of literary prose? The answer to this question is arrived at by comparing those examples of modern poetry in which the *maximal* conditions of metrical organization are observed.

The example of Bal'mont quoted at the beginning of the book ("Ona otdalas' bez uprëka...") demonstrates the possibility of a metrical organization close to such a maximum. The stresses are repeated after every two syllables in keeping with a metrical rule; the number of syllables in the line is constant; each line has an end rhyme, which clearly denotes the end of that line and its relationship to others within the same stanzaic unit; syntactically, the line is coterminous with an independent sentence, linked to neighboring lines by repetition and parallelism; even in the organization of the sound pattern there appear certain secondary features of metrical order. Of course, this sort of verse too has its variations — not only in the qualitative selection of sounds but also in their purely rhythmical distribution according to semantic groups (the arrangement of word boundaries), and in the relative strength of the metrical stresses. But, in addition, it must be borne in mind that this is poetic rhythm; that is to say, the syllabic components and the interstress groups need not be absolutely isochronous: the rhythmical quality is determined by the count of the syllables, by their sequence in a definite order. This is the first violation of absolute structural equilibrium in verse, the violation of the musical principle of counting by bars, and it is a feature of all speech rhythm.

The example from *Evgenij Onegin* ("Moj djadja samyx čestnyx pravil...") exhibits a further violation, or more exactly, a modification of the original equilibrium of the syllabo-tonic line. In these lines one finds omissions of metrical stresses now on one, now on another, of the even syllables. In the poem as a whole, however, the stress tends always to fall on the even positions, and for that reason there is established in our consciousness the norm of an iambic framework, a metrical intent which determines the perception of each individual line, as subordinated to the general metrical pattern. Here also the overriding isosyllabism, the break-down of syntactic divisions into lines, and the use of rhyme as a terminal signal play an essential role in creating the impression of the line as a metrically organized unit. We know, however, that the syntactic equili-brium can be disrupted (or rather, modified) by the presence of enjamb-ment, that within the stanza end rhymes can unite lines of differing length, which may not only alternate according to a strict rule within the stanza but also follow each other in a purely arbitrary fashion, as in the free iambics of Krylov's fables or Griboedov's *Gore ot uma*.

A further sort of disruption of the original equilibrium arises when the number of unstressed syllables between stresses becomes, as in purely tonic verse, a variable quantity. Here there is established an equality between accentual groups united by a stress but varying in the number of syllables. In the so-called *dol'niki*, where the number of interstress syl-lables is more or less constant (from one to two), it is considerably easier to feel the equivalence of such groups (regardless of how such equivalence is achieved in oral recitation). In those cases where each accentual group comprises a large and at the same time arbitrary number of unstressed syllables, our rhythmical sense is faced with a more difficult task: that is why we feel the presence in such verse of something like rhythmical interruptions, which make it resemble the unequal "rhythm" of colloquial speech. But our rhythmic *consciousness* can overcome this obstacle and learn to build an artistically composed rhythmic whole out of complicated and contradictory material; we can even take special pleasure in the difficulty and internal complexity of such a new form. Here, of course, an especially important role must be played by the secondary factors of metrical composition: the precise coordination of lines and syntactic units, the type of metrical clausula, and especially rhyme as a means of uniting the rhythmical lines into a structural unit of a higher order (the stanza).

If one admits in principle the possibility of a line in which a sequence of metrically even stresses, dominating uneven accentual groups, is felt to be *rhythmically equivalent*, then one should find nothing surprising in the fact that it is also possible to have stanzas which, composed of lines based on this same (tonic) principle, permit — precisely as in the free iambics of the eighteenth and early nineteenth century — the alternation of rhythmical sequences of uneven length, e.g. three lines of four stresses each, followed by a shorter fourth line having only two or three stresses. And this is exactly what we have in the verse of Majakovskij or in the *Skazka o Balde*. Our feeling that such verse is rhythmical is based on our lengthy acquaintance with poetic form, which has gradually taught us to get along without a great many of the most elementary features of rhythmical equilibrium — syllable counting, equal number of stresses in adjacent lines, and so on. As a result of such training we can learn to accept as rhythmical a form of speech that has been systematically deprived of all those signs which originally served as the basis of our rhythmical perception.[1] True, there remain certain important secondary elements of metrical organization: the syntactic divisions used to underscore line boundaries, and rhymes as a means of separating stanzas. In many poems of Majakovskij, if we were to throw out the rhymes without changing the syllable structure, and shift the syntactic boundaries around by the use of enjambment, we would lose the last support for any perception of rhythm, and the whole edifice, thus deprived of its equilibrium, would disintegrate completely.

Thus, if we approach Majakovskij or *Skazka o Balde* with a view to the external, objective criteria of rhythm, we must recognize that the secondary elements of metrical organization have usurped the place of the primary elements, of "meter". "Meter" is indicated only by the presence of a certain sequence of accentual groups which our rhythmic instinct accepts as equal ($x \perp x \perp x \perp ...$). There is no doubt that the prose of Gogol', Turgenev or Tolstoj might yield passages which, as regards number of syllables and placement of stresses, would coincide with an excerpt of Majakovskij's verse, e.g., with a loosely constructed stanza

---

[1] We find a similar disruption of external equilibrium in, for example, French verse, which does not have constant stresses, and which, moreover, in actual pronunciation, frequently ignores the mute "e" and thereby discards the prime feature of the "syllabic system", the constant number of syllables. Cf. Landry, p. 273. The same thing applies to English "iambic pentameter", where one finds not only "omissions" and "displacements" of stresses (approximating the "syllabic" system of the Romance languages), but also fluctuations in the length of the interstress intervals and, consequently, in the total number of syllables per line (disruption of the syllabic principle).

having a sequence of lines in which the stresses number $4 + 3 + 2 + 1$. It would, of course, be more difficult to find such parallels for a whole group of stanzas, inasmuch as the verse of Majakovskij (like that of *Skazka o Balde*) undoubtedly shows a marked preference for the three or four-stress line — its "norm" to a certain degree. If, however, we limit our comparison to one stanza, we discover a distinction not so much in the objective accentual features of the material itself as in the different *orientation* of our perception. Where we feel constrained to relate a certain alternation of stresses to an ideal norm, conceived as a sequence of identical elements, we have poetry, though it be poetry of the loosest possible construction. Where we feel no such constraint, we have prose. One could undoubtedly interpret a sample of artistic prose by Gogol' or Turgenev, even a newspaper article, as free verse, analyzing it into syntactic groups of unequal length, and reading them as a series of shorter and longer rhythmical lines. That it is possible for a developed rhythmic consciousness to see a rhythmical strain in any sample of prose has been shown by Ed. Sievers, for example, and by others investigating spoken language.[2] In the prose sample itself, however, no objective features constrain one to do this if the syntactic groups vary sharply in their number of stresses and syllables. A slight compulsion appears in so-called rhythmical prose under the influence of syntactic parallelism, which marks the first signs of a rhythmico-structural grouping of the verbal material.[3] In Majakovskij's poetry and in Puškin's *Skazka* there is such an objective necessity principally thanks to the rhymes and the syntactic grouping and also thanks to a certain levelling of the rhythmical sequences (the "norm" being the three or four-stress lines): for a reader brought up on the verse culture of our century, these features immediately indicate the metrical composition and the measures of a poem.

[2] Cf. Ed. Sievers, *Grundzüge der Phonetik*, § 721 (p. 266), where he speaks of the "tendency of prose to fall into rhythmic patterns", which appears in the urge "to break speech up into fragments which are approximately identical in their temporal length." Landry, pp. 77-78, on the "illusion" of isochronism; cf. note 12.

[3] On the role of syntactic grouping in "free verse", cf. *Kompozicija liričeskix stixotvorenii*, p. 87 ff. On the same question cf. in particular M. Liddell, p. 155 ff. (with regard to Whitman); and also A. Potebnja, *Ob"jasnenija malorusskix i srodnyx narodnyx pesen*, II (1887), p. 5 and 17 ff. (on the "syntactic foot").

BIBLIOGRAPHY

The author has had at his disposal the following works on the general history and theory of verse:

German Metrics:

H. Paul, "Deutsche Metrik", *Grundr. d. germ. Philol.*, Bd. II (Strassburg, 1905²), Abt. 2, Abschn. VII, 39-140.
J. Minor, *Neuhochdeutsche Metrik* (Strassburg, 1902²) (with detailed bibliography).
Fr. Saran, *Deutsche Verslehre* (Munich, 1907).
Rud. Westphal, *Theorie der neuhochdeutschen Metrik* (1870).

English Metrics:

J. Schipper, *Altenglische Metrik* (Bonn, 1881).
J. Schipper, *Neuenglische Metrik*, Bd. I-II (Bonn, 1888).
G. Saintsbury, *A History of English Prosody*, Vols. I-III (London, 1908 ff.).
G. Saintsbury, *Manual of English Prosody* (London, 1922).
Mark Liddel, *An Introduction to the Scientific Study of English Poetry* (London, 1902).
T. S. Omond, *English Metrists* (Oxford, 1921) (a review of metrical theories).
L. Abercrombie, *Principles of English Prosody* (London, 1923).
Robert Bridges, *Milton's Prosody*, revised edition (Oxford, 1921).
The articles of Prof. J. B. Mayor and Alex J. Ellis dealing with English metrics in the *Transactions of the Philological Society*, 1873-74, 75-76, 77-78.
W. Skeat, *The Complete Works of G. Chaucer* (Oxford, 1894), "General Introduction", §§ 98-119 on versification.

French Poetry:

L. Becq de Fourquières, *Traité général de versification française* (Paris, 1879).
Ad. Tobler, *Vom französischen Versbau alter und neuer Zeit* (Leipzig, 1903⁴).
L. E. Kastner, *A History of French Versification* (Oxford, 1903).
M. Grammont, *Le vers français, ses moyens d'expression, son harmonie* (Paris, 1913).
M. Grammont, *Petit traité de versification française* (Paris, 1908).
Fr. Saran, *Der Rhythmus des französischen Verses* (Heidelberg, 1904).
Thieme, *Essai sur l'histoire du vers français* (1916) (with bibliography).
A. Cassagne, *Versification et métrique de Ch. Baudelaire* (Paris, 1906).
Edm. Stengel, "Romanische Verslehre", *Grundr. d. roman. Philol.*, Bd. II, 1 (1902¹).

Old Germanic Poetry:

Ed. Sievers, *Altgermanische Verslehre* (1893).

A. Heusler, *Über germanischen Versbau* (1894).
A. Heusler, *Zur Geschichte der altdeutschen Verskunst* (Breslau, 1891).

Experimental Phonetics:

E. Brücke, *Die physiologischen Grundlagen der neuhochdeutschen Verskunst* (Vienna, 1871).
Paul Verrier, *Essai sur les principes de la métrique anglaise*, Vols. I-III (Paris, 1909-10) (also contains a general theory of English verse).
Eugene Landry, *La théorie du rythme et le rythme du français déclamé* (Paris, 1911).

Experimental Psychology:

W. Wundt, *Grundzüge der physiologischen Psychologie*, Bd. III (1905), Kap. 15, 16 (pp. 1-94, 154-175).
E. Meumann, *Untersuchungen zur Psychologie und Aesthetik des Rhythmus* (= *Philos. Studien*, Bd. X) (Leipzig, 1894).

The most important works on the theory of Russian Verse:

Theoreticians of the eighteenth century:

V. Tred'jakovskij, *Novyj i kratkij sposob k složeniju Rossijskix Stixov* (1735) (quotations from the edition of A. Kunik, *Sbornik materialov dlja istorii Akademii Nauk v XVIII v.*, 1865, p. 17 ff.).
M. Lomonosov, *Pis'mo o pravilax rossijskogo stixotvorstva* (1739).
V. Tred'jakovskij, *Sposob k složeniju Rossijskix Stixov protiv vydannogo v 1735 g. ispravlennyj i dopolnennyj* (quotations from the edition of A. Smirdin, Vol. I, p. 123 ff.).
Of Tred'jakovskij's other writings cf. in particular: *O drevnem, srednem i novom stixotvorenii rossijskom* and *Mnenie o načale poèzii* (*op. cit.*, vol. I); cf. also his prefaces to *Tilemaxida* and *Argenida*.
Prince Antiox Kantemir, *Pis'mo k prijatelju o složenii stixov russkix* (*Sočinenija*, ed. P. Perevlesskij, 1849, p. 55 ff.).
A. Sumarokov, *O stoposloženii* and *Otvet na kritiku* (*Sočinenija*, Vol. X, p. 50 ff. and p. 96 ff.)
A. Radiščev, *Apologija Tilemaxidy i šestistopov* (*Sobr. sočinenij*, Moscow, 1811, Vol. IV, p. 74 ff.) and *Putešestvie iz Peterburga v Moskvu* (the chapter entitled "Tver'").

Theoreticians of the early nineteenth century:

A. Vostokov, "Opyt o russkom stixosloženii" (first published in the *Sanktpeterburgskij Vestnik*, 1812, part II, p. 39 ff., p. 68 ff., p. 271 ff.; quotations from the second edition of 1817, which was augmented by *Kritičeskoe obozrenie stoposložnyx razmerov, upotrebitel'nyx v Rossijskom stixotvorstve*, pp. 34-65).
Dor. Samsonov, "Kratkoe rassuždenie o russkom stixosloženii", *Vestnik Evropy*, XCIV (1817), p. 219 ff.
Slovar' drevnej i novoj poèzii, ed. N. Ostolopov, parts I-III (1821).
D. Dybenskij, *Opyt o narodnom russkom stixosloženii* (Moscow, 1828).
N. N. Nadeždin, the article "Versifikacija" in *Enciklopedičeskij Leksikon Pljušara*, vol. IX, (1837), pp. 501-18.

Of the scientific investigations of versification during the second half of the 19th century, the only outstanding ones are as follows:

R. Vestfal', "Iskusstvo i ritm", *Russkij Vestnik*, vol. 147 (1880), p. 241 ff.; "Teorija ritma v primenenii k russkim poètam", *Russkij Vestnik*, vol. 154 (1881), p. 154; "O russkoj narodnoj pesne", *Russkij Vestnik*, vol. 143, (1879), p. 111 ff.

P. Goloxvastov, "Zakony stixa russkogo narodnogo i našego literaturnogo", *Russkij Vestnik*, vol. 156 (1881), and also in *Pamjatniki drevnej pis'mennosti*, vol. 45 (1882).

F. A. Korš, "Vvedenie v nauku o slavjanskom stixosloženii", in *Stat'i po slavjanove-deniju*, published by Akademija nauk no. II (1906), pp. 300-78; "O russkom narodnom stixosloženii", *Izv. otd. r. jaz. slov. Akademii nauk*, 1896, vol. I, Bk. 1; "Razbor voprosa o podlinnosti okončanija 'Rusalki' A. S. Puškina", *Izv. otd. r. jaz. slov.*, 1898, vol. III, Bk. I, pp. 633-785; "Plan issledovanija o stixosloženii Puškina i slovarja Puškinskix rifm", *P. sovr.*, III (1905), p. 111 ff.

The following books are school textbooks:

V. Klassovskoj, *Versifikacija* (1863).
P. Perevlesskij, *Russkoe stixosloženie* (1853).
M. Brodovskij, *Rukovodstvo k stixosloženiju* (1895).

The Most Recent Studies:

A. Belyj, *Simvolizm* (1910).
S. Bobrov, *Novoe o stixosloženii A. S. Puškina* (Moscow, 1916); *Zapiski stixotvorca* (Moscow, 1916).
Božidar, *Raspevočnoe edinstvo* (Moscow, 1916) (edited with commentary by S. Bobrov).
Val. Brjusov, *Nauka o stixe* (Moscow, 1919) (in the second edition: *Osnovy stixovede-nija*, Giz., 1924; *Opyty* (Moscow, 1918) (Preface and notes); *Stixotvornaja texnika Puškina* (in the collected works of Puškin, ed. S. A. Vengerov, vol. VI, p. 349 ff.); "Ob odnom voprose ritma" (à propos Belyj's *Simvolism*).
D. G. Gincburg, *O russkom stixosloženii. Opyt issledovanija ritmičeskogo stroja stixotvorenij Lermontova* (with a preface by G. M. Knjazev) (Petersburg, 1915).
V. Žirmunskij, *Kompozicija liričeskix stixotvorenij* (Petersburg, 1921); *Rifma, eë istorija i teorija* (Petersburg, 1923).
N.V. Nedobrovo, "Ritm, metr i ix vzaimootnošenie", *Trudy i Dni*, 1912, No. 2.
B. V. Tomaševskij, *Russkoe stixosloženie* (1923); "Problemy stixotvornogo ritma", *Liter. Mysl'*, 1923, II, p. 124 ff.; "Ritmika četyrëxstopnogo jamba po nabljude-nijam nad stixom Evgenija Onegina", *P. sovr.*, XXIX-XXX, (1918), p. 144 ff.; "Pjatistopnyj iamb Puškina" (in the collection *Očerki po poetike Puškina*, Berlin, 1923); "O ritme *Pesen zapadnyx slavjan*", *Apollon*, 1916, II; "Stixotvornaja texnika Puškina" (à propos an article by V. Brjusov, *P. sovr.*, XXIX-XXX, p. 131 ff.
V. Čudovskij, "Neskol'ko myslej k vosmožnomu učeniju o stixe", *Apollon*, 1915, VIII-IX; "Neskol'ko utverždenij o russkom stixe", *op. cit.*, 1917, IV-V; "O ritme Puškinskoj *Rusalki*", *op. cit.*, 1914, I-II; "Zametka o *Putnike* Brjusova", *op. cit.*, 1911, II.
G. Šengeli, *Traktat o russkom stixe* (Odessa, 1921) (quotations from the second edition, 1923).
R. Jakobson, "Brjusovskaja stixilogija i nauka o stixe", *Naučnye izvestija*, No. 2 (Moscow, 1922), pp. 222-240; "O čéšskom stixe, preimuščestvenno v sopostavlenii s russkim", 1923.
N. Šul'govskij, *Teorija i praktika poètičeskogo tvorčestva* (Petersburg, 1914) (a school textbook).

B. Jakubs'kij, *Nauka viršuvannja* (Kiev, 1922) (in Ukrainian; contains the most complete bibliography of Russian metrics.)

For the years 1900 to 1922 cf. I. Ajzenštok and I. Kaganov, *Ukazatel' literatury po poètike* (in the appendix to *Poètika* by Müller-Freienfels, translation edited by A. I. Beleckij, Kharkov, 1923).

The bibliography of works dealing with Russian folk poetry, the hexameter, and logaoedic verse will be found in footnote 23 on p. 212, and 29 on p. 228.

SLAVISTIC PRINTINGS AND REPRINTINGS

Edited by C. H. van Schooneveld

22. NIKOLAI DURNOVO: Očerk istorii russkogo jazyka. Photomechanic reprint. Second printing. 1962. 384 pp. Cloth.　　　　　　　　　Glds. 24.—

23. PETER K. CHRISTOFF: An Introduction to Nineteenth-Century Russian Slavophilism. Volume I: A. S. Xomjakov. 1961. 301 pp., 2 plates. Cloth.　　　　　　　　　Glds. 33.—

24. JOVAN BRKIĆ: Moral Concepts in Traditional Serbian Epic Poetry. 1961. 177 pp. Cloth.　　　　　　　　　Glds. 24.—

25. JOSIP VRANA: L'Evangéliaire de Miroslav. Contribution à l'étude de son origine. 1961. 211 pp., 10 plates. Cloth.　　　　　　　　　Glds. 48.—

27. Studies in Russian and Polish Literature. In Honor of Wacław Lednicki. Edited by Z. Folejewski, †M. Karpovich, F. J. Whitfield, A. Kaspin. 1962. 250 pp., portrait. Cloth.　　　　　　　　　Glds. 36.—

28. WACŁAW LEDNICKI: Henryk Sienkiewicz. A Retrospective Synthesis. 1960. 81 pp., 7 plates.　　　　　　　　　Glds. 15.—

29. A. M. VAN DER ENG-LIEDMEIER: Soviet Literary Characters. An Investigation into the Portrayal of Soviet Men in Russian Prose, 1917-1953. 1959. 176 pp. Cloth.　　　　　　　　　Glds. 16.—

30. HENRY KUČERA: The Phonology of Czech. 1961. 112 pp. Cloth.　Glds. 18.—

31. Taras Ševčenko, 1814-1861. A Symposium. Edited by Volodymyr Mijakovs'kyj and George Y. Shevelov. 1962. 302 pp. Cloth.　　Glds. 32.—

32. MICHAEL SAMILOV: The Phoneme jat' in Slavic. 1964. 172 pp. Cloth.　　　　　　　　　Glds. 28.—

33. ROBIN KEMBALL: Alexander Blok. A Study in Rhythm and Metre. 1965. 539 pp., portrait. Cloth.　　　　　　　　　Glds. 80.—

34. V. ŽIRMUNSKII: Voprosy teorii literatury. Statej 1916-1926. Photomechanic reprint. 1962. 356 pp. Cloth.　　　　　　　　　Glds. 28.—

35. CHARLES E. PASSAGE: The Russian Hoffmannists. 1963. 261 pp. Cloth.　　　　　　　　　Glds. 30.—

36. VSEVOLOD SETCHKAREV: Studies in the Life and Works of Innokentij Annenskij. 1963. 270 pp. Cloth.　　　　　　　　　Glds. 32.—

37. A. I. SOBOLEVSKII: Lekcii po istorii russkogo jazyka. Photomechanic reprint. 1962. 308 pp. Cloth.　　　　　　　　　Glds. 26.—

38. GEORGE Y. SHEVELOV: The Syntax of Modern Literary Ukrainian. The Simple Sentence. 1963. 319 pp. Cloth.　　　　　　　　　Glds. 48.—

39. ALEXANDER M. SCHENKER: Polish Declension. A Descriptive Analysis. 1964. 105 pp., 38 figs. Cloth.　　　　　　　　　Glds. 17.—

40. MILADA SOUČKOVA: The Parnassian Jaroslav Vrchlický. 1964. 151 pp., plate. Cloth.　　　　　　　　　Glds. 20.—

41. A. A. ŠAXMATOV: Sintaksis russkogo jazyka. Redakcija i kommentarii Prof. E. S. Istrinoj. Photomechanic reprint. 1963. 623 pp. Cloth.　Glds. 48.—

42. CHARLES A. MOSER: Antinihilism in the Russian Novel of the 1860's. 1964. 215 pp. Cloth.　　　　　　　　　Glds. 22.—

43. RENÉ WELLEK: Essays on Czech Literature. Introduced by Peter Demetz. 1963. 214 pp., portrait. Cloth.　　　　　　　　　Glds. 23.—

45. Dutch Contributions to the Fifth International Congress of Slavicists, Sofia, 1963. 1963. 162 pp. Cloth.　　　　　　　　　Glds. 36.—

46. American Contributions to the Fifth International Congress of Slavists, Sofia, September 1963. Vol. I: Linguistic Contributions. 1963. 384 pp. Cloth.　　　　　　　　　Glds. 69.—

47. JU. TYNJANOV: Problema stixotvornogo jazyka. Photomechanic reprint. 1963. 139 pp. Cloth. Glds. 18.—

48. Russkaja Proza, pod redakčiej B. Ejchenbauma i Ju. Tynjanova. Sbornik statej. Photomechanic reprint. 1963. 265 pp. Cloth. Glds. 28.—

50. American Contributions to the Fifth International Congress of Slavists, Sofia, September 1963. Vol. II. Literary Contributions. 1963. 432 pp. Cloth. Glds. 69.—

51. ROMAN JAKOBSON and DEAN S. WORTH (eds.): Sofonija's Tale of the Russian-Tatar Battle on the Kulikovo Field. 1963. 71 pp., 49 plates. Cloth. Glds. 20.—

52. WACŁAW LEDNICKI: Tolstoj between War and Peace. 1965. 169 pp., 4 plates. Cloth. Glds. 25.—

54. A. V. FLOROVSKY (ed.): Georgius David, S. J.: Status Modernus Magnae Russiae seu Moscoviae (1690), Edited with Introduction and Explanatory Index. 1965. 135 pp., 4 figs. Cloth. Glds. 28.—

56. N. S. TRUBETZKOY: Dostoevskij als Künstler. 1965. 178 pp. Cloth. Glds. 28.—

57. F. C. DRIESSEN: Gogol as a Short-Story Writer. A Study of his Technique of Composition. Translated from the Dutch by Ian F. Finlay. 1965. 243 pp. Cloth. Glds. 36.—

MOUTON & CO · PUBLISHERS · THE HAGUE